No Touch Monkey !

and other
travel lessons learned too late

Ayun Halliday

SEAL PRESS

No Touch Monkey!: And Other Travel Lessons Learned Too Late

Published by Seal Press
A member of the Perseus Book Group
1700 Fourth Street
Berkeley, CA 94710

"On the Road" originally appeared in *The Unsavvy Traveler* as "Carry Me Out of Africa," published by Seal Press in 2001.

"On Local Custom" originally appeared in *A Woman Alone* as "Dog Master," published by Seal Press in 2001.

Library of Congress Cataloging-in-Publication Data:
No touch monkey!: and other travel lessons learned too late/ by Ayun Halliday.—1st ed.
        p. cm.
ISBN-10: 1-58005-097-2 (pbk.)
ISBN-13: 978-1-58005-097-5 (pbk.)
1. Halliday, Ayun—Travel. 2. Travel—Anecdotes. 3. Voyages and travels. I. Halliday, Ayun.

G465.H345 2003
910.4'09'049--dc22

15 14

Designed by Paul Paddock
Printed in the United States of America by Berryville Graphics

For Greg, India and Milo

contents

FOR YOUR ENJOYMEN AND SAFETY PLEASE OBSERVE THE FOLLOWING INDIKATION!

- DO NOT TOUCH OR TEASE THE MONKEY AS THE MAY REACT WITH UNPREDIKTABLE MANNERS.

- FORBIDDEN FED TO THE MONKEYS. SUPPOSING YOU HAVE SOOM FOOD FOR THEM. PLEASE LEAVE TO OUR MONKEY'S EXPERT.

- IF THERE IS NO MONKEYS EXPERT WITH YOU TOSS THE FOOD TO THEM FROM A SAVE DISTANCE.

- DO NOT HIDE FOOD ON YOU. THEY WILL FIND IT, EVEN IF IT IS IN YOUR POCKET OR A BAG.

- NEVER GRAB A MONKEY. IF A MONKEY GETS ON YOU, DROP ALL YOUR FOOD AND WALK A WAY UNTIL IT JUMPS OFF.

We Trust Your Visit Will Be Memorable One.

—sign in Ubud, Bali

Introduction

I thought I'd get to write this introduction in a small hotel in the Dominican Republic. The owner was going to let us have two rooms for fifty bucks a night, but by the time my two-year-old son's passport arrived in the mail, return flights were booked solid for the entirety of Easter week. So I'm stuck in exotic Brooklyn, though I suppose every hour my husband spends with the kids so I can write is a kind of vacation, for me if not for him. Compared to hauling little Milo and his five-year-old sister around the subways of New York, the years I spent traveling on a shoestring budget seem about as difficult as locating a carved wooden frog for sale on the island of Bali. I keep threatening to pull up stakes and take the family on any number of adventures, but considering that it often takes us five hours to get to the playground across the street, I wouldn't hold your breath waiting for us to turn up at that Guatemalan Spanish-language school I read about in the *New York Times* Travel section anytime soon. Still, I can dream.

Whenever I think about hitting the road with Inky and Milo, I remember Sky and Summer, a couple of Australian urchins I last saw careening unchaperoned through the streets of Solo, Java, in a bicycle rickshaw, urging the driver to go faster by spanking him with palm fronds. Their exhausted parents were my guesthouse neighbors. Financing their trip by collecting the dole in absentia, they had gotten divorced solely to up their benefits, each claiming to be the full-time single parent of one child. I admired their resourcefulness, but had no idea how intrepid they were. The children were crazy, unfettered hippie kids with tangled locks and smart mouths—in short, exactly the kind of kids I wanted as long as I didn't have to take care of them. The boy—I think he was Sky—spent an hour bedeviling me with a feather duster he'd picked up somewhere, screeching, "I'll fluff ya!" My torment ceased only when his father, passionately discussing college radio with my then-boyfriend, stopped in midsentence, having misheard the little boy's threats as something a tad more hardcore than "fluff." I've always thought I'd like to write about Sky and Summer—and look: now I have. If it weren't for this introduction, they'd exist only in my memory and, presumably, Australia, where they must be teenagers by now.

As long as I'm rolling down memory lane, I'll seize the opportunity to mention the leaf pile where I slept in Portugal, the civet I ate in Thailand, and the outhouse three hours from the peak of Kilimanjaro, which looked like someone with a particularly propulsive case of Montezuma's revenge had stood on the seat and aimed their ass at the ceiling. There. Now they're in the book, too. Traipsing through dozens of countries on the extreme cheapie-cheap, I accumulated anecdotes aplenty to tide me over during this dry spell, cooling my heels until Milo is old enough to hold his water, walk long distances without whining, and remain seated during takeoff with his belt securely fastened instead of squirming free and breaking for the aisle. If only reminiscences counted toward frequent flyer miles, all four of us could celebrate Milo's fourth birthday in Sulawesi without having to spend a dime on airfare. Instead, I shoehorned as many of them as I could into a book, discovering in the process why people who believe that beauty is in the smallest details spend their entire lives scratching out twenty-volume treatises on the Civil War, only to die exhausted and penniless soon after publication. I have little kids, carpal tunnel syndrome, and a fondness for knocking off at the end of the day. Realizing that only a fraction of my low-rent gadabout memories would make it into the finished product was a travel-related shocker to rival the time my then-boyfriend Isaac and I got off the plane in Tokyo and I discovered that Issac's good buddy who'd be hosting us in the small village where he taught English was none other than the black belt who had kicked a foot-shaped bruise into my chest during my one semester of karate at Northwestern University. Dang, I think that's the only mention of Japan you'll find here, though I did manage to squeeze in two other ex-boyfriends, not counting my husband Greg. Really, what is a husband if not the final boyfriend of a serial monogamist? Call me sentimental, but I wish there were a way to pack it all in: seeing cell phones for the first time on a ferry full of Hong Kong businessmen; in Madrid's Plaza del Sol, running into friends from school, who then sprang for paella; snorkeling in Nha Trang with an Australian guy who impaled himself on a sea anemone . . . Some names got changed but many more were left out. Also, I'd like to thank everyone Greg and I mooched cigarettes off of in Vietnam and India; we were so appalled by our obnoxious behavior that we quit cold turkey in Calcutta.

It's true that travel broadens the mind. It also wreaks havoc on the digestive tract and can make one awfully weary of the T-shirt one's been wearing every other day for months. That might not hold true for the suite-at-the-Ritz crowd, but the kind of budget on which I saw the world set me up for lots of memorable, if stinky, experiences. In the quest for authenticity, whatever that is, I ended up smoking doobie, watching Arnold Schwarzenegger videos and eating a lot of banana pancakes with other Westerners in Chinese pants. Which reminds me, if you've never seen *Octopussy*, there are at least four screenings every day in Udaipur, where it was filmed. And if you're tempted to order an "Australian Pizza" in Lovina Beach, don't: It's a pancake smothered in ketchup with half an uncut raw onion plopped on top. If you find yourself in rural Tanzania, don't get carried away by an impulse to wade in standing water unless you want bilharzia, an infestation of microscopic snails beneath your skin. Don't expect anyone to be able to break your one-hundred-thousand-dong note in rural Vietnam. Don't forget to call your mother once a month.

Thus concludes the unsolicited travel advice of one who's logged many miles on laughably little money, except for this final suggestion: Bring a lot of plastic bags with you when you travel so you can compartmentalize everything in your backpack, keep your clean clothes safe from contamination by the dirty ones and, the tampons separate from the traveler's checks. Nate and I fought about money, Isaac and I fought about what happened in the Gulf of Thailand with that handsome Swede, and Greg did everything within his power to get me to throw away the plastic grocery sacks from Chicago erupting like milkweed out of my pack. Eventually I agreed, but only after I had amassed an impressive supply of their Indian, Thai, and Vietnamese counterparts. On my budget, plastic bags stamped in exotic script counted as souvenirs, as authentic as any memory.

Greg, having his own memories, insists that several of mine are inaccurate. Even though I've noticed a recent trend in introductions whereby authors ask forgiveness, citing the subjectivity of their recalled past, I'm claiming that every word is 100 percent true, especially the bits that Greg wasn't there for. At least that's what I'll tell the kids when they're old enough to read this book but still too young to ditch their vagabond mother at the departure gate.

Happy trails to you. Happy trails to me.

Ayun Halliday
Brooklyn, New York
May 2003

On Hygiene

Things really went to shit in the Munich train station men's room.

Nate and I had failed to plan carefully for our first trip abroad without parental supervision. My theater degree from Northwestern University still warm, I had spent the summer in Scotland, acting in the famous Edinburgh Fringe Festival. The experience left me feeling worldly, despite the fact that the company under whose auspices I performed was a barely disguised con, casting every starry-eyed undergraduate who auditioned back in the States, provided she could cough up airfare and the inflated rent for a short-term apartment. Ten of us lived crammed in a rundown flat with no phone and no living room. But the bedroom I shared with three others—four if you count Nate, who rarely slept in the B & B where his band was billeted—boasted a romantic view of the Edinburgh Castle, so I loved it. Nate had arrived in Scotland with two hundred dollars, a briefcase of harmonicas, and no backpack. His unpreparedness for our upcoming tour of Europe provoked feelings of anger, which I quickly squashed when he suggested that maybe, since he had no money, he should return to Chicago and let me do the trip alone. What did his reluctance signify? If the shoe had been on the other foot, I wouldn't have let anything so dreary as under-funding come between me and Eurailing with my beloved. I was a year younger than Nate, but much more advanced in my determination to force reality to conform to the future I envisioned. "Why would you want to back out now?" I argued, conserving our resources by eating packets of unrefined sugar in lieu of dessert in a vegetarian cafeteria near the theater. "Don't worry about your Eurail pass. I'll buy it and you can pay me back later. We can save money by sleeping in the train stations. As long as you have a ticket, they won't arrest you!" Alarmed by Nate's frown, I pressed hurriedly on, "Or you know, we can work it so we only take overnight trains. That way we never have to pay for a hostel. Look!" I dug in my bag for *Europe through the Back Door,* a budget guidebook authored by an intrepid, bearded fellow photographed with chopsticks shoved in his nostrils. "According to this guy, Rick Steves, what you do is find an empty compartment, spread out all your stuff, and pretend to be asleep whenever another passenger comes by looking for a seat. Another thing he recommends is pretending you're a Hare Krishna!"

Nate ran a hand through his already-thinning blond curls. "I don't think I'd want to do that." I stifled the impulse to choke him.

"Why not?! If it gets you a private train compartment for the night, it's worth it. You'll see. Instead of eating in restaurants, we'll go to markets and buy stuff for picnics—you know, bread, olives, sardines . . ." Nate wrinkled his nose. "Or not sardines," I blurted. "We're under no obligation to have sardines! I only suggested them because they're nutritious and cheap, but if you play harmonica in the town square, we'll make enough for an entire day's food in an hour, easy. I can buy some chalk and do sidewalk drawings for money! Come on, baby, it won't be any fun if you don't come."

The only thing more painful than remembering the hack productions in which I performed that summer is reflecting on what might have happened had I not been such a naive young monogamist. Barely twenty-two, I was too inexperienced to know that the kind of shoestring travel I contemplated offers endless possibilities for memorable adventures, but only for those unburdened of penniless, fearful boyfriends. If only Nate's father had prevailed! A successful funds manager, he co-opted the term I used so enthusiastically—"bumming around"—to express disapproval. It really frosted his ass that his son would quit his restaurant job and allow his Chicago acting career to lose momentum, in order to gallivant around Europe with no forwarding address, a dozen harmonicas, and a hippy-dippy girlfriend. Maybe if Nate had gone home directly after the Edinburgh festival, he'd be famous and I'd have tales of nightclubs, abandoned seaside cottages, and ancestral villas. Oh, the motorcycle rides I'd have taken with the boy I met at the hostel/on the train/on the steps of the Trevi Fountain: the crazy northern Italian, the adorably sarcastic Welshman, the passionate Greek, the artsy Belgian, the handsome Spaniard whose doctor had given him just two months to live!

Instead, I grew fat and Nate skeletal from a diet composed largely of bread. In less than two months, we visited thirty cities in nine countries. It would have been eight, but we slept through an intended stop, awakening not in Venice, but in Vienna on a cold, rainy Sunday when all of the moneychangers were closed. I have yet to sample the mouthwatering sweets of Vienna's fabled coffeehouses, but I did eat a sandwich made from half an avocado, the dregs of our peanut butter, and a stolen onion.

• • •

Germany started auspiciously enough. The second our train pulled in, we swung by the left-luggage room to check my big backpack and Nate's little daypack, to which we had bungee corded a now filthy blanket liberated from my furnished Edinburgh flat. Bolstered by the fresh stamps in our passports, we allowed ourselves a sit-down meal, ostensibly to get warm after waiting nearly forty-five minutes for the Marienplatz's clock tower to chime the hour, triggering its anticlimactic but free-of-charge carillons. I'd never been a fan of Germany's heavy cuisine, but the monotony of our diet lent an unexpected piquancy to the splurge, further buoying my mood. I even consented to try a bite of Nate's sausage, rationalizing that one bite didn't make me *not* a vegetarian, any more than eating sardines would have. The grudge that increased every time he slunk away to squander some of our dwindling nest egg at McDonald's evaporated. We were in this thing together! Hand in hand, we set out to discover any part of Munich that didn't require admission fees or mandatory purchase. "Look, there's a ferris wheel!" I cried, pointing to a festive semicircle visible above the rooftops of the business district. Navigating by its neon spokes, we found the entrance to the carnival grounds, a lettered arch framed in greenery. "Oh my god, Nate, Oktoberfest!" What wonderful blind luck to hit Munich just as its biggest and best-known festival was going into full swing!

This wasn't the first regional holiday we'd stumbled upon, but Siena's Palio—a bareback horse race that's been an annual Italian tradition for centuries—did not spark imitative shindigs in the American Midwest. I'd steered clear of the annual beer blast in Chicago, but only because I feared legions of drunken Cubs fans in fraternity sweatshirts, the same guys who lurched up Clark Street on St. Patrick's Day, vomiting green. In its place of origin, Oktoberfest seemed to have more in common with the Indiana State Fair, a Teutonic honky-tonk complete with rides, civic displays and sucker booths baited with inflatable cartoon characters and lurid, polyester teddy bears. We spent a long time admiring the façade of Geisterschlucht, where a ten-foot-tall robotic ape toadied up to a King Kong–type three times his size, who periodically interrupted to boom, "Geisterschlucht!"

"That means 'haunted house,' " Nate told me excitedly, dredging up a not entirely accurate morsel of his forgotten high-school foreign-language training. Fifteen minutes flew by as we gaped, totally infatuated with the German-speaking cyber monkeys creaking in the chill autumn afternoon as they cycled through their limited repertoire of hand gestures. Our pleasure was heightened by the incongruity of jungle creatures pimping an attraction any red-blooded American can tell you has nothing to do with zoos or safaris and everything to do with witches, ghosts and, in some liberal interpretations, hockey-masked chainsaw murderers. The entry fee was nearly half the cost of an International Youth Hostel Association membership, much too high to consider. Had it been less, we would have squabbled over whether or not we could afford to go inside. I squeezed Nate's arm, warm in the knowledge that nothing inside Geisterschlucht could equal the complimentary animatronic display outside.

Tearing ourselves away from one of the great sights in Europe, we decided to take a peek inside a beer hall. It seemed that every brewery sponsored its own building. After cruising past the possibilities, we settled on the Hofbrauhaus, a cavernous barn filled with long, sparsely occupied tables. An oompah band played on a bare stage as waitresses in dirndls ferried an astonishing amount of beer by slipping their hands through eight mug handles at once. For decoration, a papier-mâché cherub with the face of a sixty-year-old alcoholic was suspended from the rafters, swiveling his over-sized head, a bleary smile on his face. "It seems silly to be here and not have a beer," I ventured. "Find out how much they are. Maybe we could split one."

Nate consulted with a beefy waitress and came back grinning. We could swing a mug, no problem, especially since our accommodations wouldn't cost a dime. There was a train to Salzburg at 11 P.M. We could board the moment the train pulled into the station, log a few hours of shuteye, cross the platform in Salzburg, and slumber all the way back to Munich. The brilliance of the plan called for celebration. Timidly, we took a seat on a long bench, joining an older couple decked out in full Tyrolean regalia. The man modestly fessed up to speaking a little English. Introductions were made and our travels briefly described, but conversation dwindled almost immediately. Our tablemates hadn't visited any of the places we'd been, nor did they seem wildly envious, the way I am, talking with someone recently returned from St. Bart's. More importantly, they didn't want to get in too deep with scuzzy vagabond kids, the kind of bad element they'd raised their children to avoid.

When our mug arrived, Nate and I praised its contents to the heavens, licking our lips lustily in a courteous attempt to include the non-English-speaking Frau. Before tucking into the steaming piles of sauerkraut, potatoes and sausage the waitress placed before them, they nodded politely. The manner in which they glared at their food made it clear that eating time was not talking time. I took small sips of our beer, trying not to look too Oliver Twist–like.

Unfortunately, our restaurant meal had produced an effect akin to culinary foreplay, and I was getting blue balls for lack of my own heavily laden plate. One glance told me Nate was experiencing the exact same thing. The husband had to have a fat wallet secreted in his lederhosen, full of crisp deutsche marks organized according to denomination. If we had been schoolmates of his kids, he'd have asked if we were hungry, ordered schnitzel for the table and brushed off our insincere offers to pay. Just because we were strangers whose appearance betrayed our hard-traveling lifestyle, he felt it wasn't rude to fork up all those calories in front of us, not volunteering even the tiniest taste. So what if it was a commercial establishment? The muscular waitresses kept banging out of the kitchen, hauling beer mugs and more food, none of it destined for us. Behind us, a trio of wide-bottomed ladies waddled off, groaning, leaving plenty of half-eaten grub on their plates. If only propriety would allow me to pounce on their scraps like a house cat—it was criminal that perfectly edible, paid-for chow would be scraped in a rubber dishpan while two young Americans starved nearby. After a month of roughing it, sanitation barely entered the equation, but regardless, the pantsuit-wearing matrons who had forfeited their membership in the clean plate club were dead ringers for my grandmother's sisters, Ina, Ruth, and Edith. The odds of contracting trench mouth from their leftovers seemed pretty low.

Fortunately, before I could make a move, the band struck up a prototypical German drinking song, and our tablemates, obeying some national impulse, linked elbows with us to sway for the duration of the number. This segued into the "Chicken Dance," in which the husband dutifully instructed us, correcting us when we wiggled our tail feathers instead of flapping our wings. Apparently, the bandleader, a cutup in knee socks, Alpine hat, and wraparound New Wave shades, was the only one allowed to play fast and loose with Oktoberfest tradition. The moment this awkward exercise ended, I encouraged Nate to chug his half of our beer so we could flee before I disgraced us by snitching a roll from the unbussed plate behind me.

We attempted to walk around Munich, but I couldn't shake the nagging suspicion that only squares wander around in near-freezing temperatures, pretending to admire the half-timbered architecture when the rest of their generation is whooping it up just a few short blocks away. Watching some Guatemalan street musicians, I hatched a brief fantasy in which they invited us back to their snug flat, ladled spicy bean soup into hand-thrown crocks, and insisted we spend several nights sleeping on a pullout sofa under colorful woolen blankets they'd brought from home. I angled for an in, but nothing I could say would coerce Nate to pull out a harmonica and join them. "It's not the right kind of music," he scowled. "Besides, I'm too cold to play. Aren't you freezing?" He cast a critical eye at the closest thing I had to cold-weather gear, a flea-bitten green sweater I had picked up in a Scottish thrift store. It had been knit with someone much taller in mind. When it was new—to me, anyway—it was vaguely flattering in a *Little Rascals*, sleeves-over-the-hands sort of way, but now it was unraveling, and the chewing gum I had inadvertently slept on in Charing Cross Station had turned black and hard. I jumped up and down irritably as a cold wind entered via my frayed elbows. "What do you want to do?" Nate demanded.

"I don't know. What do you want to do?"

"We could just bag the whole thing and push on toward Belgium or something."

"I thought we were going to Dachau in the morning!"

"If you want to."

"Yes, I do, since you asked. My friend Lisa Beadles said it was very moving, although she was only there for like a half-hour or something before a bee stung her on the eyelid and she had an allergic reaction and some other travelers took it upon themselves to take her to the hospital, which is a good thing, since her throat started swelling shut. The whole reason I wanted to come to Munich was to go to Dachau. You can get there on the subway."

"Okay, we'll go to Dachau. No need to bite my head off."

"I didn't bite your head off—I'm just cold! And I don't want to go hang around the train station for five hours, waiting for the train to Salzburg to roll in."

"So, what do you want to do?"

"I guess I wouldn't mind going back to Oktoberfest so I could get a picture of Geisterschluct."

It wasn't long before we found ourselves back in the Hofbrauhaus, now packed with young people, waving cigarettes and hubcap-sized pretzels as they shouted over the oompah band. Recklessly, we ordered two beers and squeezed in opposite some pleasant Irish guys, next to some gussied-up local girls who didn't seem particularly thrilled to have us horning in on their territory. In short order, our shared mother tongue sent the girls off in search of other quarry. Our conversation veered from the early Rolling Stones to the playwright Brendan Behan to the atrocities of the Nazi regime. "I'll be fucked," Jim declared. "Sure I wouldn't of figured they'd know the name of Brendan Behan back where you come from."

"Our school did a production of *Borstal Boy*," I told him. "A friend of ours played the transvestite."

"Did you hear that, Pete? They know fuckin' Brendan Behan!"

"There's a great bar near where I lived," Nate intimated. "O'Rourke's. They've got these giant blown-up photographs of Brendan Behan, James Joyce, Samuel Beckett . . ."

"O'Rourke's, Jesus," Jim laughed, pretending to reel off of his bench. "Who'd've thunk it?"

Our new friends flagged down a waitress to order four beers and Wiener schnitzel all around. The food came out of the kitchen ungarnished, meat cakes the same shade as Pepto-Bismol. I could tell from Nate's expression that he'd been expecting links, too. Oh well, down the hatch! It was delicious in a livery, Braunschweigery, goes-good-with-beer-and-didn't-cost-me-a-dime sort of way. I polished mine off and started on Nate's. "Ayun's a vegetarian, as you can see," he remarked dryly.

"So, is it mostly meat the people eat where you come from, then?" Jim inquired.

"It's mostly McNuggets," I said, making a face. "The national cuisine. Nate loves it, but I think it's disgusting. People call it Mickey D's."

"Mickey D's," Nate crowed.

"All right, here's something I'd like to be knowing," Jim said. "What's in a goulash, anyway?"

"Goulash?" I asked, blinking.

"You'll have to excuse him," Pete snickered. "The truth is we know fuck-all about your country."

"What's there to know," Nate shrugged. "Mickey Mouse. New York. MTV."

The Irishmen roared in disbelief. "Mother of God, you're a Yank?" Jim cried.

"Where the fuck did you think we were from?"

"Her too?" Pete asked, jerking a thumb at me.

"Of course, isn't it obvious?"

"We thought you were starving Hungarians," Jim howled. "Because of the looks of you, see. No offense, but I'd never heard tell of an American as dirty as the two of you. And that big hairy sweater and your long hair and the little wire specs. Are you sure you're American?" Flushed with the pleasure of being mistaken for a European, I had to fight the impulse to tear off my shoes to display the blackened, cracked soles of my feet. I was dying to tell them I hadn't shaved my pits in years.

"I wondered why you complimented us on our English," Nate said.

For the next few hours, Peter and Jim plied us with one mug after another, refusing to let us reciprocate, telling us that, for all they knew, we had spent the last decade behind the Berlin Wall. I lost count of how many beers I had drunk, as I staggered happily back and forth from our table to the ladies' room. The later it grew, the less I wanted to travel all the way to Salzburg and back just to get some sleep. If only one of the guys would offer us the keys to their rental car so we could crash in the parking lot of their motel. I didn't want to come right out and suggest it, afraid they might think I was fishing for an invitation to spend the night on their floor. The car would have done fine, but neither Peter nor Jim took the hint. Maybe our shoddy hygiene made us look untrustworthy as well as Hungarian. Getting us totally blitzed was no assurance that we'd refrain from stealing their ride. Before I knew it, we were exchanging open invitations to spend a few weeks in Chicago and Dublin, me forgetting that I had given up the apartment that went with the phone number I scrawled on the flap of Jim's cigarette box.

We made it to the station with minutes to spare, just a few steps behind several hundred crocked Austrians hoping to make it home to Salzburg before their hangovers hit. The left-luggage room was closed for the night. No matter, we'd be back in a few hours anyway. "Shit, it's packed," Nate groused as we boarded the train. We walked through several cars, sliding open the metal doors to every unreserved compartment. They were all stuffed to capacity with sloppy, singing drunks. Finally, we came upon a trio of girls who had claimed an entire compartment for themselves à la Rick Steves, their backpacks and sweaters fanned across the unoccupied seats. "Pardon," I gurgled with a crisp French intonation. The girls gave no indication that they had heard, though their eyes were squinched shut with more energy than a genuine sleeper would expend. I begged their pardon a little louder. The one nearest me produced a seven-part sigh, fluttered her eyelids and curled into fetal position. What an actress! Shrugging impotently, I turned to Nate.

"This is bullshit," he said, shoving past me into the compartment. "Excuse me, can you move your legs please? We need a place to sit down." The girls flicked open their eyes to glare. "Do I need to get a conductor? The train's full, so deal with it. You want to give us some room here?"

Muttering darkly, they consolidated their belongings, their hiking boots thudding accusingly as they swung their feet down from the seats. Trying to take up as little space as possible, I meekly thanked the girl opposite. She flared her nostrils in reply. The one next to her dropped her head onto her friend's shoulder, a petulant frown on her kewpie-cute face. I was glad when a few minutes later they had to move the rest of their stuff to accommodate a gangly Brazilian, even though my own legroom was severely impinged by his gargantuan backpack, which sat between us like a coffee table. The train chugged out of the station, sending the revelers still partying with hip flasks and open containers sprawling against the outer walls of our joyless compartment. Someone kept farting silently. The world spun when I closed my eyes.

I was awakened some time later by the mournful blast of the train whistle, a sound I never grew sick of, even when the only air available was poisoned with hostile strangers' breath. I'm not saying I didn't contribute to the oppressive atmosphere. Flatulent rodents nested in my mouth. I cursed myself for failing to pull our toothbrushes from our bags when we checked them at left-luggage. The sinks in the tiny toilet cabinets claimed *l'eau non-potable*, but this was an emergency situation. If I couldn't brush, at least I could swish and spit. Still lurching a bit from the Oktoberfestivities, I fumbled toward the door of the compartment, treading on several unidentified insteps in the process. The corridor was bright but eerily quiet. Bracing my hands against the walls on either side, I started toward the WC, keeping my eyes fixed on a point in the distance, a tip my mother had taught me years ago, when I used to get nauseated from riding in our station wagon. Suddenly, my feet hydroplaned out from under me as I stepped in a generous puddle of someone else's vomit. "Could be worse," I told myself as I took a moment to recover on hands and knees. Somebody could've witnessed my disgrace. I could've broken my arm in the fall.

Have you ever been to Salzburg? If it's anything like its train station at four in the morning, I'd say give it a miss.

By the time we got back to Munich, I was a mess. Every time I thought back to the night before, an involuntary abdominal contraction threatened to push a tidal wave of bodily fluids out of every orifice, including my eye sockets. The station was alive with commuters, fortifying themselves against the Monday morning frost with pastry and coffee. "You want some breakfast?" Nate croaked.

I shook my head miserably. "I just want to go to Dachau." I pulled my sweater tight against my cramping guts, hoping to truss them back toward solidity. "But first I've got to spend some time in the bathroom."

"Poor baby," Nate crooned. "You should clean up. You'll feel better." I nodded, desperate to believe that soap could erase the previous night's excesses. We waited for the left-luggage room to reopen and then repaired to the main entrance to divvy up our communal toiletries. "Here," he said, squeezing some Pepsodent onto his toothbrush, "you take the tube." While he poured shampoo into my rarely used camping mug, I divided a packet of shower gel I'd taken from the cheap hotel room we'd splurged on in Paris. "Okay, I'll meet you back here in a little while." He strode toward the men's room, while I crossed the terminal in search of the ladies'.

A hulking attendant stationed at a card table near the entrance saw my toiletries and waved me toward a doublewide stall with a real door. It cost nearly a dollar to enter, but seated on the clean toilet, my head on my knees, I felt I was getting my money's worth. Every time I thought it was safe to stand, I realized I was mistaken. Staring woozily at the black crescents below my nails, I swore I would never drink again. Had I made a fool of myself in front of Peter and Jim? I had trouble recalling the last hour of our acquaintance, let alone how we made it to the train station. Oh, if only I could spend the whole day in my little rental bathroom. It was cold, but clean, cleaner than it would have been in one of the sunny Mediterranean countries. Maybe I could curl up on the floor the way I would at home. Groaning, I nuzzled the toothpaste tube like a teddy bear.

Eventually, I struggled to my feet, slowly stripped off every stitch above the ankles and wedged my head beneath the taps of my private sink, attempting to wash the cigarette funk out of more than a foot of hair. The water was tepid at best, and when I straightened up, rivulets from my tangled locks raced for my socks, raising goose pimples in their tracks. Shit, Nate had the towel. Moving very slowly, I crouched alongside my pack, hunting for something that could double as a washrag. A crinkly gauze skirt seemed like the best bet. It hadn't been washed since Florence, but at least it would dry quickly.

I was glad the only mirror in the stall was a small square mounted at face level. I knew I was not a pretty sight, gingerly swabbing my flabby, sour-smelling body with a sopping hippie skirt. Through the thin walls, I could hear other American backpackers, chattering brightly as they tried to decide what outfits to change into.

"Oh my god, that is so cute! Did you get that here?"

"No, the Gap."

"You are kidding me!"

"Does anybody have a brush I can use? I swear I won't give you cooties!"

"It's okay, I don't care. This is going to sound crazy, but are you from Oklahoma?"

"Texas, but we both go to Tulane."

"Sorry, I thought maybe you were this girl I met a few years ago at choir camp."

"God, that would have been weird! I do choir, too, though. Church and school. I'm a soprano, but I wish I were an alto, because I get so sick of singing the melody. It's not challenging enough, you know?"

"Nicole, you know what would look really cute with that vest? My white pants."

I put a foot on the edge of the sink, the better to wash my malodorous vagina.

"Pardon me," called a proper English voice. "Is there an Annie in here?"

"Uh, me, sort of," I called back, my voice as shaky as my hands.

"Your boyfriend's wondering if you're all right. He says you've been in here for almost an hour."

"Yeah, can you tell him I'll be out in another minute? I've just got to get dressed."

"He said to tell you to hurry."

Still feeling leprous but somewhat purified externally, I pulled on the least soiled garments I owned, fixed my snarled, wet hair in a loose braid and forgave my ratty sweater all its sins, so grateful was I for its warmth. My pert countrywomen fell silent as I emerged from the stall, refraining from further prattle until the untouchable was out of earshot.

Nate was standing just outside the entrance, hugging his daypack to his chest, his hair frozen into little soapy points. He saw me and burst into tears.

"Oh my god! What's wrong?"

Nate wiped his nose on the back of his sleeve. "I d-didn't want to pay for one of those special stalls," he gulped raggedly. "So after I took a whiz at the urinal, I took my shirt off and started washing my hair in one of the regular sinks. It was no big dee-hee-heal! There were at least a dozen of them in a row! It wasn't like somebody couldn't wash his hands because of me. So, I'd just lathered up when this stupid fucking female bathroom attendant the size of a house started screaming at me, '*Ist verboten! Ist verboten!*' "

"They have a woman working in the men's room?"

"Yeah, but she was really dykey," he snuffled. "And I'm shouting, 'Just lemme rinse! Just lemme rinse!' but she won't stop screaming '*Ist verboten! Ist verboten!*' like a fucking broken record!" He stamped his foot in frustration, unable to staunch the tears. "So, this business-suit guy who's just come out of the crapper thinks the problem is that I don't understand what she's saying and takes it upon himself to educate me. 'These sinks are for hands only, after the toilet. Everything else, you must pay a fee, for which she will give you a private chamber with toilet and sink.' So I say, 'Okay, tell her next time I'll do that, but would she mind if I rinse the goddamn shampoo out of my hair first?' He starts to translate what I said, but she just keeps screeching that it's *verboten,* at which point, I think, 'Lady, enough! Fuck you! I get it!' and stick my head under the faucet so I can get the shampoo out. The next thing I know she's got me by the arm, trying to drag me away from the sink, like she's forcibly removing me from the premises. So I grab my pack and sort of take a swipe at her, like this." He demonstrated, swinging his daypack by the straps in a horizontal arc. "And then, before I could get away, she takes this broom from the corner and cracks me over the back with it. She wouldn't stop hitting me. She just kept banging away until I managed to get out of there. I left our shampoo on the side of the sink." He covered his face with his hands and sobbed.

I noticed that passersby were giving us a wide berth. With different clothes, Nate's hair might have passed for punk, but by the light of day, he looked less a filthy Hungarian than a pampered son of Westport gone to seed under his girlfriend's stewardship. My toxic blood was cleansed by a surge of maternal compassion. "Would you like to go to McDonald's?" I asked gently. He hiccupped in assent. Taking him tenderly by the hand, I led him to the familiar golden arches, and bought him a complete breakfast menu while he washed the stiff suds out of his hair in the single-seater lavatory. What the hell? It didn't kill me to dish out a little prefab TLC, even if it did blow half a week's budget.

On Commerce

I wasn't willing to admit it just yet, but it looked like my hippies had decamped. No one answered my knock and the place had a seedy, uninhabited look. According to a slightly out-of-date *Europe on $25 a Day*, they were running a guesthouse on a houseboat near Centraal Station. Their beds were cheap, and their breakfasts large and vegetarian. The boat was named *Wu Wei*, after the Taoist concept of going with the flow. Sounded good and vaguely familiar to me. Most likely I had run across the name while researching yin-yang symbols, before having one tattooed on my ankle as a reckless college junior. (The permanent modification of my young flesh had not impressed the Vietnam vet wielding the needle as reason enough to discontinue a spirited conversation he was having about motorcycles. I ended up with a yin ya: The dark half's white, or more accurately, flesh-toned dot is entirely blotted out by its black field. That I am marked for life with an out-of-balance symbol for balance is an irony not entirely lost on me.)

It was starting to snow. It was, after all, a few days before Christmas. I shoved my hands into the pockets of my parka and squinted at the chipped garden gnomes and Day-Glo mushrooms bolted to the houseboat's flat roof. They were depressing and creepy, like fairy-tale characters in untended roadside attractions. Maybe they would look more cheerful in bright sunshine. I had reset my watch to Amsterdam time as the KLM flight began its descent: a few minutes past 6 A.M. The sun would be rising soon. Maybe the hippies were still asleep. The city was just coming to life. Cyclists dinged bells mounted to the handlebars of their one-speeds as they obeyed traffic signals in their own specially designated lanes. Delivery trucks rumbled along the canal. The air was scented with wood smoke. I shrugged off my heavy backpack and sat on it, keeping my eyes fastened on the faded cardboard blocking the *Wu Wei's* portholes. Any minute, a red-cheeked Dutch hippie would emerge in wool socks and Birkenstock sandals to fetch an armload of firewood, polish the mushrooms, and welcome me aboard what would be home base for the three days I had arranged to spend in Amsterdam en route to Tanzania.

"You are looking for a room?" I turned around. A man old enough to be my father called to me from the deck of another houseboat. He had aviator glasses and a bad haircut.

"No thanks! Got one!" I turned back to the *Wu Wei.* Her paint was peeling. The man picked his way across the decks of several houseboats tethered together. When he reached the pier, he took out a pipe, which he filled from a leather pouch. In silence, we contemplated the desolate hippie boat, a sorry spectacle compared to the trim vessels surrounding it. The puffing pipe made me think of my grandfather comfortably ensconced in his red rocking chair with the patriotic upholstery, monitoring the comings and goings of the wren house he had hung in the redbud tree outside the family room window. It was an awfully cozy image, complete with homemade chocolate chip cookies, slices of pepperoni and little cubes of cheddar cheese arranged on one of my grandmother's apple blossom plates. Goddamnit. All over Amsterdam, citizens were settling into their breakfast nooks for similarly high fat, homey meals. Meanwhile, my feet froze in the cheapest hiking boots Sportmart stocked. I was homeless and impotent.

Breaking up the long flight to Tanzania by extending a two-hour layover to three days had seemed exactly the sort of thing an experienced solo world traveler would do. I had never traveled alone, but while bumming around with Nate a year earlier, Amsterdam had impressed me as the kind of town where one could have a free-wheeling, memorably fun time if one wasn't saddled with a mopey boyfriend and no money. My decision to go to Africa had confounded my grandmother. Why on earth would I want to spend Christmas chasing a bunch of dirty, overgrown monkeys around a volcano in a country she had never heard of? Dutifully, I had driven to Indiana in early December so the family could shower me with gifts in a semiprivate hospital room, where my grandfather was recovering from prostate surgery. Unlike Africa, Amsterdam would be cold and Christmassy. I was looking forward to a merry three days celebrating the secular aspects of the season with my new friends, the hippies and the international cast of fellow travelers availing themselves of the cheap beds and vegetarian meals.

The man gestured toward the gnomes with his pipe stem. "If it's them you are waiting for, they left in February."

"Oh, uh, do you think they're coming back?" Like in an hour or two?

He chuckled and shook his head. The other boats had clean lace curtains. The names painted across their bows were well maintained, and although I don't speak Dutch, I doubt that any of them referenced Eastern religion. Several had circular plaques nailed to their doors, Scandinavian mandalas with recurring patterns of flowers, peasants and hearts. We had one on the back porch when I was growing up. My mother called it a hex. I was scared of it, ever since that Sunday when, reading the funny pages, I came across an episode of *The Phantom* in which, as best I could figure, a beautiful woman is discovered dead with a colorful circular design carved into her back. From then on, any time my parents lowered their voices on the back porch, I knew they were discussing the latest grisly hex murder. The ones on the houseboats were just as folksy and welcoming as the one in my childhood home, but I couldn't escape their sinister implications. Give me the long-tongued Hindu goddess Kali trampling a corpse in her necklace of skulls any day!

"If you are looking for a place to stay, my wife and I have a house-boat also," the man offered. "It is very reasonable, twenty-five guilders. This includes a big Dutch breakfast. My wife is a good cook." He puffed on his pipe, calmly awaiting my reply. I considered my options. Plan A had been to stay on the much-fantasized-about *Wu Wei*, practicing yoga, eating lentil stew, lounging with my hippie hosts on batik pillows, singing Christmas carols and passing around bottles of homemade berry wine. There was no Plan B.

The hostel where Nate and I had stayed a little more than a year earlier was nearby, but it was tainted with memory. When the junkies in the main square and the marijuana imagery in the cof-feehouses spooked Nate so badly that he curled like a steamed shrimp on the top bunk, refusing to leave our dorm room, I went exploring on my own. In a coffeehouse, I made friends with a middle-aged, off-duty doorman. He asked me if I liked tulip bulbs and wooden shoes. Politely, I answered in the affirmative.

Although my new friend was Pakistani, his pride outstripped a native's regarding the symbols of his adopted land. "I tell you what I am going to do! I am going to buy some wooden shoes for you, very high quality, with windmills painted on the toes. Also some for your friend. And tulip bulbs for you to take home and give to your mother. You will have nice souvenirs to remember your visit to Holland."

I thanked him uneasily. This tourist junk was expensive, especially on a doorman's salary. If I had met him on my home turf, I wouldn't have offered to treat him to a Chicago Blues T-shirt and a paperweight replica of the Sears Tower. On the other hand, Nate and I were on such a tight budget, the prospect of free souvenirs was alluring. The doorman told me that he had to take care of some business at the hotel where he worked but he would come by the hostel's lobby at seven o'clock to take Nate and me out for a fancy dinner. He asked for a goodbye kiss. I proffered my cheek. Pinning me between his plump thighs, he stuck his tongue down my throat. Prying him off me in what I hoped was a friendly but firm manner, I exclaimed, "No, no!" and "How about a hug?"

I found Nate huddled where I had left him, and told him all about my afternoon, leaving out the skin-crawling slobbery goodbye. "So, this guy wants to give us Dutch shoes and stuff just *because?*" He was skeptical, but enticed by the prospect of a good meal. "Did he say where he was taking us for dinner?"

"I don't know," I murmured, feeling ill. I had whored myself for the promise of wooden shoes. If I was that desperate for tourist kitsch, why not hold out for a T-shirt from the Bulldog, a slick coffeehouse chain featuring space cakes, Ziploc baggies of marijuana, and a marketing plan on par with the Hard Rock Cafe's? Did I plan to clump around Chicago like Hans Brinker? When other women traded their bodies for shoes, they had a good reason, like surviving another winter of forced labor on the frozen steppes. I was so gullible that a college friend once convinced me that an organ-grinder's monkey had spoken to him in English. Only now did I realize that the doorman had no intention of showing up. He'd gotten what he wanted, the bare minimum, but still, better than nothing.

The next day, Nate and I were on our way to blow most of our remaining cash on Anne Frank's secret annex when we passed a luxury hotel. There, in epaulets and a hat trimmed with gold braid, was my friend from the coffeehouse, opening and closing doors for a well-dressed crowd. I told myself that if Nate hadn't been there, I'd have marched right up and slapped him, shouting, "What happened to my *shoes*, Mr. Big Talk?" He was reaching for the handle of a Mercedes when he saw me. Immediately, we both dropped our eyes, scuttling to the safety of our respective roles, me a seedy backpacker without reserves or wits, him an immigrant dolled up in the unmistakable finery of the servant class.

That encounter hadn't soured me on Amsterdam, just the hostel, which wasn't much of a hostel anyway, not the kind where you linger over the breakfast table, the beneficiary of a Swiss youth group's chocolate. It was more like a holding pen where hollow-eyed strangers padlocked their backpacks to the rickety bunk beds before slinking away to pursue some solitary vice. I had nothing against vice if it was communal. For my three day layover, I'd been entertaining visions of the epicurean Christmas Eve party Dickens's Mr. Fezziwig throws for his employees with an Aquarian Age twist. Red cheeks, wineskins, libertine new friends, constant clamor, red-and-green hookahs trimmed in holly. Dang, I had been looking forward to that cozy, hippie houseboat, with its Bob Marley posters and its promiscuous striped cat.

I was cold. My backpack was too heavy. I followed the man from the pier across his neighbors' decks to the *Prudencia*. It too had a hex. Inside, it was as solid and respectable as a midwestern retiree's recreation vehicle. Brown plaid curtains hung at the windows. His-and-her easy chairs were stationed near the TV, a basket of knitting within easy reach of one. "This is where you eat breakfast," the man said, nodding at a chunky wooden table. A prim vase of silk flowers was centered on a doily. The flowers were apricot and Wedgwood blue. "Sausages, toast, eggs, bacon, porridge, butter, jam, coffee or tea, juice, cereal," the houseboat owner enumerated as he led me to the bow, where the guest rooms were located. "This was my son's room. Now, he is grown." I poked my head into a tiny cabin containing a bunk bed made up with flowered sheets. It bore no trace of its former occupant's personality. "This is the toilet," he announced frankly, stepping aside so I could inspect a room no bigger than an airplane's WC.

"All right," I said, handing him a sheaf of brilliantly colored money. The fifty-florin note had a bright yellow sunflower on it. My host asked if I would eat breakfast now. I told him that I would. His wife started ferrying jam pots, butter dishes, and small pitchers of cream and syrup from the kitchen. She was a vigorous if silent woman in her forties with sensibly short hair and a pretty apron tied over her T-shirt and khakis. Smiling modestly, she presented me with half a dozen bright red wieners, split lengthwise. Her husband followed hard on her heels with a toast rack. They were like the rotating figures on a Bavarian clock. When one disappeared behind the swinging doors that led to the kitchen, the other emerged bearing another heaping platter. The toast rack was not allowed to remain empty. The traditional Dutch breakfast is one hell of a bargain, but I doubt that the fit specimens pedaling around Amsterdam partake of this bacchanal more than once or twice a year, probably at Christmas when they go visit Great Aunt Thumbelina in her windmill. I stuffed myself methodically, as outside the window the sky lightened to pearl gray. Flurries tinked against the glass. I was in no rush to get going. When I started on the giant apple pancake that goes by the name "Dutch Baby" in Evanston, Illinois, my hosts finally took a break. Making pleasantries about the weather, they stationed themselves in their armchairs. I felt conspicuous and awkward, as though I were driving cross-country and an acquaintance had insisted, "Don't waste money on a motel room in Cleveland! You can stay with my parents!" I complimented the food repeatedly. I asked their names, but did not seek clarification of the answer. Art and Tal? Arn and Torl? Something like that. I volunteered my name. They nodded noncommittally. They asked what brought me to Amsterdam. I told them I was spending a couple of days on my way to Africa. "Africa!" they exclaimed, as expected. "Isn't that something?" The man said something to his wife in Dutch, cocking his head toward me. She made noises of agreement, her expression one of noninterfering maternal benediction. I shoveled in scrambled eggs, wondering if they were refraining from turning on the television because I was in the room.

"Well, that was delicious," I announced for the twentieth time, patting my overstuffed abdomen. "Guess I'll go wander around the city now, see what there is to see!"

The man raised a finger in warning. "Yes, there are many interesting things to do in Amsterdam. The Anne Frank house. The flower market. The Vondelpark is very nice. But, you must take care not to go to the red-light district. Do you know what this is?"

I shrugged. "I saw some of it the last time I was here."

"There are some very bad people there," he said emphatically. "Many young tourists do not know. They think, 'I will go just to look, for fun.' It is not fun. There is much crime. Drugs."

"Drugs," his wife echoed, her face grave.

"There are cafés where they are selling drugs one street over from where families are living with young children." My host's face darkened. "Just last month, my wife and I are having a young guest who went there and got into trouble. The police came. You must promise me that you will not go there. There is nothing there but bad people and drugs."

"Sure, sure," I swore, eager to get away from the squares. "It's not my thing at all."

"That is good that it is not your thing. It is a disgrace. Those of us who live in Amsterdam are ashamed that such a place exists in our city."

"Well, again, thank you for breakfast. It was really good."

I spent the next two days tromping in and out of museums, street markets, and sidewalk cafés decorated for the upcoming holiday with evergreen garlands and fake snow. I drank many cups of cocoa as a measure against the unrelenting cold. After the frenzied preparations for my trip, shopping for gear, getting vaccinated against tropical diseases and taking leave of my restaurant job, Art and Tal's son's old room felt like a cradle. So, Amsterdam wasn't shaping up to be the hootenanny I'd envisioned. Soon, I would be having a bang-up time in Africa. Until then, I would write in my journal, take photographs of bicycles parked alongside the freezing canals, and consume several thousand calories every morning at breakfast. On the day of my departure, I popped around to the Bulldog but imbibed nothing stronger than coffee. I didn't want to freak out and lose my sense of direction, forget the name of the houseboat, miss my plane. A Dutch soldier on the next stool mocked the American method of smoking joints in flawless English. He inhaled through pursed lips as if trying to suck a bowling ball through a straw. "They look so stupid," he pronounced, nonchalantly dragging on the biggest blunt I'd ever seen like it was a Virginia Slim.

Like Benedict Arnold, I betrayed my country and agreed that Dutch potsmokers accomplish the task with admirable sang-froid. I was glad I had an excuse to decline the puff he offered. If I didn't smoke, I wouldn't fail his test by bogarting and babbling like a dorky freshman. His barely cocked eyebrow communicated his opinion that only an American would be so infantile as to refrain from getting stoned just because she had a plane to catch. The Bulldog's warmth was more inviting than the chilly streets I'd meandered for three days, but the soldier's company was insupportable. I ducked back outside.

Five o'clock in the afternoon and it was already dark as midnight. I still had several hours to kill before leaving for the airport. A few blocks' wander took me to an area strung, as was most of Amsterdam, with Christmas lights. Here, though, the lights were a uniform red and women in cheap lingerie lounged behind plate glass windows. The windows were edged in red neon, as if one might mistake a teddy-clad occupant for a housewife buffing her nails in what Ellie Mae Clampett used to call her skimpies. These women were obviously for rent. They looked bored. As a waitress, I recognized the ennui of a slow shift. Some rowdy young males shoved each other along the sidewalk, joshing loudly. The women ignored them, sensing that they didn't mean business, at least not yet. A few older men scuttled along, their shoulders hunched, their eyes avid. I was the only woman on the outside of the glass. Bespectacled, makeup-free, my twenty-three-year-old curves hidden beneath a sleeping bag's worth of down, I was invisible. It made no difference that my coat was the color of a traffic cone; as long as I stuck to the background I was free to observe. I checked the women out obliquely, pretending to study the lurid bongs, two-headed dildos and *Fabulous Furry Freak Brothers* posters displayed in small shops adjoining the women's windows.

There was something heartwarming and un-American in that smorgasbord of female flesh. Rolls of fat, flat breasts, cellulite, birthmarks, scars, bad perms, and eccentric teeth had not been airbrushed out of this sexual display. Women of all skin colors and an age spread of at least thirty years presented themselves as if they were empirically desirable. The system seemed egalitarian in a way the junior prom had not, though it would have been *more* egalitarian if men were in the windows too, or at least in their underwear. Very few of the working girls seemed interested in a hard sell. They perched on stools, leafing through magazines or chatting if they shared a window. Those actively engaged in trolling for customers looked like they wanted to murder someone, baring their teeth and thrusting their crotches as if hoping to trigger hidden switchblades behind the zebra-print triangles of acetate. A few of the windows had curtains drawn across them to prevent potential customers and the odd female backpacker from getting a free show in the form of a transaction taking place on the other side of the glass.

Fascinated, I stooped to fumble with my bootlaces so I could observe one postcoital pair at my leisure. The woman stood in the doorway to her cubicle, a white cotton sheet wrapped toga-style around her naked body as she bid goodbye to her customer. The two appeared comfortable with each other, if not exactly intimate. It was the genial camaraderie of the hair stylist and the fellow who's been coming to her for a trim every three weeks for the last three years, the guy who tips well, never cancels at the zero hour, and shows just enough friendly interest in her life outside the salon to distinguish himself favorably from the rest of her clients.

I crisscrossed the narrow alleys, comparing the virtues available for hire, but I burned out after a few dozen windows. It was like going to a department store and trying on too many perfumes. Everyone seemed sullied by the lurid light: White teeth glowed purple. White bras and panties took on a tawdry sheen. I tried taking in the scene with a photographer's eye. I'm no great shakes with a camera, but I've leafed through enough coffee-table books to know what makes a good composition. The snow swirling past the street lamps was certainly atmospheric. The brightly lit, nearly nude bodies were a nice contrast to the shrouded figures in the street. On the outskirts of the district, I looked across a canal to a second-story window where a surprisingly glamorous girl with long hair lounged on a stool, intent on her nails. Just as intent were a group of fraternity boys, who stared up at her from beneath black umbrellas that they had opened as light snow turned to light sleet. The girl worked an ice maiden angle, refusing to glance down even once, but the large German shepherd at her feet followed the boys with unflagging interest. I wondered if the girl and her dog worked as a kinky team. Maybe he was her bodyguard. It seemed a safe bet that he helped her command top dollar in one way or another. They seemed frozen in that tableau, the clump of worshipful boys, the uncaring girl, and the attentive, smiling dog. If I were a real photographer, I would have had plenty of time to set up a tripod, screw on a high-powered lens, and make several exposures at the slowest setting. Alas, I had to content myself with a mental image. There was no way my borrowed point-and-shoot could do justice to a scene that far away.

Finally, my watch indicated that I could head back to the *Prudencia*, collect my stuff and leave for the airport. Renewed purpose put a spring in my step. I was on my way to Africa, man! Crazy. In less than a day, I would trade my parka for shorts and a T-shirt, the northern European snow giving way to the dust of East Africa. Wondering what Tanzania held in store made me sentimental about dear old Amsterdam with its flower markets, its big breakfasts and its legalized prostitution.

Ooh, there was a good shot, right there! If I had been looking the other way, I'd have missed it. A couple of alleys opened into a broader boulevard, creating a small triangle of public space. Someone had erected a Christmas tree in a bucket and trimmed it entirely in red decorations and lights. Behind the harlot evergreen, a couple of girls were at their posts in their underwear. This seemed to be within reach of a beginning photographer armed with a thirty-five-millimeter autofocus Pentax. I resolved to be sly. Heaven forbid I be mistaken for a goggle-eyed innocent abroad, unabashedly shutterbugging, too big of a bumpkin to notice the sophisticated citizens snickering openly. If only I had a real camera! I didn't know my ass from an f-stop, but with serious equipment I might be mistaken for a photojournalist. How's that for a swinging assignment? Our spunky twenty-three-year-old freelancer gets the scoop on the red-light district for *National Geographic*. Next up: the Dark Continent and a drink at the international press club, where she catches the eye of a dashing, semialcoholic correspondent played by Mel Gibson.

I had to remind myself to feel grateful for the camera I had with me. A well-funded college friend, seeing the dime store piece of jay I was intending to pack had insisted on loaning me his tiny Pentax for my trip. Stealthily, I stuck my hand in my pocket to unwrap the cotton hankie that I felt offered adequate protection for the delicate lens. Pretending to be deep in thought, I sauntered around the perimeter of the triangle, until the ideal vantage point presented itself. I checked that no oncoming pedestrians would spoil my composition. Then, *bam!* I whipped out the Pentax, released the shutter and dropped it back in my pocket in one unbroken movement, cool as jazz, Daddy-o. The automatic flash had gone off in response to the late afternoon dark, but I doubted that would affect the photo adversely. A small white starburst reflected in one of the windows would be no big deal. Satisfied, I stepped off the curb.

Immediately, a small hand shot out and dragged me back by the hair. It felt rather like a bird of prey had landed on my head, convinced that I had stolen one of her eggs. I bent my knees as my attacker tugged downward.

"You cannot do that!" she shouted in a West Indian accent, a lilt that prior to this encounter connoted only reggae music, jerk chicken, and Northwestern ZBTs getting stoned. "That is not allowed! Don't ever do that!" She was livid, her face as tight as a fist. Her nostrils flared in abject fury. Her eyes prepared to bolt straight out of their sockets into my brain, dropping me like a pig on the slaughterhouse floor. Where had she come from? She was on me so quickly she might have materialized from thin air. Her hair was short and untended. She wore jeans, sneakers, and a thin, acrylic sweater machine-knit with snowflakes and reindeer. She seized my arm with the spring-loaded strength of a pit bull, shrieking, "Give me the film!"

Animals in my predicament have a fight-or-flight response. I instinctively chose a third route, casting myself in the role I had struggled so hard to avoid, that of the naïve hayseed who's blundered in where she doesn't belong. "I'm sorry! I didn't know!" I cried, raising my eyebrows in the winsome oops-I-didn't-mean-to Girl Scout smile that had gotten me off the hook on several prior occasions. I quickly gathered that techniques that work just fine on suspicious midwestern private-school teachers don't cut the mustard with apoplectic West Indian madams or off-duty hookers, whichever she was.

"Sorry mean nothing to me," she spat, shaking me with one arm as she grappled with my parka's various zippers and snaps. "Where is the camera? Give it to me!"

Oh no! If she got her hands on my friend's little Pentax, chances are she wouldn't give it back. She'd probably rip out the film and hurl it to the ground. My brain scrabbled off in several different directions. She was going to break the borrowed camera! I'd have no way to take pictures in Africa! She was going to take my film! If size counted, I'd have been able to shake her off like a bear dispatching a bothersome Yorkshire terrier. Even without the Michelin bulk of my parka, I had plenty of padding, having taken liberal advantage of the free-food-for-staff policy while waitressing at Dave's Italian Kitchen. I was at least half a foot taller, but she was steely where I was doughy, and much more experienced in the ways of the world. My adrenaline had the tang of real fear, hers of the terminally pissed-off pink-collar worker sick of dealing with clueless college girls. I'd seen it before, albeit in infinitely milder form, in my co-workers, the veteran waitresses at Dave's. As a child, I had managed to provoke a few spankings, but never before had my actions elicited this much fury. In my recent experience, people who were mad at me spent hours analyzing the shortcomings of our relationship. This little woman possessed the fighting prowess of a crazed ferret, a wild ferret, not the domesticated kind who travel in fanny packs worn by lumpy zealots whose T-shirts proclaim, "I'm a Ferret Fan!" I tried to seize her wrists, but she was way too fast for me. It was like fighting off bats. She squeezed my puffy coat at random, searching for the fist-sized lump nestled over my right hipbone. Frustrated at not finding anything, she tangled her fingers into my hair and yanked. Acutely aware of the dangers posed by my dangling earrings, I knew I'd better think fast. Too panic-stricken to cry, I put my heart and soul into pretending to cry. In this circumstance, a three-hour self-defense course would have served me better than a theater degree from the most expensive school in the Big Ten, but you use what you've got.

"Please, no," I begged. "I'm sorry! I didn't know! I won't do it again!" Looking back on the situation, I think I turned in a fairly credible performance as Terrified Midwestern Backpacker, probably because that's exactly what I was. I didn't really look the part of damsel in distress in my sturdy hiking boots and my giant clown-colored coat. If anyone could've used a white lace bra and matching panties in the red-light district that day, it was me. Maybe I've seen too many bad movies. In truth, I think there was no remorse, real or hammed-up, that would have worked on my pintsized attacker. She was remarkably focused in her intent to remain "on message."

"Give me the camera!" she screeched, bending me nearly double, steering me with my own hair. "Give the film to me!" She was near boiling point.

"No! No, it's, it's—" My mind raced. "It's got my high school graduation pictures on it!" Did I think this would garner her sympathy? Her family had probably sold her to a pimp at the age of fourteen, when they discovered her dallying with the neighbor boy in the banana grove! She was a wraith, bound to be bitter about anything that constituted my life of privilege.

"Give it to me! Give me the film! Give it to me! Give me the film!" The repetitive chant was a really bad sign. She was getting into a groove, like a prizefighter. She showed no signs of wearing down. She would keep it up until she got the camera or beat me to a pulp, whichever came second. I pictured myself lying broken and bloody on the sidewalk, my orthodontia smashed. Detained in a police station, no one to bail me out but Art and Tal, the owners of houseboat *Prudencia*. Unconscious in a hospital bed, robbed of all identifying documents! I was going to miss my plane to Africa!

A circle of onlookers had formed around us. They were all men. Their jaws slack and eyes glassy, they watched our struggle impassively. "Help!" I screamed. "Help me!" None of them moved. Their faces swam in and out of focus as the tiny West Indian shoved me in a rough dance, never letting go. It was worse than the short Humane Society film we had watched in second grade, which showed a cat's perspective as her owners scooped her up, swung her around and flung her onto the furniture. "Please," I pleaded. "Please!"

All of a sudden, another woman appeared, pulling at my attacker's elbow. Like the first, she was small-boned, with brown skin and an island accent. Her shoulder-length hair was adorned with a floppy, girlish bow. She had raced coatless into the cold, clad only in a black camisole and panties. Waves of mounting excitement emanated from the men. "Let her go," the woman with the bow urged. "She don't mean anything."

My hero! I was doggedly grateful for her selfless attempt to save me. In my mind, she was as incredible as the beautiful, straight-A senior who tells her fellow cheerleaders to stop harassing the chubby, pimpled boy they've nicknamed Boobie. What did she stand to profit from defending stupid me, a freeloading gawker? Nothing. She was probably getting herself in a lot of hot water just by leaving the window. She was like a goddess in our midst! "No! Not without the camera," the madam hissed, thumping my goose down.

"She didn't know," my hero cajoled. I nodded as emphatically as I could with those clawlike fingernails snarled in my hair. Yes, that was right, I was stoop-stoop-stupid! I would have eagerly put on a silly hat and done a little dance if it would have bought my way out of this mess. The one with the bow wrapped her arms around her body and shivered, a representative from a warm climate, affronted by the brutality of a northern European December. "Leave her. It's so cold."

Exasperated, my attacker turned and rapped out something in their mother tongue. The woman with the bow responded in soothing tones. My attacker loosened her grip to gesture angrily. I didn't need a translator to get the gist. *She took a photograph of us with a camera that she's stashed somewhere in that ridiculous goddamned coat! You think she should get off scot-free for that?*

I was shifting nervously from foot to foot, waiting for my sentence to be handed down when—*whooom!*—someone tackled me from behind. The force of the blow propelled me at least twenty feet before I could get a bead on what was happening. A tall man with brown hair had his arm slung tightly around my shoulders, hustling me up the sidewalk. I looked back. The two tiny women faced off, arguing in the silent ring of men. "Just walk away," the man muttered in an English accent. "Just keep walking."

"Thank you," I gasped, struggling to keep pace with his long legs. "Thank you so much. Thank you for helping me. I don't know what—"

"You really shouldn't photograph them," he admonished.

"I know," I said. I wondered if I'd dare tell him that it wasn't me. It was a case of mistaken identity. Some other idiot had snapped a picture and disappeared. I was an innocent bystander.

"They're not doing this for fun, you know. They're in it to make money." Abruptly, he dropped his arm. "Keep going," he said and disappeared down a small alley. I was disheartened to see him go. Shouldn't his daring rescue mean that we were bonded, at least for an hour or so? I could have made time for a cup of coffee and maybe even a space cake before I absolutely had to leave for the airport. I knew I was deserving of his contempt. He was the veteran fireman. I was the harebrain who insisted on darting back into the burning building to save her pet goldfish. I wouldn't want to have coffee with me either, especially if I'd come here for the sole purpose of procuring a reasonably priced blowjob after a long hard day as a foreign correspondent or a ticket agent at the local British Airways bureau. But still.

Alone and ashamed, I made my way back to the *Prudencia*, to reclaim my backpack from Art and Tal. My scalp tingled from the hair pulling, but there wasn't so much as a scratch on me that might tip them off. Their vehement warning to avoid the red-light district had struck me as so frumpy and unwarranted that first morning at breakfast. They were like my grandmother, disparaging punk rock and the shopping mall on the other side of town, things she feared but knew nothing about. For most visitors to Amsterdam, the red-light district offered nothing more dangerous than government-sanctioned sex for hire. Seedy though it may be, it's a bona fide tourist attraction even for those interested in looking only, bizarre primarily because it's such an open spectacle. No doubt it could become dangerous if you tried to skip out on payment for services rendered or sought unadvertised shady dealings involving piles of cocaine or cockfighting, but did I really impress Art and Tal as the type to stiff a hooker or gamble on bloodthirsty roosters? If only their counsel had been less general, something more along the lines of what my lanky British rescuer and, indeed, the tiny, livid West Indian had insisted: *You must never take photographs of the women sitting in the windows. It is simply not allowed.*

The borrowed camera rested in my pocket like a hand grenade, a reproachful reminder of my lack of experience abroad. I collected my pack, boarded the airport shuttle and tried to put the incident out of my mind. Only after I was aboard a KLM flight bound for Dar es Salaam, watching the lights of Amsterdam dwindle to tiny pinpoints, did it occur to me to wonder if my attacker's accent wasn't possibly *East African* instead.

Rwanda Photo Op

On The Road

The mosquito must have bitten me the first night. Lots of mosquitoes bit me that first night in Tanzania, but this one was special. This one had a snoutful of malaria, or some jungle crud that caused me to stagger across our campsite two weeks later like a lion-felled gazelle, erupting at both ends.

When I planned the trip, I was looking for any excuse to get away from Nate who'd become as irritating as a sinkful of dirty dishes. Attracted by an advertisement prominently featuring a baby gorilla, I signed on to travel through East Africa for two months with an adventure trucking company. It turns out that I needn't have spent thousands of dollars and traveled thousands of miles to be free of him. By the time I left Chicago, Nate was gone, squeezed out of the apartment we shared in Chicago's Boys Town by my crush on a fellow waiter, Isaac. The hefty deposit for the trip was nonrefundable, though, so I went. Unlike Karen Blixen, I had no desire to penetrate deepest Africa, but I am a member of the clean plate club. Having based my choice on little more than the sex appeal of a newborn ape, I had picked Tanzania, Rwanda, and Kenya from a wide menu of travel options. Now the time had come to get my money's worth by licking the platter clean.

The first night, I was full of hope. There were eighteen of us, from seven countries. We sat in a circle near the truck, introducing ourselves by name and nationality, sizing up potential tentmates. Later, one of the frat boys from Wisconsin told me that I'd had food all over my teeth.

Elsie, a stout, capable Swiss girl, asked to tent with me. I was delighted to reject her, having already hooked up with Deborah, who bore a passing resemblance to Ally Sheedy. Coming from kibbutz, she seemed to know what was what. I'd learned a thing or two Eurailing around with Nate. I had learned to sleep on the floor of a train station and to ante up for a private stall when shampooing your hair in a public washroom. Belatedly, I had figured out not to brag that you're starving to death when really you're gaining twenty pounds from eating nothing but bread. And I now knew not to take photographs of the hookers in Amsterdam. Even so, I feared I wouldn't know how to set up a tent. Deborah seemed like she'd be able to get the job done. Elsie did, too, but she was so formal. I wanted to share my tent with a booty-shaking funmaker. Experience had not yet taught me that the booty-shaking funmakers are inevitably Australian.

At bedtime, Deborah told me that she and Arnold had decided to splurge on a hotel room. Arnold, the last of our group to arrive, had swaggered in from Zimbabwe, full of himself in a tank top and Panama hat. He was prematurely balding, but he had eyes like a jungle cat. Arnold wanted a break from the bush and Deborah wanted a hot shower, so just for tonight they had rented a room at the hotel adjoining our campsite. They extended no invitation to join them. I stood around uncertainly. The rest of the group was busy unfolding tents and fitting metal legs into canvas cots. Elsie expertly whacked iron pegs through the rings of her fly sheet as her wan Canadian tentmate watched.

"Maybe I'll just sleep in the truck," I announced, stretching and scratching as if I, too, had been roughing it for the last few months. "Why deal with the hassle of setting up a tent?"

The truck had two long rows of dusty velour seats that looked more comfortable than any train station floor. In lieu of glass windows were sheets of plastic that could be untied and dropped down in case of rain. I correctly figured that the truck would be cooler than a two-man tent with a black fly sheet. I lay on top of my sleeping bag, telling myself that mosquitoes prefer the open air to semi-enclosed spaces.

The next day we rolled out, headed across the horrible pitted roads of Tanzania toward Rwanda. The civil war that resulted in the slaughter of hundreds of thousands was a couple of years away, and *Gorillas in the Mist* had just been released. Few Americans had heard of Rwanda. I hadn't either until I was leafing through the adventure trucking company's brochure. I hoped to become part of a crew, a wild, piratey lot, rumbling around Africa having adventures only dreamed of by our friends back home. I found out that everybody else on the truck signed up because they liked gorillas.

We had a few hours to kill in Dar es Salaam as we waited for the Rwandan embassy to issue our visas. I watched in awe as Elsie haggled for vegetables in the market. She looked prepared to shiv the guy who tried to charge her four dollars for a bushel of carrots. I wanted to seem tough, too, so I volunteered to join the black-market money-changing expedition. The black market turned out to be a Muslim housewife's spotless kitchen table.

Our first full day on the road was not unlike every other day in the weeks ahead, except that manners were still cordial, no one had malaria, and the storage containers under the velour bench seats had not yet begun to stink of decayed mango. The rutted dirt roads made for a bumpy, irritating ride with lots of red dust flying in the windows. We passed settlements of small thatched huts, but did not stop. When it was time to make a pit stop, we pulled over so the men could pee on the side of the truck and the women could walk far across the savannah in search of a modesty bush. Our taciturn English driver confirmed the horrifying rumor about another group traveling with the same adventure trucking company: While stopped on the shoulder of a narrow mountain road so that the men could pee, the dirt under the wheels gave way and the truck rolled over, squashing them all. There was one death for every year the company had been in business, he told us, including a mass execution and one decapitation by hippo.

Lunch was a constant drag: white bread sent over from England, along with dehydrated curry and some stale Weetabix. And Blue Boy margarine, which was murder on a butter snob like me. It tasted like petroleum, but I loved the bright blue can with its wide-mouthed schoolboy rendered in mid-chomp. (I am still kicking myself for passing up a small ladle made from a can of Blue Boy—an actual household implement for sale in a hardscrabble, middle-of-nowhere market. I was so green that I bypassed that truly worthy souvenir, amassing instead countless Masai necklaces, thumb pianos, and salad forks carved to resemble giraffes, none of which have Blue Boy's Proustian ability to recall my Africa.) We had bananas. The Australians on the trip had jars of Vegemite, an oily black substance they claimed was their national peanut butter. Basically, we had shit, and we fought over who had to prepare it and who had to pack it away.

Every time we stopped for lunch, a crowd of locals gathered. They stood at a slight distance, watchful as we choked down the unappetizing grub. The villagers who came closest were the children, and they were never shy. My long hair went over particularly well with the little girls, most of whose heads were shaved for lice prevention. They handled my locks like antique silk and admired the very stinky pink T-shirt I'd been wearing all week.

My hair was nothing compared to Pete's Polaroid camera. He was smart to bring it. Pete was just smart in general. A research scientist for Miller Brewing Company, he confided that they'd had the formula for dry beer for four years before unleashing it on the public. They could have started selling it right away, but they waited until the zeitgeist was ready for dry beer. No wonder he'd thought to bring a Polaroid camera. What overjoyed astonishment when he handed a small gaggle of children their photograph and gestured for them to keep it! These children had never seen themselves in a photograph. They lived alongside a red clay canyon too remote to attract busloads of day-trippers on photo safaris. Unlike their Masai countrymen, they had no exotic necklaces or stretched earlobes or ceremonial face paint. They wore rags approximately the color of the canyon. No one was going to seek them out anytime soon, and here was Pete, passing out Polaroids as if Polaroid film grew on trees. For those kids, we were about as exotic as it gets. I hope they're still alive. I hope that all of the children in my photographs are alive.

Rwanda came as a great relief. For one thing, it had paved roads. Our driver explained that this was because the Rwandan government used foreign aid for its intended purposes, whereas the Tanzanian government used it to throw lavish parties. Rwanda was green and hilly. Elsie confirmed that it looked something like Switzerland. After the dusty brown monotony of Tanzania, photogenic Rwanda's tightly packed vegetable gardens seemed the very model of Swiss wholesomeness and industry. It even had sweater weather in the evenings. The land was farmed in terraces, and the cash crop—pyrethrum, a common ingredient in most insecticides—smelled like pot. In the early morning, we passed women in bright headscarves with babies slung across their backs, harvesting the daisy-shaped pyrethrum in misty fields reeking of doobie. I imagined myself capable of painting this pastoral scene and told the others I would render it in oils. I jabbered about stretching canvas and gallery openings as if I knew what I was talking about.

We spent Christmas Eve in an Episcopal church in Kigali. The church had a washtub and enough hot water for all of us to bathe, as long as we went two by two. I had my bath with Agnes, a prim-looking Canadian who shouted, "Whoo, time to wash the old snatcheroo!" Her high spirits set the tone for the holiday. Cleaner than we'd been in weeks, we hit the market, where I scored a handful of "hash" from a nervous man in a madras shirt. We bought a plastic bag of popcorn as a Christmas gift for Bradford, the frat boy, who had stayed behind, running a fever. We bought rake-shaped bamboo combs and bananas to give to each other. We used paper money printed with gorillas to buy postage stamps printed with gorillas. I stepped on an eyeball in the meat section. It was a wild hedonistic spending spree. Whacking each other with giant banana leaves, we marched back uphill with our purchases. We burst into the church's Spartan dormitory shouting "Ho! Ho! Ho!" and shaking the bag of corn in our fevered friend's face.

"Jesus Christ, what the fuck is that?" he screamed, scuttling to one end of his bunk.

"Popcorn," we crowed, pleased with our own magnanimity and resourcefulness. By this point, food had assumed totemic status on the truck, and we were well versed in who would order what, should a genie appear in this culinary wasteland. Our frat boy's first choice was a twice-baked potato. Given the circumstances, we figured popcorn was almost the same thing.

"No, I mean what the fuck is *that*," he groaned, pointing to a black exoskeleton disappearing between the kernels. We held the bag up to the bare bulb. Dozens of hard-bodied bugs were marching purposefully in the corn.

That evening, after the little bald girls who'd been invited in to admire my hair finally dispersed, the Old Snatcheroo and I broke out the hashish. We invited Elsie to join us, and to my surprise, she immediately rolled a cigar-sized joint with typical Swiss precision. Before we could light up, the rector of the church poked his head in the door, determined to pad his Christmas Eve service with as many cleaned-up travelers as he could hunt down. Episcopal Mass proved no more exciting in Africa than in Indianapolis, Indiana, where I was once awarded a lime-green polyester prayer pillow for being the child with the best command of Bible verse.

The next day we drove up a volcano to the Mountain Gorilla Project. By this time, I was tenting with Madge, a forty-year-old Australian nurse. She'd noticed my solo fumbling at each new campsite and delicately suggested that we'd both save time if we threw in together. So Madge set up our tent by herself while I rushed to the equipment box to score us as many of the dwindling cot legs as I could. She was a classic good egg. Efficient and cheerful, Madge never complained about the silent, toxic farting I unleashed in our tent every night. My bowels grew more rebellious with every passing day, but childhood conditioning is a stern master. Rather than ask Madge, a nurse, if she cared to speculate on the medical nature of my agonized intestines, I remained ashamed and silent. After all, the one who smelt it dealt it. One night it got so bad, I burst out of the tent and planted a caramel-colored loam behind the frat boys' tent pitched next door. There was no way I could make it to the campsite's toilets a quarter-mile down the road, especially in the dark. When the frat boys put up an understandable squall early the next morning, I held my tongue. They quickly blamed Deborah and Arnold, who were roundly despised for making camp as far from the rest of us as possible.

We spent nearly a week at the base of the volcanoes where the Mountain Gorilla Project was headquartered. I enjoyed the respite from the daily grind of making and breaking camp. I hung around the fire for hours, writing postcards to Isaac, reading *One Hundred Years of Solitude,* and chewing the fat with anybody who happened to draw up one of the mildewed campstools.

We were taken to see the gorillas in shifts. They were awesome, well deserving of the A-ticket status. They behaved just as they did in *Gorillas in the Mist,* so I tried to act like Sigourney Weaver—an attempt spoiled by a wealthy American tourist who would not stop talking about California real estate. Actually, as cool as the gorillas were, I preferred the bamboo along the walk to the gorilla nesting area. To me, reared among maple and oak, bamboo was more exotic than the great apes I'd been primed to see.

Things really went to hell back in Tanzania. Bradford had never fully recovered, and now the other frat boy fell ill, too, both of them shivering under the African sun even when they pulled on all the gear they'd brought to climb Kilimanjaro. Bradford started hallucinating under the jacked-up truck as our driver struggled to jury-rig it for the third time that day. This slapstick routine was sheer delight to the gaggle of children watching every move. It seemed possible that Bradford might die while the rest of us perished of boredom waiting for a mechanical miracle. I pretended to be Sigourney Weaver tending a sick gorilla.

With the truck finally fixed, we rolled on, down to rotting

mangoes, Cremora, and some dehydrated curry. When Deborah and Arnold dumped an inedible amount of Tabasco into the communal curry pot on their turn to cook, it almost came to blows. As we passed great herds of gazelle and zebras, I barely glanced up from my book. My friend, the Old Snatcheroo, was eager to swap for *Interview with a Vampire*, which she'd found wedged under a seat. It was only missing the first forty pages or so.

The only break in the monotony came courtesy of my intestines. Whenever the driver successfully got the truck going, he was loath to stop it for any reason, even a bathroom break. Clenching every muscle in my body against the impulses of my ravaged bowels gave me something important to do. My thoughts were evenly divided between Isaac and the clean porcelain toilet bowls of my youth. How I longed to rest my cheeks against their alabaster coolness!

The road seemed to stretch on forever.

We heard the chosen ones before we saw them. With "Born to Be Wild" blasting from big speakers, they exploded from a cloud of dust, tan as hell. Most of them lounged on the roof of their truck, cloth wrapped around their heads like guerilla commandoes. The same company owned our trucks, but they'd been traveling on theirs for almost a year, driving through Europe and the Middle East before hooking down into East Africa. I could see they were a lean, groovy unit. These campers didn't wander off to photograph the sunset or fight over cot legs when they stopped for the night. They didn't throw their forks in the bushes to avoid washing them. They loved each other; they finished each other's sentences and sprang about like monkeys. One of the group had died a few months back, but otherwise the trip was great! Endless summer, mate. If they considered us flabby wieners, irritable and weak, they didn't show it. We socialized for fifteen minutes, while the drivers gossiped and exchanged crucial driver-type information, and then they bombed away, like the commandoes they were. That was the trip I thought I was signing up for. My wild, piratey lot. We lumbered away in the opposite direction, soiled and surly, past endless, identical lines of wildebeest.

Finally, the incubation period was over and I got sick, too. The mosquito that nipped me on that first night got me good. At last, a justification for my terrible bowels, even if it did come with a high fever and vomiting. On New Year's Eve, our driver left the rest of the group squabbling around a fire that wouldn't catch, and drove me and the frat boys to a fancy hotel on the edge of a game preserve. Leaving us sprawled on the seats, he told the desk clerk he had three "very sick people" in his truck. The clerk took one look at his filthy shorts and his tire-tread sandals and told him there was no doctor on staff. Bless the English-speaking maid who overheard the conversation and fetched the doctor before the truck could turn around in the driveway. She held a flashlight while the doctor examined us. "Malaria," he pronounced.

In my fog I was half-happy to hear it. What an exotic souvenir to take back to the States, far more interesting than a bamboo comb. Then the doctor produced an enormous hypodermic full of procaine penicillin and asked us to lower our pants. Bradford went first. "It feels like somebody's shooting peanut butter into my ass!" he howled. I blacked out.

I woke in relatively posh quarters. Madge had sprung for a hotel room with two twin beds. The frat boys occupied a room on one side of us; Arnold and Deborah were on the other. The walls were so thick I couldn't even hear their coupling, if they were still coupling. They seemed to like each other only slightly better than we liked them. Several group members availed themselves of the hotel's helipad to buy their way out of this mess. The others camped on the grounds. In the mornings, they ventured into the preserve on the truck, returning to the cocktail lounge at night. The frat boys and I slept, the hotel's clean sheets and firm mattresses a pleasant hallucination.

Madge made me take three tablets of Fanzidar to carpet bomb the malaria. A doctor back in Chicago had prescribed them for me, along with chloraquine, but he warned me not to take them unless I was dying because they caused blindness and kidney failure. When I protested to Madge, she scoffed, "That's why you Americans are the only ones getting sick. That chloraquine they gave you is worthless. These mosquitoes are old hands. Chloraquine means nothing to them. I take my Fanzidar every day, and I'm a nurse!"

I swallowed the Fanzidar and wrote Isaac a postcard saying that I had malaria and I'd taken a dangerous drug but not to worry—I was sharing my tent with an Australian nurse.

In the morning the frat boys and I felt well enough to venture into the hotel dining room, a baboon stole our toast rack. That big old monkey bounded through the huge glass doors and snatched it off the table before anyone could get a slice. I remember him far better than any gorilla. We'd waited forty-five minutes for that toast.

There were no tearful goodbyes. When "good" people like Madge or the Old Snatcheroo left, I made pleasant noise about staying in touch. When Deborah and Arnold took their leave, I made myself scarce. Elsie and I met a yacht captain in the bar, and he invited us to join his crew. She would be the scuba instructor. I would be the cook. I went home, like an idiot, because I had a boyfriend. Elsie, sensible, stolid Elsie, sailed to the Seychelles on a yacht. For a year, I received postcards extolling the islands' indescribable beauty and describing her swims alongside whales and shark. I slipped Elsie's postcards in the back of my African photo album. Elsie's adventures sounded genuinely exotic, not to mention glamorous. I can't imagine she had to fight it out for cot legs on a yacht. Still, there's something about my blurry, faded photos that makes the mundane, uncomfortable details of our unexceptional trip seem kind of fun, in their own way. The monochromatic expanses of Tanzania look more interesting in the background of shots starring my fellow travelers and me than they did in person. Reliving a Kodak moment of Madge muscling our tent poles into position, it sounds kind of fun, camping outdoors, cooking our communal meals over an open fire, buying mangoes and bananas in bulk in little flyblown markets. When I look at that group photo from one of our last nights together, all of us perched on the roof of our orange and blue truck, I can almost convince myself we had a pretty good time, even if I have to strain to come up with the names that go with some of those faces. I remember how Deborah and Arnold had refused to pose for that photograph and how the rest of us had laughed, feeling united in our hatred of them and their hatred of us. That wasn't so bad. I wonder what Deborah thinks when she looks at her pictures of Arnold. Surely they aren't still in touch.

I have pictures of people carrying things on their heads, and of raggedy children, clumped together in fascination. I have pictures of a skinny bendable Santa wrapped around a bottle of Johnnie Walker Black Label from our post-Mass celebration in Kigali. I have pictures of distant wildebeest and one real standout, a lucky shot of a silverback gorilla roaring, his fangs glinting in a wide-open mouth. If I didn't know better, I'd say he was yawning.

On Etiquette

Onscreen, a tailored Asian gentleman ran through safety procedures in a voice of pure buttercream. If your safety vest fails to inflate when its cord is pulled, he discreetly informed us, simply place your lips on the tube and blow. I peeled the complimentary hot towel off my face for a peek. The camera cut to a beautiful woman wearing the official Singapore Airlines' flight attendant's uniform, a long, figure-flattering batik dress. Following Mr. Buttercream's order, she applied her heavily glossed lips to the inflation tube and . . . well, fellated it, basically. Isaac and I pounded our armrests with approval, tears streaming down our cheeks. If Singapore was anything like Singapore Airlines, we were in for one hell of a trip.

Twenty-two hours later, we landed. At one in the morning, the ultramodern Changi Airport was even deader than anticipated. The buses to the city wouldn't resume service until six-thirty. "No problem," I told Isaac. "We'll just crash on a bench for a few hours." The reticence that had seemed so sexy when we were Platonic co-workers kicked in, as I'd feared. Bumping along those rutted Tanzanian roads with my peevish truck-fellows, I'd daydreamed about how wonderful it would be to travel with him, just the two of us, intrepid, romantic, our bowels unbothered by their expatriation. Now, right off the bat, Isaac balked at sleeping in a public place. He crossed his thin arms, raising one eyebrow obstinately, the way he had when I told him there was no way he could bring his guitar. Was this what backpacking around Southeast Asia was going to be like? "Come on, it's no big deal," I insisted, tugging him up the escalator to a food court that had shuttered its operations for the night, though the padded banquettes were still accessible. Compared to some of the places Nate and I had slept in Europe, the corner table we selected seemed like pretty plush digs. It would have been nice if Isaac could have showed some appreciation by lying down, but he remained upright, looking around nervously as he listened to his Walkman. "You're going to be sorry when jet lag clobbers you later today," I murmured into the spotless upholstery. "You should take this opportunity to reset your body clock to our new time zone."

"I'm not sleepy," he prickled. I didn't feel tired either, but in my role as the veteran traveler, felt it imperative to practice conventional backpacker's wisdom. Scrunching my eyes against the fluorescent lights, I endeavored to lose consciousness, an impossible assignment, given the hypothermia-inducing air conditioning. Rifling through my pack for a sweatshirt, I consoled myself that the Chinese hotel I had read about in Lonely Planet's *South-East Asia on a Shoestring* would not have air conditioning. We would head there as soon as the buses started running.

Isaac went to the men's room and returned with a local couple. They looked to be about our age, Asian, neatly dressed in conservative clothes. The man, Pete, was wild to drive us to our hotel. After all the touts who swarmed around the truck in East Africa, the oft repeated anecdotes of Mickeys slipped in Eurailer's drinks and the wooden shoe incident in Amsterdam, I wanted to know what his angle was. Was he a gypsy cab driver, a hustler in search of a hotel commission, or a villain who slaughtered backpackers like fatted calves? If the latter, his girlfriend provided him with an ingenious cover. Demure and nearly mute, she fiddled with the dainty gold cross at her throat, as bland as a Nilla wafer. If they'd been dreadlocked guitar players in Bob Marley T-shirts, I'd have leapt at Pete's offer, understanding how our company would seem desirable and rare in a place so fastidious that there were laws against public gum chewing. What these goody-goodies stood to gain was beyond me. Maybe they were proselytizing missionaries! That would explain why they were hanging around the airport at three in the morning. Boy, wouldn't Isaac just love it when his new pals started in on the Jesus talk, driving us in circles in a fervent attempt to coax him away from Judaism. It was odd to see him converse so willingly with strangers, particularly a man who'd introduced himself at the urinal. Maybe traveling was bringing out his sociable side. My misgivings not laid entirely to rest, I acquiesced to the free ride, displeased that Isaac seemed so much more open to the experience than I was. When I gave Pete the address of the hotel, he said he'd never heard of it, though he knew the area around Bencoolen Street. Zipping along in his tidy compact sedan, he supplied civic commentary as the boondocks flanking the expressway gave way to city streets. He pointed out the foreign embassies, and which international corporations had offices in which gleaming modern buildings. He taught us how to say "Happy New Year" in Chinese. That's why he was so intent on giving us a lift: to start the Year of the Horse making merit by selflessly aiding strangers.

The sky was lightening as we pulled up before a two-story, yellow stucco building. The painted sign hanging over the latticed double doors read Tai Loke Hotel. I sucked in my breath. It was even better than I had pictured it, with wooden shutters painted aqua and a potted flowering tree set beside the tall, arched entrance. Raised on the cookie-cutter dependability of Holiday Inns, I now craved the decrepit and funky. The Tai Loke looked like something out of Tennessee Williams. A place as moist and seedy as this would spawn intrigue like mildew. "Singapore," I whispered, in a voice informed by repeated viewings of *Casablanca*. Pete escorted us as we went to check in, but the lights were out in the big, unadorned lobby. We stood around on the checkerboard linoleum, wondering if we should tap on one of the many doors lining the room on either side. There was a battered wooden schoolteacher's desk set at the far end, with a telephone and a ledger, but no bell to summon the concierge. Pete, looking skeptical, went to investigate. "This is amazing," I whispered, squeezing Isaac's hand in excitement. Pete returned with an elderly Chinese man, very grumpy at being roused by prospective guests. I bowed politely. Unmoved, he scratched the potbelly protruding under his stretched-out sleeveless undershirt. Pulling an old-fashioned iron key from a desk drawer, he scuffed across the linoleum and unceremoniously unlocked one of the doors. The furnishings were Spartan—a solid double bed, a wooden ceiling fan, a chair and a huge barred window—though there was plenty of room for more. Three feet shy of the lofty ceiling, the walls stopped and the same wooden latticework that formed the heavy outside doors took over. Perfect.

Pete stood in the center of the room, shaking his head. "I think this is a crummy hotel," he frowned. "Why not stay at the Strand with air conditioning and TV?" No, we insisted, air conditioning and

TV were exactly the kinds of things we were trying to get away from. He continued to lobby for more suitable lodgings as we returned to the car for our backpacks. We bid goodbye to his girlfriend, who had remained in the front seat clutching her pocketbook while the rest of us inspected the hotel. Shaking Pete's hand, I felt chagrinned that I'd been so suspicious of his intentions. "You guys should come by before we go on to Malaysia. We can go out to dinner together!"

"Oh, yes, maybe," Pete replied vaguely, putting on his sunglasses as he slipped behind the wheel. "I hope you have a pleasant stay in Singapore, but I do not think you will like this hotel so much."

How little he knew me. I had no use for his precious Strand, with its sanitized drinking glasses and private bathrooms! We thanked him again for the ride. *"Gung hay fat choy,"* I said, haltingly wishing him a Happy New Year, using an approximation of the words he had taught us.

The old man had shuffled out to the front of the hotel, his flip-flops announcing his whereabouts as effectively as a bell on a cat's collar. Ignoring the pleasantries we attempted on our way back to the room, he dislodged what sounded like a prodigious hairball from the back of his throat, hacking it into the potted tree. Quietly, because of the lattice, we consummated our arrival on foreign soil then, too discombobulated to sleep, lounged around reading *Rolling Stone* and a supermarket tabloid with a cover story on Roseanne Barr's wedding. "Do you think you should call that friend of your mother?" Isaac asked, naming a man who had held a high-ranking political office in Indiana before his current gig as U.S. Ambassador to Singapore.

My mother wasn't at all tight with the ambassador, though she had met him on a couple of occasions, mostly professional. Someone

Mom knew was good friends with him and his wife, though, and when this woman heard that Singapore was part of our itinerary, she had insisted on passing along the phone number to the ambassador's residence. "Oh, Bippy would be delighted to hear from Ayun," she assured my mother, perhaps thinking that the ambassador was one of the many Hoosier muckety-mucks with whom my class had posed for group photos on visits to the state capitol building and my eighth-grade trip to Washington, D.C. He was supposed to be an affable guy, though I reminded myself that people said the same about his fellow party member, Ronald Reagan. His wife, Bippy, was well known in Indianapolis, mostly for the sort of unconfirmed rumors that could get someone in a lot of trouble if she repeated them in a book. Isaac laughed as I regaled him with some of the wilder ones, saying that he hoped her husband tipped those service industry workers well for keeping mum about her mania.

"Everybody knows," I told him. "It's an open secret."

"She sounds like a lunatic. Are you sure you want to get together with them?"

"She is a lunatic, but word is she's pretty fun, too. You know, sort of a live wire, doesn't give a damn what anybody thinks." I was picturing Zelda Fitzgerald in Barbara Bush's inaugural outfit. "Anyway, they're expecting me to call. I think I'd rather wait until tomorrow, though, so we won't be all jet-laggy when we meet them."

After cleaning ourselves up with a spray hose and pans of water in the hotel's only bathroom, we set out to explore the city. In a hawkers' center on Albert Street, we sampled Singapore noodles, star-fruit juice, and a spicy carrot pancake that was delicious, despite looking like the joke vomit advertised in the back of comic books. The stall ladies got a big bang out of it when, trying to be helpful, I returned our empty dishes. They showed me that each stall had its own signature color, for bowls, cups, everything, even the plastic chopsticks. A couple of men zoomed around, bussing the tables as soon as they were abandoned, repatriating dirty dishes segregated by color.

Back in the street, we walked for hours, less mindful of avoiding blisters than amassing postcard-worthy descriptions. We removed our shoes to investigate Buddhist and Hindu temples and a gold-domed mosque where we were herded to the balcony to observe the men genuflecting below while, nearer to us, white-swathed women prayed behind a screen. We were pissed off to discover the famous Raffles Hotel completely boarded up for a two-year, head-to-toe restoration, which meant no high tea on the lawn or Singapore Slings, whatever those were. Lonely Planet had insisted that the Raffles was an imperialist treat not to be missed, and no doubt that's why the hotel had closed, to get rid of the hoards of inappropriately attired, thrill-seeking backpackers colonizing their lawn furniture. Undeterred by a torrential rainstorm, we plodded along the quay to Chinatown, where we admired red decorations set up for the Year of the Horse, and plumbed narrow alleys that made the rest of the city's spacious layout seem uninteresting. When jet lag hit like an anvil, we stumbled back to the hotel, getting lost several dozen times before finally collapsing at four o'clock in the afternoon. Good thing we'd held off on calling Bippy and the ambassador. Nodding off as the butler served tiny cups of palate-cleansing sherbet would have been a faux pas indeed.

The next day, after procuring moleskin, Band-Aids and headphones to replace the ones Isaac had snapped when he should have been sleeping on an airport banquette, we braved one of the boxy yellow pay phones in Serangoon Road's Little India. The ambassador answered. I fought the temptation to assert my liberal adulthood by using his first name, addressing him instead by his former title. "Oh yes," he replied, pleasantly. "Bippy's been expecting your call. Now I'll tell you what, we've got dinner plans this evening, but I'm sure she'd love to have you and your friend over for cocktails before that. We've got to clear it with her first though, because you know, she's the boss." I laughed politely, familiar with the style of jest favored by my elder tribesmen. "She's out shopping now, but why don't you give me the number where you're staying so she can call you back to confirm."

"Oh," I said, gesturing to Isaac to drop another coin in the slot. "I don't have the number with me, but maybe you could look it up in the phone book." The ambassador assured me that this would be no problem, so I spelled Tai Loke. He wasn't familiar with it. Most of the folks he knew who came to Singapore stayed at the Strand. How was the Tai Loke, anyway? Were they taking good care of us there? "Oh, yeah, we love it. It's really neat. Hey, listen, I'd better give you our room number, too, because I've noticed there are a lot of different people who answer the phone so she might get somebody who wouldn't know us by name."

"All right, Ayun, just a moment." He grunted like a lumberjack, picking up his pencil. It occurred to me that taking down phone messages was a novelty for him. He had a secretary, of course, along with the uniformed housekeeping staff I'd been imagining. I gave him the number. "Well, that's just super, Ayun, thanks for calling. Bippy's going to be thrilled." I hung up.

"What's the story, Annie-baby?" Isaac asked.

"They invited us over for drinks."

"What time?"

"Don't know. Bippy's going to leave a message at the hotel. I'd reckon cocktail hour is about five or so. He said they were expected somewhere for dinner." We poked around Little India some more, went to a restaurant that served vegetarian curries on banana leaves, watched a shirtless fortuneteller on Arab Street, bought stamps, gawked at caged pythons outside a temple, took refuge from the rain in a bird market, and cracked ourselves up with a bag of rambutan, plucking all but two of the fuzzy red fruit from a two-pronged branch, which we dangled in front of Isaac's khakis at testicle level.

Back at the hotel in midafternoon, I asked the old man if there were any messages. He blinked behind lenses as thick and greasy as Canadian bacon. "Did my friend call?" I asked, pointing to the black rotary phone on top of the desk. Still nothing. "American Ambassador?" I pointed to myself. "Ayun Halliday. Telephone. Paper. Pencil. You write." Despite supplemental mimed visuals, nothing struck a chord. A marginally younger fellow was summoned from the cement courtyard out back where the dozen or so men who sporadically worked the desk congregated, squatting, to spit and gamble. After I repeated my patter, the two conferred in Mandarin. The one with the glasses fished out a stubby pencil, scrawled a figure, and spun the pad around to face me.

"Okay, you call," the younger one explained. "This much call America."

"No, uh, I want to know if anyone called for *me*. Did an American lady call today?"

"Okay, today, you can call." He picked up the receiver, waiting for me to supply the number.

"No, uh, can you ask if anyone took a message for me, for Ayun, for room two?"

"Room two," he agreed.

"So you do have a message for room two? Hey, Isaac, can you check if maybe someone slipped a message under the door?" The men waited stoically for Isaac to fetch some object that might shed light on the thus far baffling line of questioning.

"Nothing there, Annie-baby."

Shit. "Uh, paper? Write message?" I tried again, not holding out much hope as I scribbled on my palm. The man with the glasses immediately obliged, holding out his pencil and pad. "Man, if only there were a way to draw a picture of someone taking a message so they'd get it. You got any ideas, Isaac?"

Isaac looked at the ceiling as he blew his long bangs out of his eyes. "I think it's time to concede defeat."

"Yeah, okay. Besides, maybe she hasn't called yet. You want to rest up for a few hours and maybe she'll call?"

"Why don't you use their phone to call her?"

I looked at the two old men, standing there in their stained, baggy undershirts. Overloaded with information in an unfamiliar language, they remained as impassive as river stones. For all I knew, this was their version of freaking out. "No, the ambassador said she'd call us. Maybe he meant she'd call us if it was convenient for us to come for a visit tonight."

The idea of calling to see why Bippy hadn't called brought out the shy only child in me, especially since it would involve further interaction with the old men. Though I struggled to suppress the memory, I couldn't help thinking of an embarrassing screw-up from my trip with Nate. An old friend of my father had mentioned in a letter that we would be welcome to visit him at his home in the English countryside, an hour from London by train. Worrying that the vagueness of the invitation meant it was not to be taken literally, I forced myself to call Tom shortly before the end of the Edinburgh festival. He seemed enthusiastic to hear from me, though as I recalled from our only meeting eight years earlier, he was generally bluff, as cheerful as the son my age was sullen. Yes, yes, we should come by all means, he insisted. Trains ran every hour from London, and he would expect us a few days hence on the one that arrived at six o'clock. He would invite some friends over for a little dinner party and take the next day off work to give us a tour of the surrounding area. He hoped we would stay on for a few days, before returning to London to activate our Eurail passes. It sounded great, until we arrived at the station, a half-hour before the agreed-upon train was due to depart. Two round-trip tickets would set us back nearly a hundred dollars, an amount that according to my calculations was expected to last us four days if not five. I was aghast. Accustomed to traveling far and wide on Chicago's extensive subway system, I had assumed the fare would be no more than a few pounds. Fighting back tears of shame, I rang Tom's house to say we wouldn't be coming after all. I left a message with one of the dinner guests since Tom had already left for the station. He seemed sympathetic, but confused, and kept asking if we were in any trouble. It was humiliating, though fortunately, our would-be host regarded the fuckup with his customary good spirits, ribbing my father about my bleached-bones budget. The incident held enormous appeal for Daddy, who likes to repeat amusing anecdotes of my thriftiness and cockamamie reasoning the way other proud parents display their children's athletic trophies.

What time was it in Chicago? Suddenly, all I had energy for was lying prone under the ceiling fan, exhausted from my failed charades and the shameful memory of the time I failed to materialize at Tom

Boyd's country house. I didn't want to jump through hoops to call Bippy. It would have been different if she were an old family friend, but I'd never met the woman. Ugh, I just wanted to sleep through until morning. Why had I committed us to a situation where we'd have to dress up and make small talk with senior citizens, who given their political affiliations were probably pro-life, anti-welfare and opposed to taxpayers' dollars funding foul-mouthed, chocolate-smeared performance artists. If Bippy really did call the shots, she was probably none too pleased about her husband inviting the rabble over on the spur of the moment. Maybe she was pretending she hadn't gotten the message, to save herself the embarrassment of uninviting us. It was probably a blessing in disguise that she hadn't called. I lay crosswise on our bed, read three words about Roseanne's new hubby, and slipped from consciousness.

When I came to, Isaac was dead to the world, a half-finished postcard to his sister creased beneath his cheek. Poking my head into the hall, I surprised a young woman washing the baseboards with a rag and a basin of soapy water. She looked up in alarm as I smiled, pointing to the phone. "Did an American lady call for room two?" She frowned, shaking her head. "Okay, thanks," I said, closing the door, pretending that I had just witnessed a grimace of "Sorry, no messages," knowing full well it was an admission of "No speak English." Crouching beside my backpack, I tried to determine what combination could pass for a dressy outfit, in the unlikely event we were still on. The Indian bedspread-print wraparound with the hot pink T-shirt? The sleeveless cotton blouse that showed my hairy armpits? My white Tretorns looked more demure than the chunky Birkenstocks I had been tromping around in. Isaac could wear a shirt with a collar and his khakis. The curry stain from lunch wasn't too visible.

"Still no word?" Isaac yawned, rolling onto his side. "Those guys probably hung up on her. No English! Bang!"

If this was the case, I didn't think much of Bippy's resourcefulness. Surely, she had someone on her staff who could speak Mandarin, or whatever dialect the old men used on the rare occasions when they did speak. I imagined the Singapore Airlines safety-video man in an immaculate white houseboy jacket wrapping a hankie around the telephone receiver before dialing the Tai Loke. If efforts to get through by phone were thwarted, she should have sent her chauffeur around to deliver a message in person. She was the one who lived here, not us! If she really wanted to get together, she would have tried harder to make contact. Having gotten out of many obligations myself by simply not returning phone calls in time, I got the message loud and clear. Welcome to Singapore, dear, but really, you can't expect us to entertain every young vagabond whose parents once voted for my husband. Five o'clock came and went. Six. "I'm getting hungry," Isaac complained at seven. "How much longer do we have to wait?"

"Yeah, so much for cocktails. Let's blow this popcorn stand." Wandering aimlessly, we eventually selected a Chinese restaurant with sidewalk tables set in a gloomy canyon between two skyscrapers and an extensive menu priced in the birthday/anniversary-celebration range. "It's okay to splurge once in a while," I rationalized, and ordered turtle soup. Ha ha, who needs the ambassador we sneered, regaling each other with tales of extraordinary things we had eaten while waiting for our food to arrive. I licked my chops anticipating a creamy French concoction, like vichyssoise but hot, with puréed terrapin standing in for potatoes. After nearly an hour, an unapologetic waiter spanked down a bowl brimming with what looked like dishwater. Dipping my spoon below the filmy surface, I tried a tentative sip.

"Can you taste the turtles?" Isaac asked.

"No, it tastes like anise. It's good," I proclaimed, a bit too heartily. I fished up a gyroscope-shaped nugget of gristle and bone: an oddly lopped section of vertebrae was my best guess. The only way to eat it was to pinch it between thumb and forefinger while nibbling what few scraps could be dislodged from the crevices of the razor-sharp skeletal fragment. "Mmm." *This* was a delicacy to be consumed in polite society? Beneath the oily licorice flavor, the stringy meat was less inspired than my grandmother's pot roast, and whoever had butchered it needed to return to the abattoir for remedial lessons in reptile anatomy. I realized with dismay that I had been thinking of a turtle as something like an oyster, an invertebrate aphrodisiac easily scooped from its shell.

"You want to share mine?" Isaac asked, considerately shoving a plate of greasy ramen studded with scallions and small frozen shrimp to the center of the table.

When we returned to the Tai Loke, there was, from what I could gather, still no message from either the ambassador or his wife. That struck me as a bit impolite, to invite someone tentatively over for drinks and then never bother to confirm. It dawned on me that the ambassador's residence may have been run like Gertrude Stein's salon, a sort of open house that one could attend—or not— on whim. If that was the case, the ambassador should have been more explicit. That sounded like a lot more fun than talking Indiana with some stodgy old Republicans, the kind of thing I might still consider attending if they could bring themselves to issue a proper invitation, but no calls came.

After a couple more days, we were sick of skyscrapers. Hindu temples and curbside fortunetellers aside, Singapore seemed too modern, too convenient. It wasn't nearly as exotic as the Tai Loke, which was proving itself far less accessible than any of Tennessee Williams's oeuvre. The morning we left for Malaysia, the police stormed the place following a wee-hours disturbance that sounded like something between a grand mal seizure and attempted murder, or possibly the discovery of Mr. Rochester's first wife. Even though it was a bit terrifying, I experienced a sensation of smug satisfaction, knowing that this was exactly the sort of colorful incident one would miss out on by staying at the Strand. The old man didn't look up from his newspaper as we lumbered away beneath our big backpacks, in search of an unspoiled beach upon which to cultivate our tans.

Halfway up the west coast of Malaysia, we decided it was time to check in with our parents, in case the postcards we had sent soon after landing hadn't made it yet. The guy who ran our guesthouse directed us to the local long-distance telephone bureau. Isaac went first and was charged the full three-minute minimum when he reached an answering machine. My mother was home with some upbeat local news about the dog and a Cantonese restaurant that had opened near the Castleton Mall. Unprompted, my stepfather picked up the extension in the upstairs hall. "What the hell did you do to the ambassador's wife?" he growled.

"Oh now, Art," my mother chastised with a nervous giggle. "This call is on Ayun's nickel!"

"She was coming out like a biting sow," he continued. "Sent your mother a four-page fax! Demanded to know how she could have raised such an 'ill-mannered, thoughtless little bitch'—"

"Art!" my mother protested as I simultaneously exclaimed, "She's the one who didn't call us!" The nerve of her! She couldn't figure out how to get a message through to the Tai Loke, but she could fire off an international fax simultaneously damning my character and my mother's abilities as a parent. If she expected contrition, she'd have done well to ape Tom Boyd's bemused diffidence. Tom had knocked himself out, preparing a special meal and inviting friends, all of whom were rumored to have gotten quite a bang out of my flakiness. What had Bippy done? Ordered the butler to make a pitcher of martinis? When we didn't show, she probably drank them all! Dozens of excuses and accusations boiled on my tongue, but before unleashing them, I checked my watch. Forty seconds more, then I'd be charged by the minute.

"Jesus Christ, that woman was pissed," Art chortled. "Couldn't believe anyone would be so rude! Said they were two hours late to an official dinner because they'd been sitting around waiting for you and you never showed!"

"Is it warm there?" my mother broke in, eager to avoid conflict at all costs. If I had offended the ambassador's wife, Mom was prepared to take the fall for me, a fact that further prejudiced me against the intemperate Bippy.

"Yeah, we just spent all week on this gorgeous island. I don't think I wore my shoes once. Did she say if she tried to call our hotel?"

"Well, now, I wouldn't worry too much about Bippy," my stepfather drawled. "You know what they say about her, don't you?"

"Yeah, I heard," I said, gazing out the glass door of my phone cubicle at a poster of a blow-dried hussy vamping for Bintang beer. "As far as I'm concerned, it's all true."

On Local Custom

Ubud, Bali is renowned almost as much for its foul-tempered homeless dogs as it is for those cute wooden carvings of frogs and monkeys and striped cats holding fishing poles. The crafts attract droves of Western tourists to Ubud's many guest-houses and luxury hideaways. The dogs are the wild force keeping the tourists' needs and desires from overrunning the place entirely. As a cat person, I'd never had to bend over backward to accommo-date a dog's agenda. Isaac, for all his reticence around his own species, was the kind of guy who laughs when an acquaintance's Irish setter knocks him down and starts lapping his face. But the diseased-looking mongrel hordes unsettled him too, until he was felled by a gastric tsunami that trapped him in our guesthouse for the remainder of our stay in Ubud. Everyone figured me for a solo traveler and probably wondered why a person who looked so healthy needed to buy two or three rolls of toilet paper a day.

Many Western tourists seem to have a take-charge attitude toward the balding, growling curs that slink around the edges of Ubud's Central Market. It's clear that the dogs belong to no one, but you'll be hard pressed to find one with Benji's hobo charm. Since they're not pets, argue the ambassadors from a different canine model, they should be rounded up and euthanized en masse, before they become more of a public health hazard than they already are. "It's kinder than letting them suffer any more in these miserable conditions," the tourists add, guiltily thinking of beloved, healthy Rover back home, picking at his pricey Eukenuba kibble in a kennel whose rates rival those of a first-class Balinese guest house.

The citizens of Ubud are in no rush to do away with the dog population. Instead, they teach the tourists their trick of pretending to hurl a rock at a threatening dog. The dogs usually fall for it. It's not that different from that old standby "Who's got the ball? Who's got the ball? Where did the ball go, boy?" The guesthouse owners and the guys who make their living selling wooden frog sculptures cluck their tongues in sympathy when a tourist comes to them with a bad dog story. They know that the dogs are potentially bad for business. I, on the other hand, would argue that the dogs are potentially good for business. Ubud, once a sleepy inland town surrounded by rice paddies, has become so heavily touristed that it feels only slightly more "authentic" than Kuta Beach, that sexy, surfin' destination most visitors to Bali hit first, to work on their tan. You can get M&Ms and Diet Coke in Ubud. You can receive faxes and check email and arrange for your cratefuls of flying frogs to be FedExed anywhere in the world. Abbreviated performances of traditional dances are staged nightly. They're beautiful but, for the audience, the experience is not much different from taking in a live show at Disneyland, and the number of camera-flashes-per-minute are enough to convince you that you're at an *NSYNC concert. Sure, Mick Jagger and Jerry Hall got married in Ubud, but as a tourist destination, it's lost its edge. Now that Western-style toilets are widely available, there's nothing to stop your grandmother from loving the place.

Except for the dogs. The dogs, feral and threatening, are like nothing you'd run into back home.

Balinese women spend a part of every morning placing beautifully constructed offerings of fruit, flowers, and incense to the gods in various locations around their homes and businesses. Bali's indigenous religion is a unique spin on Hinduism, with numerous deities, demons, and characters who seem to exist purely for comic relief. As boggling as the pantheon is to most Western visitors, it's a cinch to even the smallest Balinese child because everyone on the island shares the same faith. Temples are everywhere, festivals are frequent, and ritual observance is embedded in the fabric of daily life. I remember how long it took me to weave a single one of those palm frond crosses we wore pinned to the front of our blouses on the Palm Sundays of my childhood. In the time it takes a Dutch tourist to roll a cigarette, a Balinese woman and her kids can knock out a half dozen delicate palm baskets to contain their offerings to the gods. Well, of course they're good at it. They do it every day. The demons get presents too, nothing fancy, just a few spoonfuls of cooked rice on scraps of banana leaf left on the ground. The dogs are always ready to pounce on the offerings intended for the demons. As reported in that most venerable of guidebooks, Lonely Planet's *South-East Asia on a Shoestring*, this is just another part of Balinese theology. The dogs, being minions of the demons, are welcome, and indeed expected, to gobble the rice from the ground. No problem. This is the sort of easy-to-comprehend detail that tourists love to repeat to their less well-traveled friends, and since every Westerner in Ubud is packing a copy of Lonely Planet, it's not uncommon to overhear someone who's been there a week explaining the relationship of dogs and demons to someone who's only just arrived.

A tourist doesn't have to wander too far afield to score her own personal Ubud dog story. The miserable beasts are omnipresent and will obligingly raise their hackles and growl at anyone who smells like sunscreen. If the tourist has yet to be briefed on the imaginary rock-throwing ruse, a local is sure to hear the barking and come to the rescue before the dog can attack. A story about a tense standoff with a mangy, potentially rabid mongrel is a good story. A story about the fourteen shots you had to get in the stomach after the sucker bit you is not, which is why there are many If The Monkey Grab Your Camera Let Him Have Your Camera signs in Ubud's fabled Monkey Forest. The monkeys are pretty irresistible, particularly the baby ones who sit in your lap and have yet to grow the huge yellowed fangs of their parents. There's a reason there is no Dog Forest in Ubud.

The peanut vendors of Ubud congregate near the tourist entrance to the Monkey Forest. Accordingly, the monkeys also congregate near the entrance. The tourists congregate near the monkeys, and, if monkeys are what you've come to see, there's little reason to plunge deeper into the forest. On the other hand, there's little reason not to plunge deeper into the forest. Few tourists have anything more pressing than another banana shake and several thousand flying frogs requiring their immediate return to town. One afternoon I wandered to the back of the Monkey Forest and out into the rice paddies. At a crossroads, I met a local man who was on his way to Ubud with a couple of baskets of souvenirs slung milkmaid-style on a pole across his shoulders. He told me that if I walked another mile or so I would come to a small village where a wedding was about to take place.

Now, every visitor to Bali, well, maybe not the Australian college students whooping it up on spring break, but every other visitor to Bali wants to stumble onto a funeral. An enormous funeral pyre shaped like a bull that cost the bereaved an entire year's wages? Now that's something to tell the folks back home! Don't forget your camera! If you can't score a funeral, a wedding's a not-too-shabby second. I sped off, thrilled at the possibility of an authentic experience. I came to a gorge spanned by a fallen tree. The locals were zipping across it in rubber flip-flops, balancing bundles on their heads, their arms swinging at their sides. I froze, overcome by memories of third-grade gym period humiliations involving the balance beam. Finally, a local guy offered me his hand and crossed the log backwards, cooing encouragingly as I inched along behind him. There was no charge for this service, though he no doubt went his way pleased that he had a good story to regale his family with at dinner, how he helped a doughy, whimpering tourist across the bridge.

There was nothing shaking in the alleged wedding village, a few dogs skulking around the perimeter, some young men drinking Cokes. There were a couple of other Western tourists acting on the same hot tip I was. I waited around on what I hoped were the sidelines for an hour or so, trying to exude a sort of Peace Corpsy nonchalance, lest I be mistaken for a mere tourist. Eventually I attracted a man eager to practice his English. After answering the by-now-familiar battery of questions concerning my age, hometown, and marital status, I asked him about the wedding. He told me to come back around midnight, when things should be in full swing. "Yes, yes, wedding," he promised, and, if I liked, a puppet show. Puppet show! All right! A wedding and a puppet show in a dusty settlement reachable only by fallen log—if that didn't constitute authenticity, nothing did. I couldn't be any more in the swim if I was a field reporter for Lonely Planet. I re-crossed the rudimentary "bridge" on my hands and knees, flush with excitement, determined to rest up for the all-night party ahead of me.

Eight hours later, I entered the dark Monkey Forest with my flashlights and my camera, dressed in a backpacker's facsimile of wedding finery. The forest was kind of creepy. The monkeys were off duty, apparently sleeping off the daily peanut binge. I padded past the tumbledown temple and a small cemetery, and then out into the ricefields where I walked on a narrow track, banked on either side with piled earth that must have been serving some irrigation purpose. A full moon rose high in the sky. Elsewhere in Southeast Asia, Western tourists were getting blind drunk on rice wine and shaking their shamefully clad booties at Full Moon parties staged on beaches that still resembled paradise. What would they take home with them? I was on my way to an authentic experience, I reassured myself, trying not to let the deathly quiet get the best of my imagination. The walk seemed longer than it had that afternoon. Then, suddenly, I heard a low rumbling coming from one of the dark banks. A one-eared silhouette rose into view like the Great Pumpkin arriving at last. It was a dog, his short fur bristling, his single ear a hard-won souvenir of past battle. He was growling, but they all growled. He would probably growl until I passed by his particular rice paddy, as a matter of dog principle. Pretending that I hadn't noticed him, I marched a little further along the path.

The dog trotted along the bank, growling louder. I hesitated. Should I try the old invisible rock trick? What if he could tell I was faking and lunged for my throat? That damn dog. Couldn't he see

I was no ordinary tourist? I was there because I wanted to learn more about his culture! I wasn't the type to claim I'd been to Bali just because I'd seen some regularly scheduled dance performances and had a backpack stuffed with wooden frogs! I was after the authentic experience!

Suddenly the growling rang in both ears. I looked to the opposite bank. The first dog had summoned one of his confederates, a muscular piebald number with half a tail. When he growled, his lips rode up over his gums. I thought about shouting for help, sheepishly wondering if the souvenir salesman I'd met earlier in the day would be the one to rescue me from two local dogs he knew to be no more dangerous than a couple of tough-talking second-grade boys. I was prepared to eat a big helping of humble pie at the gorge, where I'd have to waylay a local to lead me across the log in the dark. I didn't like the idea of playing the cowardly, helpless American twice in one night. Neither did I like the idea of disease-carrying fangs ripping into my soft unprotected belly.

What I really didn't like was the idea of me, alone in the middle of nowhere, surrounded, as I now was, by half a dozen snarling, unloved dogs who didn't speak my language. I turned my head slowly, pleading silently with them not to hurt me. I remembered that time in Amsterdam when I was attacked by the furious madam who thought I'd taken a picture of her wares. I'd been surrounded then too, not by dogs, but by titillated men.

One of the dogs bounded down the bank. I squeezed my eyes shut and gripped my flashlight, knowing that they would probably get the best of me even if I'd had a machine gun. If only I'd stayed at the guesthouse, soothing Isaac's fevered brow! I braced myself to be knocked down, but when I opened my eyes, the dog was standing about five feet in front of me, blocking the path. He barked and the others took up his cry. I had no idea what this meant. I knew what to do if my stepfather's well-trained Labrador retriever made the moves on a plate of toast and I knew that you were supposed to clap your hands if you met a bear in the woods, but I didn't know what to do about a gang of dogs who, from all appearances, were on the verge of Clockwork Orange-ing me. At any moment the horseshoe could close into a ring and that's when the fangs and fur would really start to fly.

I chose the bear-in-the-woods route, without the clapping. I backed up. Very slowly, I backed down the path, toward Ubud, away from the wedding and the authentic Balinese experience. The dogs stood their ground, growling, ready should I attempt a fast one. As if I'd back up only to plunge into their midst like some cocky invisible rock! The dogs receded in the distance, their warning sounds drowned out by a chorus of frogs, genuine amphibious ones. I kept walking backwards. The dogs had been very clear about that. When I got to the edge of the Monkey Forest, I turned around and hurried as quickly as I could without running to the entrance. Surely the monkeys would not bother to teach me the same lesson the dogs had hammered home with such eloquence.

Balinese faith is a form of Hinduism, but the lesson learned here is closer to the famous Zen koan that exhorts: "If you meet the Buddha on the road, kill him!"

If Dog meets Traveler on the road, he is inclined to mistake Traveler for Buddha. Dog's nature, demonic though it may be, is also very pure, very Zen. Dog will not hesitate to kill Buddha. Better for Traveler to back up slowly thanking Doggy for sharing his wisdom. The only authentic experience is the one Traveler is experiencing. Weddings are not feathers for a cap, even if they involve crossing a fallen log by moonlight. Monkeys are not on call round-the-clock. Invisible rocks are only good weapons when nothing more than dignity is at stake. Traveler cannot return home with any stories if Traveler's throat has been ripped open for her on the journey. The folks who fly home with backpacks full of flying frogs have been to Bali just as much as Traveler has. Perhaps Traveler should start leaving rice on the sidewalks of Brooklyn.

FOR YOUR ENJOYMEN AND SAFETY
PLEASE OBSERVE THE FOLLOWING
INDIKATION!

• DO NOT TOUCH OR TEASE THE MONKEY
AS THE MAY REACT WITH UNPREDIKTABLE
MANNERS.

• FORBIDDEN FED TO THE MONKEYS.
SUPPOSING YOU HAVE SOOM FOOD FOR THEM,
PLEASE LEAVE TO OUR MONKEY'S EXPERT.

• IF THERE IS NO MONKEYS EXPERT WITH
YOU TOSS THE FOOD TO THEM FROM A
F DISTANCE.

HIDE FOOD ON YOU. THEY WILL
IT. EVEN IF IT IS IN YOUR
OR A BAG.

GRAB A MONKEY. IF A MONKEY
ON YOU, DROP ALL YOUR FOOD
WALK A WAY UNTIL IT JUMPS OFF.

TRUST YOUR VISIT WILL
MEMORABLE ONE.

Monkey Forest

On Beauty

Judging from appearances, Mom and I had no business attending the spring fashion shows in Paris. Even though she had press credentials and I hadn't lived in Indiana for seven years, when compared to the streamlined, expensively dressed whippets circulating outside the I. M. Pei pyramid where the collections were shown, everything about us screamed Hoosier imposter. Mom's first overseas assignment for the *Indianapolis Star* was also her first trip abroad, not counting day trips into Nogales for cheap liquor and Polaroids in donkey carts when we visited my grandmother in Tucson. She'd have gotten to Europe a lot earlier if it hadn't been for me. She had served as the *Star*'s fashion editor in her early twenties, when attractive professional women modeled themselves on Jackie Kennedy. She met LBJ, who reportedly clasped her white-gloved hand, drawling, "Now I know why they say the girls from Indiana are so pretty." I have a photograph of her and several other fashion editors flanking gun-nut Charlton Heston, costumed as the hunky young Moses on the set of *The Ten Commandments*. Clearly, she was going places. She gave it all up to have me. In that Moses picture, she looks like she's hiding a watermelon under her pretty spring suit.

She stayed at home until I was in third grade, then returned to the part-time society beat, sandwiching stories about Junior League fundraisers and the annual 500-Mile Race hoopla between Brownie Scout meetings and the assorted weekly lessons that turned me into the dilettante I am today. When the fashion editor gave notice, my mother resumed her title, covering the semiannual collections in New York for a readership whose tastes ran to bright golf sweaters appliquéd with funny animals.

By the time we hit Paris, in the fall of 1990, the chic hats she favored as a slim young journalist had long before been sacrificed to the carelessly theatrical dress-up play of yours truly. She wore the short hair, bright lipstick, and distinctive spectacle frames of the fashion pen's reigning queen bees. But whereas they knifed their way through the crowd in expensive, body-skimming shades of charcoal, battleship, and ink, Mom's uniform ran toward pleated, pale denim shirtwaists tucked into the darker denim ranch skirts that rode high over the abdomen. There was nothing remotely sharklike about her jackets, one of which—a Frankenstein's monster of plaid flannel shirts cut into fringe and reassembled in tiers—she referred to as her "flannel fur." Further distancing herself from the Cruella De Ville crowd in the City of Lights, she'd taken to wearing Birkenstock sandals with socks, a crime against *la mode* she'd picked up from her daughter.

I operated—then as now—twenty thousand leagues below the radar of the *Glamour* Fashion Don'ts editor. My anachronistic, anti-ironing-board, kitchen-sink romanticism was perfectly suited to my Salvation Army budget. Alas, the thrift store plunder bursting from my closet never congealed into an identifiable style. I was a little bit country, a little bit rock 'n' roll, slightly ratty, rarely flattered, ever stained, mostly Shakespearean by way of Woodstock. I packed my bag with an eye toward cutting a dashing figure.

This would be my third trip to Paris. The first time, my father escorted me on a trip organized by my eighth-grade French teacher. We stayed in a two-star hotel near the Gare du Nord. Every night, we ate *omelettes, frites,* and *mousse au chocolat* in noisy bistros, where the regulars discredited the myth of Parisian hauteur by engaging us in as much friendly conversation as our midwestern-accented, academic French—mine current, Daddy's creaking with decades of rust—permitted. I had been given some early birthday presents to use on the trip: a straw purse, a high-collared trench coat that I considered far more feminine than the classic Burberry model, and some wood-soled sandals that attached via cream-colored, canvas ankle straps the width of fettuccine. I was, in a word, gorgeous: an eighth-grade woman of mystery in thick bangs cut to emulate *Mork and Mindy*'s Pam Dawber. The shop windows were bright with jonquils and chocolate molded into lambs, rabbits, and chickens. Unfortunately, the weather did not share the merchants' sunny Easter vision, treating me to my first taste of travelers' bane, the cold rain that pisses down from a pewter-colored sky for days on end. Freezing in my insubstantial off-brand trench coat, I clip-clopped from Notre Dame to Sacré Cœur, nearly breaking my tightly strapped ankles whenever my wooden soles hydroplaned on the wet cobblestones. I had a wonderful time, despite bunking with two ninth-graders who awarded themselves the choicest bathroom mirror time and both twin beds. I wheeled my rollaway cot next to our French (!) windows, dreaming of a not-too-distant future when I would return to this most romantic of cities with a handsome, artistically inclined man, temporarily played by whatever unsuspecting eighth-grade boy I felt like tapping for the fantasy. On my fourteenth birthday, the ninth-graders and I dressed up like French hookers and photographed each other posed seductively on my cot with Monsieur J.J., a worldly ten-year-old whose wealthy parents had sent him on the school-sponsored trip *sans* chaperone.

As I had predicted, the next time I saw Paris, I was in the company of a handsome, artistically inclined man, but, as shoestring travelers with only public facilities at our disposal, Nate and I were rank as goats. No doubt Paris has suffered its share of stenchy lovers. Napoleon and Joséphine come to mind. Juliette Gréco and Miles Davis had access to modern plumbing, but I'll bet they reeked of the bars in which they frisked. But with our constant stink further augmented by our poor diet, financial anxiety, and sleep deprivation, my libido didn't stand a chance of measuring up to the eighth-grade ideal.

This trip to Paris was different. Our digs in an old hotel off the Rue de Rivoli were fairly plush, food was plentiful, and this time I was wildly in love, flush with an infatuation as delicious and short-lived as the lone bead of nectar squeezed from a honeysuckle blossom. Unfortunately for my mother, she, not my lover, was my traveling companion. As soon as the *Star* gave her the green light, Mom invited me along, envisioning a fun mother-daughter escapade. We would arrive a week before fashion week, rent a car, and tour Normandy and the Loire Valley. At Giverny, we would picnic within spitting distance of Monet's infernal water lilies. Having glutted ourselves on the picturesque, we would roll into Paris, where we had a vague notion that I might tag along as a sort of barely fluent translator as Mom covered the collections.

Poor Mom. All I wanted to do was close my eyes and wake up

in the cramped candlelit bedroom of the apartment my new boyfriend Wylie shared with two other architecture majors from the Illinois Institute of Technology. If Satan had materialized on the wrought-iron balcony, I would have swapped my mother and my soul for Wylie in a nanosecond. Mom knew it, but tried to keep a brave face. Just before we rendezvoused with our rental car, we were loading butter and marmalade onto uninspired croissants in our Paris hotel's basement breakfast room. A young couple seated themselves at the next table. The woman was pretty and blond, and the man, a tall Asian guy with a long ponytail hanging down his back, looked just like Wylie. I thought I would swoon. If only I could squat beside his chair, lay my palm on his back, and feel him breathing through the thin cotton of his shirt. That was all I wanted, just a crumb, a little morsel to tide me over for the next twelve days, the hundreds of hours I would be spending with my mother instead of Wylie. We watched the couple intently over the rims of our giant coffee bowls. Their voices were pitched too low for us to hear, but they held hands and smiled at each other frequently from inside their happy love bubble. "I'll bet you miss Wylie," Mom ventured, giggling uncertainly. "Only 288 hours to go," I thought, not counting the return flight. I tore my eyes away from our neighbors, grunting an affirmative to my mother's question as I nonchalantly shook a Gauloise out of my pack. If I couldn't be with my lover, at least I could pretend to be French.

Under the cover of jet lag, I caught up on the many hours of sleep I had foregone since taking up with Wylie six weeks earlier. The humming of the rental car's wheels lulled me into unconsciousness, even as Mom freaked out from the pressure of confusing rotary exits and mileage signs posted in a language she didn't understand. These afternoon naps also served to transport me temporarily from the frenzied itching of a sudden-onset yeast infection, which, if nothing else, was expertly timed, given my transcontinental divide. Yeah, I was a real dud in the company department. Instead of lavishing me with admission to museums and gardens, and treating me to three provincial squares a day, my mother should have invited one of her friends, like Diney, her standing date for the Indiana Repertory Theater, or Ellen, a free spirit who painted watercolors of cows and Labrador retrievers. Either of those ladies would have been a livelier choice than I was, pining for Wylie's clove cigarettes and the red curtain he kept drawn across his bedroom window at all times.

Mealtimes were the hardest. In the car, I could sleep or twitch in my seat, trying to subdue the pernicious demons of my infection. Tourist attractions offered partial distraction from my Wylie-less state with their informational plaques, often helpfully translated into English. I learned quite a bit about the landing at Omaha Beach, the Bayeux tapestry, Monet's love of Japanese woodcuts, and the monk-designed formal vegetable garden at the Château de Villandry. Sometimes I got pissy, like when Mom whispered to watch my bag as we passed through a street market en route to the famous cathedral in Chartres. When one is suffering from the pangs of lovesickness, the pragmatic comments of a mother cannot go unpunished. Only lovers think that they are immune from harm, that the whole world, even the tiniest forest creatures and most hardened criminals, wishes them well.

If I couldn't have Wylie, I longed for something to take my mind off him. As it was, I was afraid Mom and I were on the verge of turning into one of those long-married and almost universally feared elderly couples who dine silently in restaurants. After so long an acquaintance, what could we possibly say to each other over roast chicken and *vin ordinaire*? It didn't occur to me to ask Mom the same questions I had posed to Wylie in the breathless recent past, or that she, too, had plenty of anecdotes relating to a time before our paths crossed.

Back at our Right Bank hotel, we found our box overflowing with invitations to the designers' shows. My mother let me play with the stack, much as she used to let me do with the bridal announcements when I was nine years old, accompanying her to the *Star* on school vacations. My "job" was to stuff the posed studio portraits that had run with the Sunday bridal announcements into self-addressed stamped envelopes the young ladies had provided when submitting their nuptial information. (I don't want to alarm any soon-to-be-marrieds, but the staff had a long-running dog-of-the-week contest, which was both cruel and almost always easy to call.) In this spirit, I pawed through the designers' invitations, ridiculing the unestablished talents' attempts to lure the press with announcements printed on T-shirts, candy bars, and oversized, brightly colored cards that the hotel maid must have hated, since they leaked metallic confetti everywhere. My mother wasn't interested in these ploys. She raked through the pile, plucking out envelopes from the real players. Not every journalist who ventures to Paris makes the cut for the hottest shows' guest lists, so every big name came as a relief. "Oh, good, here's Ralphie," she said, pushing her red glasses higher on the bridge of her nose. (To the best of my knowledge, my mother's relationship with Ralphie does not extend beyond the labels in her denim shirtwaists and her approving opinions expressed in the *Indianapolis Star*. But there's an insider-speak that goes with the territory, and my mother is fluent in it.)

The invitations were for my mother only, but she had promised to try to secure a seat for me at a few shows, so I could check out the gibbering photographers screaming the top models' names in hopes of eye contact, the celebs seated ringside and the outlandish wedding gowns that are the grand finale of each designer's spring collection. "Oh, here's one at the Ritz," she mused, picking up a large square card edged in lipstick pink. "'The Paris Lip.' I have no idea who that is. Oh, look, it says Lauren Bacall is going to make some sort of presentation. I'll see if I can get you into that."

When I checked for mail, as I did several times a day, I wasn't hoping for late-arriving invitations. Every day thus far, I had sent at least one postcard to Wylie, covering it in tiny writing and kisses before slipping it into a yellow France Poste box. I calculated that mail between Paris and Chicago should have taken approximately a week. I grew increasingly despondent as each inquiry met with a courteous *"Non, mademoiselle."* My mother discreetly pretended not to notice. Why wasn't he writing? If he had written me the day I left, I would have had that letter upon our return from Normandy.

Our second night back in Paris, we woke to the unmistakable sound of enthusiastic, extended copulation. The acoustics of the airshaft were such that our neighbors' every gasp and groan reverberated with crystal clarity. We lay rigid in our beds, my mother and I, unable to ignore what was happening so bright, early, and close at hand. Wishing with all my might that the lovers would achieve a speedy, muffled climax, I couldn't help observing that at least someone was getting her money's worth out of a Paris hotel room. No doubt she was on her knees in an expertly hand-laundered garter belt and heels, expensively moisturized and maquillaged. She vocalized without inhibition, as people do when their mothers aren't within earshot. I wondered if she was a pro. "Sounds like a chicken," Mom observed grimly, staring at the ceiling.

The next day was the Paris Lip show. My mother had told me that if I didn't want to go, she would skip it, but I had to admit I was keen to get a gander at two glamorous old legends, Ritz and Bacall. As we entered the famed hotel, a worried-looking public relations woman snuck a peek at my mother's press badge and seized her elbow. "I'm so glad you're here," she said in an accent much like my own. Mom smiled noncommittally and introduced us. The woman beamed. "We're so glad you could make it, too! Are you having fun?" I accepted the thick folder of press materials she offered with an unimpressed nod, making it clear that I wasn't some little girl with braces and Mary Janes, accompanying Mommy to work. My mother seemed pleased with my journalistic frost. Telling the PR flack we'd see her at the post-presentation reception, we entered a conference room worthy of Louis XIV.

I tend to associate conference rooms with humiliation. There was the basement space at the Holiday Inn, where I attended an obligatory three-day gathering of newly hired T.J. Maxx employees, filling out tax forms at a glacial pace set by our trainer, and watching videos along the lines of *Employee Theft: Right or Wrong?* There was the windowless cavern at the downtown Hyatt, where a weekend conference of glassware salespeople gathered for their farewell breakfast. A fellow Northwestern acting student and I had been hired to provide the entertainment. Believe me, the last thing two thousand hung-over glassware salesmen want to see at nine o'clock on a Sunday morning is mime.

Nothing in my ocher-polyester-napkin, single-serving-half-and-half-tubs-floating-in-melted-ice, coat-rack-full-of-tangled-hangers conference-room experience had prepared me for the Ritz. The enormous oils hanging between elegantly draped windows were as diverting as any in the Louvre, without the nuisance of tourist hordes shoving to get close enough to be disappointed by dark little Mona Lisa. Ten thousand dollars' worth of cut flowers towered on antique tables. The chairs arranged in rows before the small stage were of the polished wood, non-folding variety. I doubted that this was where Tati, the legendary discount chain with the ubiquitous pink-and-white gingham print bags, held their employee appreciation banquet. This room was, well, ritzy.

We took our seats midway back, on the center aisle. My mother flicked her glasses down from the top of her head and perused the press kit. I did the same. At the appointed hour, the heavy inlaid doors were pulled shut, the lights dimmed, and Prince's "Kiss" issued at thunderous volume from giant speakers flanking a large screen. Gripped by a Pavlovian response to the combination of darkness and music, the room erupted in applause at the first projected slide, a giant profile of a shocking-pink mouth with the Paris Lip logo scrawled above, as if on a bathroom mirror. A triumphant cascade of images followed, in time to Prince's beat. Scowling models with flawless skin flaunted fire-engine-red lips as thick as caterpillars. A feline teen in fishnet muscle-T arranged his queen-size maw in the kind of coy expression best practiced off school grounds, lest the spooked football team unleash a volley of wedgies, nicknames, and knuckle sandwiches. Disembodied faces, shot from the nose down, bit strawberries, suckled striped drinking straws, and licked gloss from their freakishly large lips with photogenic tongues.

Like Scarlett O'Hara pinching her cheeks before the ball, I started gnawing my bottom lip in readiness for the moment when the lights would come back up. Sidelong glances revealed that I wasn't the only one chewing my way toward the onscreen ideal. We hadn't made much headway when Lauren Bacall stepped into a single dramatic beam illuminating an old-money podium alongside the screen. It is the nature of fashion shows to attract freshly minted celebrities of questionable staying power, sitting ringside in sunglasses and platinum necklaces that identify them by their first names in diamond-studded script. In return for the tinsel their presence hangs on the designer's output, their photos are widely reproduced and, for all I know, they get free duds in the bargain. It's exciting, but still, they seem kind of tacky, not like Einstein or Mother Teresa or the other perennial biggies we noncelebrities pick when invited to compile the guest lists for our fantasy dinner parties.

Ms. Bacall was the genuine article, the girl who had asked Humphrey Bogart if he knew how to whistle, still classy and compelling in an unstructured silk suit. She paused graciously while her audience whooped it up, palms slapping together in joyous recognition of what the Academy would call her lifetime achievement. Assuming a pair of half-glasses—for the record, they made her look smart, not old—she began reading from prepared notes. "Cindy Crawford embodies the beauty of full, sensuous lips," she observed, as the supermodel's giant mug loomed onscreen. This accounting ignored Cindy's other celebrated attributes, such as her unlikely combination of weight and height, her boys' department hips, and the big brown mole that she would have had surgically removed if she were Doris in Accounts Payable. More famous lovelies followed, all of whom passed Ms. Bacall's scripted labial muster. A lusty scream arose at a slide of Mick Jagger at the height of his powers, thirty years earlier. Even Lauren Bacall—Betty, I believe she is called by her friends—catcalled the sinewy lad leering back in black and white. "Mick! Now *there's* a set of lips!" The slide carousel advanced, giving us a '70s-era portrait of Mick and his then-wife Bianca with their unsurprisingly large-mouthed daughter, Jade. "Bianca had great lips, too," Ms. Bacall confided, with the authority of one who'd probably tinkled in their powder room at some point. "And just look at little Jade! Why, we could call them the First Family of lips . . . except they're not a family anymore." The quip went over like pre-code canned tuna at a Greenpeace gathering. Several in the audience exchanged glances, as more plainspoken sorts indulged in some faint French-inflected hissing. Ms. Bacall, ever the trooper, hustled on to her next line, eager to distance herself from the bitchy joke the collagen-injection moneybags had gotten her to crack at the expense of the hopeful young family projected without their knowledge or, I wagered, permission. Lauren Bacall, of all people, should know that celebrities have feelings, too!

As the opening presentation ground on, I had to wonder how much Ms. Bacall was getting paid, and why she was so hard up for cash that she would sign on as mouthpiece for this tawdry exercise. Squinting toward the podium, I saw that her mouth seemed no larger than my own status quo model. Shouldn't the Paris Lip suits have insisted on a spokeswoman who exemplified the standard of beauty they were trying to establish, someone like, oh, I don't know, Bianca Jagger? An unmistakable note of disdain was beginning to creep into the narration. I recognized the tone immediately. Past paychecks of mine have depended on utterances that were so loath-some to me, subtle guerrilla action was required if I was to keep both income and self-respect. Balancing a cork-bottomed cocktail tray on one hand, I'd trot over to a recently arrived gaggle of thirsty sports-bar types, girding my loins for the cute opening statement John the New Manager had dreamed up all by himself: "Hi, guys! Welcome to Clubland! Can I interest you in some sex on the beach?" As I'm sure an actress of Bacall's stature appreciates, one need not play a humiliating line like that straight. A far better choice is to invest it with a subtle sneer. I got the impression that old Betty not so privately considered the super-size subnasal slashes of fuck-me red parading on the big screen to be vulgar.

Finally, Ms. Bacall fulfilled her contract and stalked offstage to a smattering of polite applause while an American employee of the Paris Lip took the podium, gushing about how it felt to share the stage with the timeless beauty who had preceded her. She talked at length about the exciting developments in the field of cosmetic sci-ence that had led to her company's remarkable new procedure, whereby skimpy lips were plumped through a series of *nearly pain-less* shots, administered in the offices of trained physicians. Thanks to this revolutionary technology, no longer would interesting, pas-sionate women be held prisoner by stingily apportioned lips. "No more faking it with a liner pencil," she trumpeted in an approxi-mation of salt-of-the-earth, you-tell-it-girlfriend frankness. She instructed us to open our press packets so we could follow along as she pointed out some of the more noteworthy aspects of the procedure. Sighing, my mother flipped her folder open as if it were the *Book of Common Household Plumbing Repair*. In the row ahead, a French journalist who resembled the young Tuesday Weld, turned to a colleague, reconfigured her mouth into a shape traditionally employed for Donald Duck noises, and wiggled the resulting orifice in a manner both mocking and obscene. If only there had been another Prince number to get us through this part of the presentation, so eerily similar to a Mary Kay cosmetics pitch. Maybe the Paris Lip was still in the theoretical phase of its development. That would explain why the lackey at the mike, for all her unbridled enthusiasm, had lips no wider than chopsticks. But no, in conclusion, she told us that we were in for a special treat. Dr. Diderot Bœuftoit, one of the Paris Lip's foremost practitioners, was on hand to perform a live demonstration. The French journalist ahead of us blanched. "Ooh, I can't watch," Mom whimpered in the queasy whine she reserves for impending cinematic violence.

The doctor bounded onstage, gathered the speaker in his arms and Frenched her, which is to say he kissed her on both cheeks as she giggled and blushed. I cannot improve upon the description my mother recklessly voiced at the reception, while still within earshot of the anxious publicist: He looked like he'd have been more at home in a gold lamé G-string on the beaches of Biarritz. He was the only medical professional I've ever seen who managed to make a lab coat look slinky. He had brown, feathered hair, a Roman nose, and the adorable grin of a highly successful rake. A gold chain glinted in the tangle of chest hair manfully asserting itself at his open collar. I think it's fair to say that he spoke English about as well as I speak French, but he turned his lack of mastery to his advantage. When he floundered describing the procedure he soon would perform, he was as endearing as a schoolboy presenting his teacher with a clump of stolen geraniums, roots still attached. The Paris Lip's American representative rushed to his linguistic aid, beaming encouragement. "*Ah, oui.* Implants. Of course, zis is ze word." He punctuated this show of abashment with a quick wink that was dazzling for being both general and incredibly specific. Swooning, the speaker staggered to the microphone and called out, "Can we bring out Christine?"

A scrawny figure emerged from a door behind the stage, took a few tentative steps on spiked metallic heels, and stopped. She had the trembling air of a fawn stumbled upon in the forest, or rather, an aging doe trying to pass as a fawn in a skintight, studded denim outfit designed for a much younger demographic. The rigors of maintaining her emaciated figure and deep nutmeg tan had left her haggard. Large, dark eyes peered from under a dry mane of unnatural ash blond. And her lips. My god, huge. Great bacon rinds, liberally frosted in bubblegum pink and outlined with pencil several shades darker. Pits and legs unshaven, my face as naked as an infant's, I found myself defaulting to a hardly constructive form of *Glamour* think: "What's the matter with you? Don't you know you're supposed to blend?" Fortunately, harsh judgment, unlike extreme heat, does not produce visible effects. If it did, poor Christine would have shimmered before our toxic gaze. The Paris Lip folk committed a grave boo-boo when they engaged a cut-rate model for an audience accustomed to *la crème*. It doesn't take a genius like Bobbi Brooks or M. Hukapoo to know that the product looks best on exquisite, sashaying sixteen-year-olds. A top model effervesces with youth, Evian, several ounces of exotic lettuce, and professionally applied makeup flecked with crushed pearls. In comparison, Christine was a terrified husk, nearly extinguished by a twenty-year effort to look as she might have at nineteen.

She didn't need the Paris Lip. She needed a fairy godmother. Gallantly, Dr. Bœuftoit rescued this lonely creature from our critical high beams, cupping her elbow and leading her tenderly to a sort of medical lounge chair that had been rolled out from behind the screen.

A uniformed nurse joined them, bearing a tray of syringes and cotton balls. A technician trained a video camera on Christine's face, which then appeared onscreen, as big as Bullwinkle's in the Macy's Thanksgiving Day Parade. The nurse swabbed her lips with cotton balls until no trace of frosty pink remained. I had to wonder how much they were paying this one—surely not as much as Bacall, but it couldn't have been pleasant to have her giant, nude lips scrutinized by strangers. "As you can see, Christine already has gorgeous, very sexy, full lips," the doctor purred through a wireless mike. "Zis is her sixth treatment. It is not necessary, she could stop now and remain happy, but after zis application, she will be even more beautiful, more sensuous." It struck me that Christine might have a compulsion on par with anorexia, a self-assessment so distorted that it led her to further inflate her already pneumatic lips. I wondered how much they weighed.

The doctor explained how he would make a series of injections at the lip line. Imagine drawing vertical stripes on your lips with grease pencil, which is exactly what the doctor did to Christine, in preparation. Got it? Good, okay, now imagine replacing the pencil with some sort of animal by-product shot straight into this super sensitive area with a surgical steel needle! Selecting a gleaming instrument, the doc bent over Christine, blocking her body, though we still had an excellent view of her giant video-projected head. Her nostrils flared and tears sprang into her eyes as the needle pierced her skin. If it had been me, I would have spilled every bit of classified information at my disposal, anything to end the torture before it got out of hand. Those of us who could bear to look writhed in sympathy, moaning. "*Shh, shh, shh,*" Dr. Bœuftoit hissed, ostensibly to his patient. He was out of his element in a situation requiring something more than gigolo charm. He fumbled with the tray, sending some surgical steel tools clattering to the floor. "Ees okay! Ees okay," he reassured us before whispering urgently to the nurse in his native tongue. I wouldn't have recognized the French for "autoclave" or "sterilizer," but I was surprised at the complete absence of basic vocabulary that seemed absolutely warranted by the recent turn of events: "floor," "dirty." *Il faut laver cette chose avant de la mettre dans les lèvres de Mademoiselle Christine.* Grabbing the needle, he applied himself grimly to the task, plunging in stripe number two. Christine yipped. She probably would have screamed if the big syringe hadn't restricted her mouth's movement. The doctor hiccupped, reflexively trying to diffuse the tension with the remains of his formerly ingratiating laugh. "It is not so bad, is it, *chéri?*" he cajoled. The enormous head bravely indicated that it was not by rotating on its neck a fraction of a millimeter to either side. The doctor turned to face the press. "You see? I told you so," he accused playfully, shaking a hairy, jeweled finger in our direction. Beads of sweat on his skinny upper lip reflected the light from the elegant chandeliers. I glanced at the American representative. She looked like she'd been shipwrecked, clinging to the podium with the expression of someone whose phobia of drowning is no longer hypothetical. "Okay, okay," the doctor muttered under his breath, psyching himself up for injection number three.

"She's bleeding!" someone in the crowd gasped. We buzzed

impotently. If only there had been a representative of Amnesty International present to step in and stop the madness. "Okay, yes, sometimes zis happens," the doctor barked, his handsome face contracting into a harassed mask of such stereotypical French indignation that I longed for a baguette and a beret to complete the effect. "It is nothing, *oui*?" The speakers crackled and popped as his body mike malfunctioned mid-rant. The video camera operator left his tripod unmanned, dug under the doctor's lab coat, and grappled with the battery pack clipped to his belt. The nurse, seemingly the only person with a handle on the demands of her profession, applied pressure to Christine's wound with a strip of gauze. Christine's eyes, as big onscreen as manhole covers, darted frantically in what was now a silent horror movie, as the technician was not wholly able to restore the doctor's mike. Once the nurse had stopped the bleeding, he completed the injections efficiently, but his narration issued forth as an alien language of gabble and squawks that frequently cut out altogether. Anyone who has ever taken part in a junior-high-school assembly would have recognized immediately that he had lost his audience for good. Contemptuous conversations sprang up like brushfires. It's amazing he wasn't pelted with spitballs.

At long last he whipped off Christine's paper drape, helped her to her feet and presented her to us as a "new" woman. She leaned weakly on his arm, hiding behind her long bangs, which had the unsettling effect of shielding everything but her much-abused lips. I was beginning to understand why we hadn't seen the Paris Lip inflicted on a higher status model, or even a fresh young face, the latest blossom to be plucked from the cornfields of Nebraska; I can't imagine that Naomi Campbell would have looked much better than Christine following such an ordeal.

• • •

At the sparsely attended reception, I wolfed down dozens of canapés from trays offered by formally attired waiters. Our mono-grammed plates came equipped with sterling claws to hold our champagne flutes. I'd never seen anything so cunning. They justi-fied the last hour far more than Lauren Bacall, who, rather than mingle, decamped to her suite to wait for the check to clear. The publicist tacked toward us, apparently trying to make it look like she was weaving her way through a great crowd. "So?" she cried, with hollow gaiety. "Have you *ever* seen anything like it?"

"No," Mom replied, cramming another canapé into her mouth to escape elaboration.

The publicist clung to us, having identified the *Indianapolis Star* as her client's last, best hope. I tried to imagine the women of my home-town driving their children to school, shopping at the Castleton Mall, and attending services at Second Presbyterian with lips the size of those wax ones handed out to trick-or-treaters. At times I've adopted a hipper-than-thou stance toward my fellow Hoosiers, but this was not one of those times. I'm happy to report that no self-respecting female Indianapolite would pay someone to inject butcher's refuse into any part of her body, let alone her lips, even if it were to help raise funds for the Cub Scout Jamboree. That publicist was *merde*-out-of-luck, as we used to say in Indiana, *pardonnez-moi mon français*.

As we left, I felt Mom's elbow in my ribs. I turned my head slowly, expecting Lauren Bacall or at least Cindy Crawford. Instead I followed her gaze to where Dr. Bœuftoit stood talking to the Paris Lip rep. Christine leaned against the wall behind them, gingerly fingering the outlying borders of her swollen gob. The rep had the air of a geeky high school overachiever, vacillating between dismay that the other kids had trashed her Homecoming Dance and elation that the coolest boy in school was teasing her about it in a nice way. The golden elevator doors opened with a suitably discreet and moneyed swoosh. The doctor slid his hand inside Christine's studded outfit via a peekaboo panel cut into the area between her shoulder blades. He steered her on, pressing a button to take them to the guest rooms on the upper floors. Mom nodded with the canary-swallowing expression of one who has not been fooled for a second. So he was a gigolo and Christine was the worn-out old showgirl who loved him! God, it was so French. I suddenly realized that I had not thought of Wylie once during my Paris Lip experience.

Later, I discovered that Mom had stuffed two pink linen cocktail napkins with the Ritz's logo into my purse while the public relations wretch was bending her ear. "I can't believe you stole these," I said, as I folded them into my backpack for the return trip.

"Well," she shrugged, pulling on her Claude Monet sleep shirt and getting into bed, "I wanted you to have something special to remember our trip to Paris." As if the Paris Lip press kit weren't souvenir enough.

On Health

Ricky attached himself to us on the outskirts of Bukittinggi, a Sumatran hill station we'd arrived in the night before. Amped up on the novelty of oatmeal and cool mist after many weeks of tropical heat, I had agreed to join Greg on a brisk constitutional in the surrounding countryside. I figured I'd have loads of time to explore the red-brick town in search of the ideal café in which to fritter away the hours, writing in my journal and consuming high-calorie, cold-weather food. We meandered through valleys and forded a small stream, accompanied by a band of five-year-olds who threw dirt clods at us when we refused to give them cigarettes. Ricky, on his way into town, heard our protests and shot-putted the little gangsters away by their ears. "Bad boys," he remarked, shrugging his thin shoulders with the seen-it-all cynicism at which fourteen-year-olds excel. Then he reversed direction to walk with us, filling us in on a few details of his life. He lived nearby with his mother, father and seven younger siblings, and he wasn't in school because "no money." He seemed like a bright kid, full of questions, including a request for a cigarette. "Marlboro," he nodded, taking two. "Cool."

We meandered around for an hour or so, cutting across fields and taking backcountry roads. Ricky took us to a cottage belonging

to a jewelry maker, where I bought two pairs of dainty silver fili-
gree earrings, figuring I could give them to someone as a present. I
didn't want our new friend to go without his tiny commission just
because I was the hippie hubcap type. He then asked us if we
wanted to see the flying foxes. Having bought the earrings and par-
ticipated in the obligatory bushwhack through nature, I was
inclined to head back to the civilized pleasures of Bukittinggi, but
Greg was intrigued. Ricky was a bit hard pressed to describe these
miraculous creatures to English-speaking visitors, since, he
reminded us, he had no money to attend school. Greg asked him
how much he would charge to lead us to their lair, while I asked
how far it was, not relishing a long tramp back. I had a hunch that
there was slim chance of the flying foxes living up to the image in
my head of the North American terrestrial model outfitted with
ruddy wings to match its auburn pelt.

After half an hour's walk further into the bush, Ricky led us
through a meadow of waist-high weeds still damp with dew. We
emerged on the lip of a gorge, a deep chasm choked with bamboo
and tangled vegetation. Pulling the checkered sarong he wore like a
shawl over his head babushka-style, Ricky indicated a dead tree rising
from the gorge floor. It was a gnarled old devil, the kind that throws
apples at Dorothy in *The Wizard of Oz*, but several stories taller.

Squinting, I could make out dozens of withered black papayas
hanging from its leafless branches, but nothing resembling a
winged fox. "Can we get closer?" Greg asked.

"Closer okay," Ricky said, picking his way a few feet downhill in
his rundown rubber flip-flops. Greg and I followed gingerly, choosing
our footing carefully on the muddy incline. Suddenly one of the
papayas opened up like a DeLorean and took to the skies. After a few

circles, it returned to the tree, wrapped itself back up in its wings and roosted beneath a branch. Flying foxes, please! These were nothing but big bats. No wonder they were all asleep. Bats are nocturnal creatures. "Flying fucking dogs," Ricky giggled. Pleased with the ring of his deftly deployed slang, he repeated himself at top volume, clapping his hands for good measure. "Flying fucking dogs!"

Pumping their leathery wings, the bats rose from the tree in a great black cloud, and I tumbled headfirst into the gorge, dislocating my knee. I came to a rest in a clump of bamboo several yards down, but the pain was so great I wouldn't have cared if I'd bounced all the way to the bottom, dashing my brains out on a jagged rock. I immediately recognized what had happened to me, even before I came to a stop. Ever since the original injury, when a rogue kindergartner darted in front of me while I was running laps in Miss Trotter's high school gym class, my knee had gone out at least once a year, but never so badly as this. Imagine your leg as a green stick. Now imagine a giant child snapping that stick in half, except the stick, being green, won't break all the way, so the kid twists it in an attempt to pull it apart. Don't forget to invest this image with all the excruciating, slow-motion, oh-god-I-think-I'm-going-to-throw-up pain you can drum up. I sprawled on my back, my wraparound skirt unwrapped, gasping like a fish in the bottom of a boat. Greg's head floated upside down in the distance. I could just barely hear him calling to me over the deafening storm of my own hyperventilation. Clutching at roots and vines, Greg managed to scramble down to my level, with Ricky skidding somewhat less urgently behind.

"Oh my god, Ayunee, what happened? Are you okay?" Wedging his foot securely against the bamboo stand, he knelt in the mud that was fast seeping through my clothing.

"My knee," I wheezed. The sky was white. In other years, my kneecap had popped back into place immediately, leaving me breathless and hurting, but able to hobble unassisted to the nearest source of ice and soothing beverages. I'd learned to milk my trick joint, claiming dislocation whenever I wanted to worm out of work at the last minute. The next day, I'd show up strapped into the bulky white cotton leg brace I'd acquired in college, smiling gratefully as co-workers forced me to sit down while they did all of my Xeroxing. What a sham! People with dislocated knees can barely stand, let alone temp, even with a removable brace! I remembered the agony when Miss Trotter had insisted that I pick myself off the floor to "walk it off." The next morning an orthopedist whose daughter had gone to camp with me put me in a cast for a month and still it killed, but not as bad as this. Bracing myself for the worst, I unsquinched an eye to assess the damage. My kneecap remained far left of its customary center. If my foot had been pointing in the same direction, I would have achieved perfect balletic turnout.

"Okay, let's get you out of here." Greg slid his arms around me to hoist me into a sitting position, which given the extremely slick conditions, was a task akin to retrieving a greased watermelon from the deep end of the pool.

"Stop! That hurts," I yelped. "Got to catch my breath."

"Okay. Okay." Greg looked a little desperate, kneeling with one arm pinned beneath me. "Do you think you can walk?"

"I don't know. Fix my skirt!"

Ricky smirked as Greg rearranged the fabric to cover my panties. "Maybe scared by flying foxes," Ricky said, seizing my arm and yanking hard.

"No!" I cried, as a deadly electric eel lit up my left leg. "Let me lie here!" We remained there for several minutes while my knee ballooned to grapefruit dimensions.

"What did you do the last time this happened?" Greg asked.

"You mean this bad?" I replied between gritted teeth. "I went to an orthopedist who reset my knee and put me in a cast."

"Did you have to have surgery?"

I shot Greg a look that said he would know all of this if he'd been listening carefully for the two years we'd been together. "No, he stuck a big needle in my knee and drained off all this fluid and then I felt better. I *should* have had surgery the first time, when I was still in school and living at home. *Owww*, this really kills."

"Flying fucking foxes," Ricky chuckled.

"Do you know if there's a doctor in town?" Greg asked him.

"A Western doctor," I interjected, imagining an elderly hot-dog-sized syringe whose rusty needle had served Bukittinggi's intravenous needs for three generations.

"Doctor, yes, doctor," Ricky sang, giving my leg a companionable poke.

When the screaming died down, Greg voiced a thought I'd been trying to avoid, namely that in order to get medical attention for my leg, we first had to get me up that treacherous, nearly vertical slope. I wasn't too keen on the idea, but the alternative—staying in the gorge while Greg returned to Bukittinggi to fetch a doctor—held even less appeal. In the absence of a rescue sled, I clung to Greg's back, while he dragged our combined weight uphill using whatever weeds and rocks offered him purchase. Ricky assisted by pushing the plumpest parts of my ass indiscriminately. White firecrackers of pain exploded behind my eyeballs every time my wayward patella came into contact with anything, even the soft, slimy mud. By the time we gained the lip of the gorge, Greg and I were basted with a thick film of mud, sweat and leaves. Ricky was tickled by our appearance, giggling as he twisted himself up in his sarong. "You like flying foxes?" he asked me.

"My leg is hurt," I replied testily. "I cannot walk."

"Look at those flying fucking dogs," he howled, slapping his own perfectly aligned kneecaps. "You no want to see?"

Greg did. "You should take a minute to catch your breath," he encouraged. "Wow! Did you see how close that giant one came?" I didn't. With my eyes rolled skyward in agony, I had no problem willing myself blind to all bat action. I consoled myself that I'd seen them already. When Isaac and I were in Java three years earlier, a fellow traveler had taken us to check out the occupant of a shrouded cage in the bird market. "Its face looks just like a puppy," he cooed accurately, pulling aside the drape to reveal the cutest bat in the history of flying mammals, a flying fucking dog.

Stumbling back through the tall weeds, leaning heavily on Greg and, less confidently, Ricky, it became clear that I was in no shape to get back to town on foot. If they let go of me for a second, the hurt leg buckled beneath me like pickup sticks. "Is there a taxi or a bemo or some way to get to Bukittinggi without having to walk the whole way?" Greg asked Ricky. Without a word, Ricky struck out ahead of us, singing, whipping trees and, when we came to a dirt road, fence posts with a tall stalk he'd uprooted from the meadow. We hobbled after him like the losing contestants in an abominable three-legged race. It's a horrible thing to be physically incapable of sinking to your knees when that gesture represents the purest expression of your despair. Instead, I galumphed on unsteadily, alternately whining and sucking in my breath sharply.

We drew up alongside a one-room store, where Ricky was already lounging on the porch, shooting the breeze in Bahasa with some older boys. He rolled his eyes slyly in my direction and made some comment that I suspected pertained to my underwear, given the reaction it got from his chums. "Where are we?" Greg asked, as he deposited me whimpering onto a low bench.

"Here, bus coming. You pay for the flying foxes now."

"The bus stops here?" Greg asked.

"Ayeeeeee." Ricky smiled, closing his eyes as he savored the tang of his drawn-out nonsense syllable. "No stop here, man. Stop there." He pointed toward a new brick school building, where dozens of uniformed children raced around kicking soccer balls behind a chainlink fence. It could have been the suburbs of Indianapolis, except all the little girls wore floor-length baby-blue skirts and matching veils. Greg paid him the agreed-upon sum, then ducked inside the little store to buy us Cokes, while I considered the implications of this newest bit of bad luck. If we didn't manage to scare up a reputable doctor, chances were I'd have to be flown out to Singapore or Australia. I groaned, imagining our whole trip budget blown on one helicopter ride, since wherever the nearest airport was, it sure wasn't in Bukittinggi.

Greg dragged me over near the schoolyard bus stop, where, filthy, strangely dressed and—they may not have known this— unmarried, we created quite a sensation among the pristine Muslim schoolgirls, who hooked their fingers in the chainlink and giggled at us until recess was over. Negotiating the steep steps of the bus was torture. The other passengers looked disturbed to see a dirty, long-haired Westerner crying, crawling, and flashing them through her gaping wraparound skirt. Until I learned the Bahasa for "knee injury," I was doomed to come off as the unsavoriest of backpacking elements, the drug casualty. We drove past cultivated fields and roadside sugarcane juice stands before the bus reached its terminus, a landmark unfamiliar to me, some sort of outdoor auto-parts market, from what I could tell.

We made it back to the guesthouse, a tidy low-slung building on a hill above the action. After spending our first night in a grubby hotel on the noisy main drag, we had gone looking for better quarters and found this place before embarking on what turned out to be the flying fox debacle. The new digs made for a pleasant enough sickroom, with clean sheets on a comfortable bed situated beneath a window that opened on a small, shaded porch. The lady of the house, seeing me limp in, made appropriate oh-you-poor-thing noises and rushed to help make me comfortable. "*Es?*" I asked, pointing to my knee, now swollen to the size of a good-sized cantaloupe. "*Ada es?*"

"*Es?*" she asked, frowning as she patted the large bun at the nape of her neck. "Oh . . . okay!" Smiling, she gestured that I should stay put on the bed. Grinning back, I mimed that I wasn't going anywhere soon.

"What's going on?" Greg asked returning from the communal toilet, located in a lean-to at the end of the porch.

"The *ibu*'s getting some ice for my knee. I think my Hoosier accent had her stumped for a minute."

"Okay, that's good. Ice ought to help with the swelling." Greg perched on the edge of the bed and I flinched in pain as the mattress sagged a quarter-inch to accommodate his weight. "So, what do you want to do now?"

I couldn't tell him that my stupid reinjury was going to cost him his trip. "Well, I think you should ask where the most expensive hotel in town is—maybe there's a Hilton or a Sheraton or something. They're sure to have a doctor on staff to treat their guests. Just explain the situation and tell him I need someone to drain the fluid, but make sure he uses disposable needles because the last thing I need is AIDS."

"The last thing *I* need is AIDS," Greg parried grandly.

"Okay, so you have a stake in this, too. Unfortunately, I don't think this is one of those problems we can fix with popsicle sticks and rubber bands."

"Don't worry, we'll get you help," Greg said, patting my leg. I screwed my eyes shut and hissed in reverse. "Sorry!"

"Okay," Ibu warbled, returning with a tray on which a thermos, a jar of sugar, two glasses, and a spoon were balanced. *"Tidak ada es"* (don't have ice). *"Ada chai."* She poured some tea from the thermos and placed the steaming glass in my hand. *"Chai* good!" she declared, beaming, unable to hide her pride in using English.

Not wanting to hurt her feelings, what could I do but agree? I took a sip of the scalding brew. "Mmm, chai good," I echoed, rubbing my belly to show just how good it was, much better than the iced beverage she thought I'd requested. "Greg, find her husband and see if you can make him understand. We need directions to the big Western hotel and a bag of ice. And get me some cookies, too, maybe some of those rice cakes with the caramel swirl if you can find them. And the Somerset Maugham stories."

"Hey, I'm reading those," Greg protested. I widened my eyes and attempted to lick my own nostrils in imitation of a deer we had once seen, lover's shorthand for "I'm just an innocent little Bambi and all I know is love."

"Oh, all right," Greg sighed, flinging the fat paperback volume onto the mattress, narrowly missing my wounded limb.

While Greg was out fetching the doctor, I received a visit from Bapak, Ibu's husband. I didn't know their real names. *"Ibu"* (mother) and *"bapak"* (father) are Indonesian terms of respect, along the lines of "ma'am" and "sir." Our hosts did seem to embody Mom and Dad, living with their unmarried adult children in an apartment behind the guest rooms. Other relatives arrived on motor scooters throughout the day, dropping off grandchildren and picking up pots of delicious-smelling food. I enjoyed the hubbub of their family life. Bapak was clearly the boss, dispatching his handsome, bashful sons on various errands and muttering as Ibu and other women I took to be her sisters laughingly did his bidding. He strutted around the property in a sarong and tank top, his comportment that of a grizzled but still strong Boston bull terrier who doesn't see the humor in his self-importance. "Ah," he rasped, glaring at my knee. "Sick. Need massage."

"Oh, that's okay, thanks, Pak," I said, as cheerful and polite as my friends and I used to be around each other's parents. "My, uh, husband is getting the doctor."

"Doctor, bah." He scowled and kneaded the air. "Massage good!"

"Maybe later. Now, just resting."

His square little head bobbed in approval. "Okay, sleep good, too. Then . . . massage!" He seemed to be waiting for something, so I closed my book and my eyes. Being careful not to disturb the injured knee resting on a pillow, he covered me with a lightweight blanket and padded out, leaving the door ajar. I stayed like that for a couple of minutes, then, feeling like a kid sneaking comics with a flashlight under the covers, I cracked open my book. Man, that Somerset Maugham! He was something! Imagine traveling around Southeast Asia by freighter, evening clothes packed in your steamer trunk, presenting your letter of introduction to a backwater Dutch government rep, drinking *stengahs* with him on the porch after dinner. . . . After the third one, the Dutchman confides that his wife murdered her lover in the bush. If only I knew what a "topi" was. Some sort of a pith helmet, I wagered. Bapak banged the door open, rocketing me back into the present. I propped myself up on my elbows, rubbing my eyes as if I'd been sleeping. He sloshed a reddish-brown liquid inside an old peanut butter jar. "*Jamu*," he informed me. "For make well."

"Oh?" I stalled. I remembered reading about *jamu*, the traditional Indonesian folk medicine, in Lonely Planet, but I had pictured it as more appetizing, like freshly ground pesto, not motor oil mixed in the open sewer. "Do you use *jamu*?"

He gave a virile grunt. "Every day *jamu*." His face clenched as if gripped by a horrible migraine, then, unscrewing the lid, he pretended to dip his hand into the foul broth and apply some to his forehead. "*Jamu* no more head hurt." Groaning, he rolled his shoulders back and forth, seeking relief from back pain. "Put *jamu*, make good, strong!" He paraded in a circle, inviting me to admire his healthy, barrel-shaped body. "*Jamu*."

"Can I see?" Bitter mentholated fumes assaulted the delicate membranes of my eyes as he thrust the jar under my nose. Little unidentified bits were floating on the brackish surface.

"Very nice. Maybe later, okay?"

"You must massage," he growled, a true believer. He stuck a paw into the *jamu* jar and seized my knee with an eagle's firm grasp.

Apparently not one to suffer torture stoically, I let out an involuntary yell that threw us both. Bapak clucked sympathetically, as if reassuring a tearful grandchild. "Ooh, hurt. Hurt a little bit." Again, he sank his fingers into the swollen fruit of my knee.

I jackknifed forward and grabbed his wrist. "Please! Please, no *jamu*! No massage! Let me sleep!"

Reluctantly, he recapped the *jamu*, rubbing the excess from his palms into the muscles of his neck. He could see that he'd have to proceed slowly with me, even if it meant I'd heal less quickly than someone like him, who bore the initial discomfort in order to get the immediate benefits of that awesome *jamu* power. "I come back. You must massage. *Massaaaaaaaaaaage.*" Sniffling a little, I curled into as fetal a position as I could manage.

Greg came back alone. "I found the fancy hotel, but they said they don't have a house doctor."

"What?! Well, did they give you a recommendation at least?"

"No, I think they wanted to get rid of me. It was more of a businessman kind of place, you know? They did give me some ice." He held up a small plastic bag half-filled and fast melting.

"Wow, so generous," I groused.

"Yeah, they weren't very happy about it. I got you some Beng Bengs though," he brightened, lining up two chocolate bars next to a bunch of bananas and a couple of sodas. "What's that weird smell?"

"*Jamu*. The old guy kept trying to massage my knee with it. Do me a favor, if you see him coming with an old jar full of reddish-brown shit, tell him I'm sleeping. He won't take no for an answer."

"So, what do you think we should do about this?" I hoisted my good leg alongside the other, so we could compare. "Jesus, that looks really bad. Is it going to be all right? Do you think maybe if you just stay off it, take it easy for a couple of days, it'll go down on its own?"

"Yeah, probably," I lied hopefully. It was sort of like hoping that finger you accidentally lopped off with the paper cutter will grow back. "If there's no doctor around, I don't see what we've got to lose by waiting around for a day or two. Why rush into things?" Greg suggested that I try to walk a little, so I didn't get too stiff. Whimpering, I inched to the edge of the bed, lowered my legs over the side and burst into tears. We decided to dine in that evening, Greg gallantly, if uncharacteristically, pretending to be satisfied by a repast of candy and bananas, even when the mouthwatering aromas of the family's dinner wafted in through the open window.

I woke in the middle of the night, my bladder full to bursting. Clenching my teeth, I lay rigid, hoping the roosters would start crowing any minute, as if daylight would make my task less arduous. When it dawned on me that the sun wouldn't rise anytime soon, I groped around for the flashlight, determined not to wake Greg for what in retrospect seems a clear-cut bedpan moment. The need to pee was urgent enough to distract from the pain as I maneuvered myself into a standing position. I took a tentative step, and the various vertical components of my leg collapsed in a configuration that had nothing to do with their customary anatomy. Stifling a yelp, I decided I'd have better luck dragging myself to the latrine in a semi-crawl, à la Andy Wyeth's *Christina's World*, the flashlight tucked into my armpit. I made it out the door of our room and onto the long porch, only slightly worried at this late hour that someone passing on the road might mistake me for a *hantu*, one of the free-ranging bad spirits in which many adult Indonesians fearfully believe.

Unused to vigorous exercise, I was damp with perspiration by the time I reached the sheet of corrugated metal that served as the outhouse door. When unoccupied, the door was held closed from the outside by a complicated hasp fashioned out of a wire hanger. Mother of God, I was going to have another accident while trying to figure out which wire I was supposed to untwist to gain entry. It was impossible to keep the beam of the armpit-tucked flashlight trained on the lock while frantically grappling with both hands. Gagging, I managed to fit the end of the flashlight between my teeth, hopping on my good leg in an effort to keep my finger in the dike as it were. Finally, I managed to figure out the lock, possibly by breaking it. The thin metal door swung open with the riotous squawk of a fully amplified nail pried from a particularly needy board. Desperate though I was, I felt that stealth was essential to this mission. I didn't want Bapak and his *jamu* jar barging in on my private moment, investigating the source of the unholy racket.

When no one came running, I hopped forward on one foot, because no matter how clean your guesthouse is, you really don't want to be crawling on your hands and knees around a squat toilet. The real dilemma was how to squat. This household had the deluxe porcelain model: a long, shallow trough with ridged footprints to either side. It's all about positioning. As long as your feet hit their designated marks, you won't sprinkle when you tinkle, or worse. Struggling to lower myself on my haunches, I realized that (a) if it were to flex, my knee would require lots of local anesthetic and several burly physical therapists, and (b) a Southeast Asian woman in my shoes would be even further up shit creek than I. They spend half their waking hours in a squat, in the bathroom, in the kitchen, chatting with the neighbors, having babies . . . No wonder Ibu had been sympathetic right from the get go. I wondered how she'd react if I hosed down her bathroom.

To get within range of my target, I resorted to a schizophrenic cheerleading move, my right side supporting all the weight in a heroic deep knee bend, the wounded leg slowly sliding to the left in a hesitant right-angled split. Just as the finish line appeared on the horizon, I lost my balance, my windmilling arms hurled the flashlight to its death on the cement floor, and I unleashed a torrent of pee on my sarong. Remembering the scene where John Malkovich dies of dysentery in *The Sheltering Sky*, I reminded myself that it could be worse.

The knee appeared no better in the morning, but we rationalized that miracles seldom happen overnight. While I delved deeper into Somerset's pre-bikini world, Greg set out to explore Bukittinggi. What little I'd seen of the town seemed tailored to my liking, what with the oatmeal and the mist, but here I was, stuck in bed, devising tactics to evade *jamu* massage. As word got around, neighbors—primarily young males—swung by the porch to peek in at the exotic wounded specimen. Other than a few who drilled me on the usual topics—what is your name, where are you from, what is your job, what is your age, why are you not married—they preferred to treat my window as a television, commenting to each other on what little action went on inside the box. Somersetted out after a couple of hours, I switched to Lonely Planet, so I could read up on all the things I was missing. Goddamnit! Bukittinggi was a hot spot of matrilineal Minangkabau culture, where everything is inherited through the female line and the boss women often dressed their hair to mimic bulls' horns, the same as the sway-backed roofs of their houses. If anyone should be soaking up all that matrilineal goodness, it was I, not Mr. Two Knees!

He returned with more Beng Bengs and a long, skinny present rolled up in newspaper. "You got me an umbrella?"

"Open it and see," he said, stretching out across the foot of the bed, reveling in the role of debonair gift lavisher. I stripped off the wrapping. It was a beautiful, dark wood walking stick carved with flowers and leaves. I'd wanted a cane since the age of four, when I amused myself by hobbling around the house with the formal silver-handled one that had been passed down through generations of Hallidays before coming to a rest in our hallway umbrella stand. As a medical accessory, my new cane was every bit as cool as a black eye patch. It certainly made going to the toilet easier.

By dinnertime, I was testy, partly due to Lonely Planet. Having read their description of *dadhi campur*, a special Bukittinggi breakfast mash involving oats, fresh coconut, avocado, bananas, molasses, and buffalo yogurt, eating Beng Bengs in bed struck me as unadventurous and dumb. The cafés serving that dish were too far down the hill for me to manage, but there was a place specializing in spicy Padang food a short walk away. Greg offered to see if they'd pack something up for carryout, but I wouldn't hear of it. After all, I had my cane.

The severity of my injury reasserted itself on the trek to the restaurant, a distance of about two city blocks on a quiet, well-paved road. Even with the stick, my knee hurt terribly. Holding on to Greg's arm did not seem secure enough. I had to hook my elbow around his neck, making him responsible for so much of my weight that he bent like a bow. "Are you sure you want to do this?" he asked, as I made my laborious way forward, inventing my own form of Lamaze breathing. I couldn't turn back now that we were halfway there.

I had worked up a powerful hunger by the time we arrived at the small, packed restaurant that had all the earmarks of a beloved neighborhood joint. The waitress, looking uneasy, tried to convince us the food would be too hot for our Western palates. Smiling broadly, I insisted that we knew what we were in for and couldn't wait to try it. The other diners regarded us with frank, none-too-friendly stares as we followed the waitress to a table placed next to the wall, me trying not to make too big a spectacle of myself as I limped along, my cane getting tangled in other people's chair legs. I understood. This was their turf, different than the banana pancake places that catered to foreign tastes. They probably thought we expected Eric Clapton cassettes and an Arnold Schwarzenegger video. Maybe it was the cane. If it was intended as a purely decorative bit of souvenir kitsch, I might appear a weirdo for actually using it, like someone wandering around Bali in Birkenstocks, a Dallas Cowboys T-shirt and a carved wooden frog mask.

Finally seated at our table, I elevated my leg by slinging my foot onto a chair in plain view of everyone else in the room. Then, because I didn't want them to think I was merely rude, I hitched my skirt high on the thigh to show off my cantaloupe joint. When our food arrived—big plates of rice covered with scraps of meat and vegetables swimming in chili paste—I eschewed silverware in favor of my fingers, the preferred method for eating Padang-style grub. Greg shook his head, holding tight to his fork as I happily shoveled it in, pausing just once to make sure I was using the same hand as our fellow patrons. Never having gone so far native that I stopped using toilet paper, I had trouble remembering which one was viewed as the wiping hand, the one you weren't supposed to offer in greeting, let alone lick the fingers of following a delicious meal.

"Wow, was this ever worth the walk," I enthused, as bits of rice and chicken fell from my grasp. By the time I finished, the floor beneath my chair looked as if a toddler had been eating in that spot. I was full of plans to eat every meal there for the remainder of our stay in Bukittinggi, but the arduous journey back to the guesthouse convinced me I might never walk anywhere ever again. Much as I enjoyed peppering my speech with a casual, shoestring-traveler, war-correspondent patois, I was still hesitant to bring up the idea of med-evac to Greg.

It seemed like the kind of thing that would take an entire day to plan, anyway, and he had a date. Two teenage boys he'd met the day before were taking him to the bullfights, something I was happy to miss, having read *The Sun Also Rises*. Even after the boys clarified that these bulls wouldn't be slain, just roughed up a little, it was still an event I had no interest in attending. I was more the flower-market type. Making sure that I had ample supplies of junk food and bananas, Greg set out with his new pals. Bapak returned so often to hector me about *jamu* that I was forced to draw the curtains and close the door to signal that I was "sleeping" and thus should not be disturbed. Sitting in the dark, stuffy chamber, I sank into an existential funk. According to the bio in the back of *Collected Short Stories, Volume 4*, Somerset Maugham wrote forty-seven books, went to medical school, and traveled the world dozens of times back in the day when you really had to work hard to get somewhere. Talk about amounting to something. By contrast, I was a late-night, low-budget actress with a degree so ridiculous I might have majored in underwater basket weaving, and now I couldn't even go to the bathroom without a cane! I had no idea what I was doing in life, just blindly trooping from one flying fox nest to another. Greg returned a few hours after dark, full of stories about how one of the boys had taken his camera and run into the ring to get close-ups of the frothing bull.

It was time for a serious discussion about how to deal with my knee, which showed no signs of improvement. My neck and lower back were developing muscular complaints of their own, from constantly torquing my body into a position most comfortable for my fragile knee. If only this had happened in Jakarta, where Greg's brother lived in an air-conditioned apartment, with a fully stocked refrigerator and dozens of hours of *The Simpsons* on tape! Sam would have known where to go to get my knee treated in a timely, Western fashion. Of course, I would never have slipped down a muddy gorge in Jakarta. Maybe I'd have fallen into a canal choked with sewage, but plenty of people lived in cardboard shanties on the banks, doing their laundry and bathing in it, and nothing happened to them, or at least they all didn't die instantly! I was beginning to realize that this type of injury is better handled by an authority figure: my parents, a personal connection in the State Department, even a physician retained to treat the hot flashes and hangovers of luxury hotel guests. Greg and I had to rely on ourselves and on an old man who thought the best medicine resided in a peanut butter jar.

The bullfight boys showed up to tutor Greg in Bahasa, but they seemed embarrassed by my infirmity, and unlikely to be acquainted with a local doctor who'd completed his training at Harvard. They did have a lot to say about my cane, however, which they spied propped against the wardrobe. Making the same guttural noises of appreciation American boys produce over the latest skateboarding innovations, they passed the stick back and forth until one of them grasped the handle and pulled firmly to unsheathe a lethal-looking dagger. Who knew? I gingerly touched the blade to the pad of my thumb. It was sharp enough to butcher a hog. No wonder the people in the Padang restaurant had given me the cold shoulder. Anyone with half a grain of sense knows to steer clear of yahoos from parts beyond who don't even bother to conceal their weapons when they enter an honest establishment. I was pleased at the discovery. Even if I lost my Swiss Army knife, I'd still have a way to core the pineapples we bought in the market. I wondered if there were some way to drain a knee by making an X-shaped incision and sucking the offending liquid out, like with a snakebite.

Since Greg was home and could prevent any assaults by *jamu*, we left the door ajar to create some cross-ventilation. We were reading in bed when a bright-eyed person with close-cropped hair, gap teeth, and a small heart dangling from the hoop in his ear poked his head into the room. "I hear you're having a bit of trouble here," he said in a thick Australian accent. "Mind if I have a look?" Most girls aren't keen on hearing "That looks nasty, all right" when they display their stems to a new acquaintance of the male persuasion, but in this instance I was glad to have validation. We explained the circumstances that had led to the injury and our fruitless search for a Western doctor. "I see. And just what exactly did you have in mind for this doctor to do?" I told him about getting the accumulated fluid drained off the first time it happened. He took a deep drag on his unfiltered cigarette. "Yeah, I don't think you want anyone sticking a needle in your knee in this country." He told us that his name was Geoff and that he'd been here for some months, studying an indigenous martial art with a family who lived in a small village in the mountains. Every Saturday, he rode his motorbike into Bukittinggi to pick up his mail and see a kung-fu movie, and spent the night at our guesthouse before returning the next day. "I don't know how you'd feel about this, but I've got a man who fixes me up when my teacher gives me too good a beating. He's not a doctor—more like an Islamic holy man who knows a thing or two about bones—but if you're up for it, I could take my bike and see if he's around. He might be able to help you.

I looked at Greg. "Up to you," he said, raising his eyebrows dubiously.

"Okay, if it's no trouble."

"No trouble," Geoff smiled rakishly, pulling his helmet on. He sped away and we waited. One hour went by. Two.

"Do you think he forgot about you?" Greg asked.

"No, he probably couldn't find the guy. He said he wasn't sure if he'd be around. Maybe it's for the best. It's not necessarily a good idea to let a witch doctor start monkeying around with your bones."

"You said it, not me," Greg testified, heading out to replenish my Beng Beng supply.

Shortly after Greg left, Geoff's motorbike roared to a stop outside the window. He came in, followed by a bashful older man half his height. "Sorry it took us so long. He had to finish his badminton game," Geoff apologized. He translated my elaborate thanks into Bahasa, while the bone setter nodded and shook his head, seemingly embarrassed by all the fuss. "He wants to know which knee it is."

"Oh, this one," I said, pointing to the left. When I'd heard them coming, I'd made an effort to pull myself together, smoothing my black chiffon skirt down modestly. Very delicately, the bone setter picked up my hem and started rolling it up like the most precious spliff on the planet.

"This is an embarrassing thing for him," Geoff whispered. "He's very devout." I was glad I wasn't wearing my wraparound skirt. When he'd unveiled the swollen eyesore, he stopped, considering. Using a touch no heavier than a butterfly's eyelash, he allowed his fingertips to isolate the area of injury, then turned to make an inquiry of Geoff. "He says it's very hot. Does it hurt?"

"I tell her she must massage," Bapak interjected from the doorway, where he stood with his jar of *jamu* at the ready.

"Well, he's not hurting me, if that's what he means. The main problem is, I can't walk without feeling like someone's twisting a giant knife around in there. I can't walk at all really."

Geoff translated and the bone setter made a face that told me he understood. He tapped the knee lightly, apparently considering the best course of action, then came around to the foot of the bed. The crowd of onlookers that had formed at the window murmured amongst themselves, eager to see what he would do. To my bafflement, he started playing This Little Piggie Went to Market, humming a little as he wiggled my toes one after another. Wanting to seem companionable, I giggled a little. He laughed good-naturedly and started over with the big toe. I glanced at Geoff. He turned his palms up, shrugging. The bone setter pulled a little harder, yanking from the bases where the toes joined the foot. It hurt a little bit, to tell the truth, and whatever the joke was, it was wearing thin. "Oww," I said, still smiling, hoping he'd realize this was a bit rougher than I liked.

"Oww," he agreed pleasantly, easing up on the pressure. I laughed to show there were no hard feelings. He hummed his innocuous little tune. My jaws ached from my good-sport grin. Without warning, he pounced, pinning my thigh to the mattress as he wrenched my shin like someone throwing the lever on a seldom-used electric chair. The dislocated knee snapped back into alignment with the resounding crack of a gunshot. The audience at the window burst into spontaneous applause while I gasped, trying to regain my composure following an exquisite blast of torture that was over almost before it had begun. "You having a party?" Greg asked, appearing in the doorway with a small sack of Beng Bengs. Beside him, Bapak looked disgruntled, no doubt thinking that his *jamu* would have done the job just as well, had I not interfered with his treatment plan. As far as I was concerned, the bone setter could have declared himself the great and powerful Oz right there, but as I suspected, he was not a man to milk it. Instead, he gestured that I should take a few steps. Having played the titular role in the Indianapolis Junior Civic Theatre's production of *Heidi*, I could appreciate the drama inherent in the moment. Weak and wary of falling, I rose to my feet and staggered unassisted to Greg, just like Clara, the lame rich girl to whom Heidi's infectious can-do spirit gives the courage to eighty-six that wheelchair! It was quite remarkable. It also made me realize how completely rat-screwed we would have been if chance hadn't placed us in the same guest-house as Geoff.

"How much should I pay him?" I asked.

Geoff said that there was no set figure, but suggested a figure so low by American health care standards, it was practically Canadian. Even doubled, it was still less than the co-pay for seeing an in-network doctor. My miracle worker tucked it into the pocket of his short-sleeved dress shirt with a courteous word of thanks, though the young men pressing against the window screen to get a gander at the wad seemed impressed. I felt like I should have offered to buy him a goat in addition, but before I knew it, he was straddling the motorbike, looking almost wizened behind the tan, tank-topped Australian. For all I knew, he'd saved me by making a house call on his day off.

Hanoi Circus Monkey

On Religion

olunteering to oversee Cambodia's first democratically held elections in who knew how long—well probably somebody knew, but unless it was mentioned in *The Killing Fields*, not me—appealed to the part of Greg that had majored in political science at the University of Chicago. I looked forward to significant interaction with locals outside the tourist trade, separating ballots with the delightful middle-aged schoolteacher who would put us up in her home for as long as it took to restore freedom. The more we talked about it, the better the idea seemed, and we had a lot of time to talk about it as we traveled all the way from Medan in Sumatra to Bangkok, where we could procure Cambodian visas. Yes, we agreed on the high-speed ferry to Malaysia, volunteering in the elections would probably be the most memorable experience of the whole trip. Before, we had been part of the herd, but now we had purpose. Our companion Danny, a chess-playing fresh-from-the-army Israeli traveling on a French passport, was not so sure. "Yes, okay, but why do these people need your help to run their country? You think they will appreciate this? You think you are welcome there?"

What could I say? The middle-aged Cambodian schoolteacher I

had cooked up was certainly glad to have us. She knew we were there because we were good-hearted believers in cultural exchange. She was grateful we hadn't followed Danny to one of those Thai islands where backpackers converged to reenact *The Bacchae* every full moon. Of course, my imaginary Cambodian friend was an educated woman, a law-abiding mother with a well-developed sense of curiosity. Maybe the Khmer Rouge would see it differently.

"You think 'maybe' is the word?" Danny asked, incredulous.

Since I enjoyed Danny's company—even if I didn't, we had a long train ride ahead of us—I decided that we had agreed to disagree. We had to remain on friendly terms so that Danny and Greg could ignore me, hunched over a tiny magnetic chessboard in one death battle after another. It wasn't until we'd boarded the dusty, second-class carriage of a Thai train that another sounding board for our upcoming Cambodian adventure presented itself. Seated across the aisle was a white-haired Italian gent dressed in a dapper linen suit and a straw hat. Behind him was an emaciated, bearded monk with an accent I couldn't quite place. His robes were Thai, but he wasn't. He was too tall and his sad eyes were closer to grapes than almonds. Neither of these old Asia hands would go down the garden path with me on Cambodia.

"My dear, do you have any idea why there is a need for volunteers?" the Italian asked, patting my hand with a condescending, perfectly manicured paw. Rather than lose face by admitting that I didn't, I treated him to the smirking, opaque shrug I, like so many other young Americans, had perfected in junior high school. "It's because the United Nations people who were supposed to be supervising the elections fled for their lives," he continued, egged on by my insolence.

"Yes, there have been shootings at the polling places," the monk confirmed. "It is not safe."

"You did not know that, did you, dear girl? I know your heart is set on it, but pursuing this plan could prove foolish and fatal. If you must go to Cambodia, stick to Angkor Wat, but even that, I would not recommend. A large tourist attraction like that most likely presents no danger, but getting in and out of the country is another matter entirely." Quite satisfied with himself, the old Italian pulled a bunch of lychees from a plastic bag and offered them around. I had a hunch that these guys felt superior because they were older. Just because the Italian could have been my grand-father, the old chauvinist thought I couldn't handle anything heavier than sightseeing, shopping, and sunbathing. How conven-ient for him to overlook that girls my age and younger had served as combat nurses in the Vietnam War! (Which I most definitely would have, had the war dragged on for another couple of decades, and had my degree been in nursing rather than theater, and had women been eligible for the draft, because ain't no way I would have volunteered. I could sing along with every word on the *Wood-stock* double album.)

"Where were these UN workers from?" I challenged.

"Being an American wouldn't save you in this case," the monk said gently.

"You're absolutely right, my friend," the Italian chortled. "The Khmer Rouge does not discriminate! They kill everyone equally! Isn't equality the foundation of your beloved democracy?"

Not wanting to give the self-satisfied old devil so much as a smile, I turned to the monk. "Where are you from?"

"Thailand is my home now. Before I became a Thai monk, I

lived in India for seven years. I was a *sadhu*, a devotee of Shiva. I was born in Surinam." I blinked. Viet was the only "nam" I knew. "It is a small country in South America. It was a Dutch colony. My parents are Dutch."

"That's amazing." I grinned to show the monk that I liked him much better than that crass Italian, cackling away to himself like Truman Capote. "So, do you live in Bangkok?"

"I live in a small monastery near Hua Hin."

"Is it right near the beach?"

"You know Hua Hin?" the monk asked, surprised.

"Yeah, sure," I told him. Truth was, the only reason I knew anything about Hua Hin was because it doubled for Phnom Penh in *The Killing Fields*. One of my favorite movies was *Swimming to Cambodia*, an autobiographical monologue in which Spalding Gray recounts his experiences as a bit player in *The Killing Fields*, how he struggled to remember his three lines and let go of his neuroses so he could enjoy the tropical location. For the next twenty minutes or so, I regaled the monk with the choicest bits of *Swimming to Cambodia*, heartily encouraging him to see it as soon as possible. The Italian, unimpressed, moved over to watch Danny and Greg's chess game, eventually provoking a heated political discussion. The old man was a Fascist and an anti-Semite they told me, when I returned to my seat.

They considered Kosiya, the monk, harmless, if a little weird. Before he got off, he invited Greg and me to visit him at his monastery, carefully writing the address in the back of my journal. If volunteering in Cambodia meant repatriating in a body bag, perhaps hanging out at Kosiya's monastery could be our "authentic" experience. He had warned me that it was nothing fancy, just a few ramshackle buildings perched on a high hill that housed him, an elderly abbot, and a Buddhist laywoman who cooked and cleaned. It sounded good to me. A couple of Thai monasteries offered meditation retreats for foreigners, but they were rumored to be somewhat woo-woo, so getting Greg there would involve chains and a very strong ox. An atheist Jew, he had no interest in becoming a Buddhist, not like lapsed-Episcopal me. I spent the last leg of our journey to Bangkok practicing the loving-kindness meditation I read about in one of the small pamphlets Kosiya had given me.

May all beings be free from harm and danger. May they be free from physical suffering. May they be free from mental suffering. May they take care of themselves happily.

I repeated the paragraph silently, unleashing global good vibes like flying monkeys. According to the booklet's author, the meditation was most effective when it concluded on a multiple of three. I tried ticking the cycles off on my fingers, but was lulled to inattention by the singsong quality of all those "may's." One minute I was encircling Mother Earth with the healing powers of my good good Buddhist lovin', and the next, I was wondering whatever happened to Melanie Brooks, the jump-rope fiend who could out–double Dutch any girl in second grade. Guiltily, I resumed the meditation, only to forget the words. What came after physical suffering, again? I imagined myself kneeling virtuously in front of a small altar trimmed with oranges, lotus garlands, photos of cross-legged, nearly naked bald men, and incense smoldering in a dragon-shaped ceramic holder. To quote Bart Simpson, *cooool*. "Greg, I think we should take Kosiya up on his invitation," I announced, barging in on their chess game.

"You are serious? You would want to do this?" Danny asked skeptically. "I mean, it is your life, but I do not think it is such a good idea, with the ears and . . ." Unable to convince me, he trailed off, still spindling his fingers out from his temples to indicate the long black hairs we all had noticed sprouting from the tops of Kosiya's ears. Greg snickered. "If I had such a problem, I would cut," Danny insisted, his furrowed brows conveying that any sane person would do likewise.

"Well, I want to go. It'll be neat, staying at a real monastery, not one set up for *farangs*."

"Didn't you tell me that the reason all the *farangs* go to that place on Koh Phangan is that it's one of the only monasteries that let women participate in the meditations?" Greg recalled.

"Who is so crazy to get up at four o'clock in order to sit on the floor doing nothing?" Danny scowled.

"I suppose cleaning toilets and making breakfast for the menfolk is a *kind* of meditation," Greg mused, happy as ever to bait me.

"Okay, okay," I said. "But listen, Kosiya said the abbot in charge of his monastery doesn't really give a flying fuck what anybody does so long as they leave him alone."

"You think this is right, that the women are slaves to the men?" Danny demanded. "An Israeli woman would not stand for it."

"Are you sure you don't want to go with us to Hua Hin, Danny?" I asked, already nostalgic for his company. "You wouldn't have to do any Buddhist stuff. You could play chess and hang out on the beach all day."

Greg looked hopeful, but Danny shook his head. "No, not with the ears and all of that. You should come with me. Where I'm going you can buy a joint and have a beer."

• • •

Two days later, with cheap plane tickets to Saigon stashed in our money belts, Greg and I again boarded the train, with nearly a week to kill before our Vietnamese visas would be ready. Kosiya had told us to stop by his friend's bar when we got to Hua Hin, and Duncan would give us directions to Wat Khow Krailat. Arriving at the Kiwi Corner around lunch, we were told that Duncan rarely arrived before two. I tried to hide my nervousness from Greg. The last time I had showed up unannounced to partake of some casually offered, noncommercial Thai hospitality, Isaac and I learned that our unsuspecting hostess, a Peace Corps worker named Elfie, had returned to the States three months earlier. Now history seemed to be repeating itself, as Duncan, a beefy, middle-aged New Zealander with a serious motorcycle and a wicked hangover, claimed that he hadn't seen the monk in weeks. We explained that we had met him earlier in the week on the train from Penang. "He probably just stopped off to see some mates, then. He does that sometimes, disappears with no explanation, but he always pops up again, Kosiya does. He knows all sorts of strange people." Duncan poured himself a shot. "I've got stuff to take care of here, but if you can cool your heels a while, I'll run you out to his wat on my bike at about five o'clock. That old abbot won't give a shit if you wait for him there. You haven't got some great bloody rucksacks, have you?" I glanced guiltily at the two thirty-pounders propped against a barstool. What I wouldn't have given in that moment to travel as lightly as an expat, just a key ring and a pair of Ray-Bans.

"No thanks, that's okay. Maybe we'll check in at a guesthouse, spend the day at the beach and then, if it's okay with you, use your phone to call the monastery and see if Kosiya's back."

Duncan turned to shout at his Thai bartender for putting too little ice in the drinks. "They smile and smile and the whole time they're just looking for ways to rob you blind," he growled.

"Okay, then, well, I guess we're off. It was nice to meet you. Maybe we'll see you again when we come in to use the phone."

"You're welcome to use my phone," Duncan smiled coldly, "but it won't do you much fucking good. Can't call the monastery if they haven't got a phone."

"Oh."

"Tell you what. When it's convenient for me, I'll pop round on the bike, see if anyone knows when Kosiya's expected back. Then you can come by here, see if it's worth it for you to stay on."

"Oh, yes please! That's a really kind offer. We'll take you up on it." Duncan rearranged some phlegm in the back of his throat and lit a cigarette. "I mean, even if Kosiya doesn't show up, there's probably lots for us to do here, right? With the beach and everything?"

"Shit hole," Duncan muttered, taking a stack of the previous day's receipts to the end of the bar.

"That Duncan is *charming*," Greg gushed as we trudged off, sweating under our giant bloody rucksacks. "A delight!" I smiled painfully. At least he was making light of the situation. Sarcasm was preferable to the grim silence I deserved for hauling us out to meet a hairy-eared, heavily bearded monk who wasn't Thai or even here. With my luck, Duncan's opinion of Hua Hin would prove accurate. Wait a minute, he hadn't been calling me a shit hole, had he? Was "shit hole" Kiwi for "asshole," like you stupid American asshole, don't I have enough trouble on my hands dealing with the thieving natives of my adopted country without having to waste bloody petrol chasing that AWOL Buddhist freak for you? "Ayun, relax,"

Greg said, catching my anguished expression. "We'll go to the beach, spend the night, decide if we want to stay longer. We'll have fun. No big deal."

Shockingly, he turned out to be right. The breezy corner room that we rented in a wooden hotel not far from the ocean was painted a calming shade of honeydew. The vast beach was clean and nearly deserted. We amused ourselves and some vacationing Thai preschoolers by clambering over the giant boulders that appeared at low tide, flicking our tongues like reptiles beneath the massive wigs we had fashioned from seaweed. We procured a delicious early dinner from a hopping night market set up in a parking lot near the Kiwi Corner. We strolled a strip lined with bars and restaurants strung with plastic Foster's Lager pennants. The sandwich boards eschewed free video triple-features, promising instead filet mignon and real Australian pub grub. We bellied up to the bar at one establishment, dazzled by our first blast of air conditioning since Greg's brother had squired us around Jakarta, taking us to the Western-style chain restaurants popular with members of the Foreign Service. We were the youngest patrons in the joint by a good twenty years, and I was the only Western woman. The gray-haired men rattling the rocks in their lowball glasses eyed my bright purple, circus-strongman-print, baby-doll frock with distaste. The mature Thai women sipping soft drinks beside them were dressed tastefully in modest pantsuits and flowered rayon dresses. So, that's why we were the only backpackers in Hua Hin! Apparently, all the other youngsters knew that it was the Oldsmobile of Thai beaches, the favored destination of British and Australian sex tourists who treated their rented Thai ladies much as I imagined they'd treated their wives.

We chugged down our gin and tonics and escaped, picking up a cheap bottle of rice whiskey to drink on the beach as the sun set. Greg trained the camera on me prancing barefoot in my ill-fitting purple shift, issuing drunken proclamations that I would love him long time. It was fun to be the only backpackers in Hua Hin, like crashing the squares' dinner party in ankle bells. On our second night, we followed the sounds of a party to a parking lot where a big screen had been erected. We lay on the pavement, captivated and horribly confused by our first Hong Kong martial arts spectacle, a costume drama complete with numchucks, superhuman jumping and star-shaped boomerangs that lopped off evildoers' heads as Thai grannies and their wakeful charges cheered. Sometime during the four-hour epic, I crawled to a refreshment cart, eager to taste one of the ice cream sundaes the other audience members were gobbling down nonstop. For a few baht, I was handed a plastic bag of chipped ice and sweetened condensed milk, studded with jackfruit, globs of gelatin, and beans. To this day I continue to pray that it will one day become as commonplace as sushi and chai in the American diet. (No doubt Starbucks is looking into it.)

On our third day's mandatory swing by the Kiwi Corner, Duncan told us that he had run into Kosiya. We settled the bill for our honeydew-colored room and boarded a public bus, showing the driver a piece of paper on which Duncan had copied the name of Kosiya's monastery in Thai script. I had resigned myself rather happily to the idea that Kosiya wouldn't show up until after we had to leave for Vietnam. Looking up at the monastery compound's red-tiled roofs sparkling under the noon sun, I had to remind myself that this was going to be great, better even than volunteering in the

Cambodian elections, and quite possibly my spiritual awakening. "You're sure he's expecting us?" Greg asked as we panted up the hundreds of steep steps cut into the hillside.

"Yes," I gasped, thanking my lucky stars yet again for Geoff and the bone setter. To think, only a month earlier, I could barely hobble to the john.

"Where are we going to sleep? Not in the same room with him."

"We'll find out." The stairs were so tortuous, I was tempted to break halfway up for a cigarette. I couldn't imagine that this was any less bad than trekking in Nepal.

"What's his name again?"

"Kosiya."

"Is that his real name or his monk name?"

"It's his porn star name, Greg. I don't know!"

"Are you going to become a hardcore Buddhist now? Is he going to expect us to chant or something, because I'm not going to." We reached the summit. Four miniature cottages with carved verandas and roofs shaped like Viking boats stood on stilts in a small pond. Frangipani and flame trees dropped their blossoms into the water. The only sounds were of automobiles passing on the distant road below. Whenever I daydreamed about becoming a devout Buddhist, I pictured myself padding around a tatami mat in a simple room furnished with a low table, a sprig of bamboo, and a bell. This was the exterior I'd never bothered to imagine! If Greg hadn't been there, I would have prostrated myself in gratitude. Leaving our backpacks at the top of the stairs, we tread cautiously onto the grounds. "Do you think we should knock?" Greg asked.

"No, they might be meditating or something. Let's just wait and see if anybody comes." I was afraid of rousing the old abbot, imagined him yanking the door off its hinges, furious to have his hermitage breached by a Western woman with unshaved armpits and a yin ya tattoo. Sighing, Greg sank onto his backpack and opened *Midnight's Children*, the Salman Rushdie epic that serves as most budget travelers' crash course on India. I explored, tentatively. There was a long, open shed with a few rotting Buddhas at one end, their gold leaf flaking and fluttering in the slight breeze. It was very picturesque but undeniably ramshackle, not like Bangkok's grand *wats*, where tourists videotaped the Buddha's garland-bedecked toes and adolescent monks armed with twig brooms continually tended the inside of the temple. Maybe I could repay Kosiya for his hospitality by sprucing up this neglected meditation room or storage shed or whatever it was. I didn't want Kosiya or the abbot thinking I was an unenlightened freeloader. There was a tatty, homemade broom propped in the corner. Surely it wouldn't be presumptuous to sweep the dead leaves carpeting the dirt floor into tidy piles. The string bundling the broom straws disintegrated on the first pass. Okay. I took a few deep breaths to calm down and decided I should try to meditate. Kneeling in the leaves, I lowered my lids to half-mast, allowing my eyeballs to drift toward each other until the Buddhas blurred into globby, gold marshmallow men. I concentrated on the whoosh of the pines rocking in the mild breeze. If I were a monk, this would be the soundtrack to my life. No phone, no radio, no burping, farting boyfriends making fun of yoga and Joni Mitchell. Just *whoosh, burrrrr, creeeeak* and that nice pinecone smell mixed with the not unpleasant aroma of crumbling mildewed Buddhas.

A generator started up quite nearby, as intrusive as a parrot squawking, "Stranger! Stranger!" and I raced out of the shed, startled, hoping that I wouldn't slam into the elderly abbot. Greg was still hunched over his book. I idled near the ruins of an ornamental fountain beyond which the ocean was visible over flowering treetops.

"So, you decided to come after all." Kosiya snuck up on me holding a shower bucket, a damp towel knotted around his scrawny waist. After all? Hadn't we just spent three days hanging around Hua Hin, waiting for him to meander home? "Give me one moment to put on my robes and I'll show you where you can stay." Reappearing in what I came to think of as monk casual, a wide strip of orange fabric that crossed his bare chest like a Girl Scout sash before descending to wrap the loins, Kosiya led us across a wooden bridge to the cottage next to his. "The monk who lived here disappeared," he announced. "It's very simple, as you can see."

"Simple's good," I said, peering over the foot-high threshold into a tiny, dark room, most of which was taken up by two straw sleeping mats. The previous occupant had left a few orange tapers affixed to the exposed beams. It was so cute, the playhouse I would have killed to have as a child.

"I can give you a sheet and some more candles. Do you have mosquito coils? Good, you'll need them. As long as you sleep with the doors and windows shut, they won't be too much of a nuisance." After Kosiya fetched the supplies, he went to inform the abbot that some Western guests were in residence. I assumed this would lead to an invitation to the head man's house, for tea if not cocktails, but glancing up, I noticed Kosiya reading on his own porch.

"What do you suppose the deal is with eats?" Greg asked quietly.

"I don't know. There's a woman who cooks for the monks, but I don't know if they eat in a mess hall or what. Why don't you ask Kosiya?"

"Why don't *you* ask Kosiya?"

"I'm not hungry."

"We didn't have lunch," Greg pointed out.

"I can live. Ask him, if you're so hungry. It's no big deal. Just ask him." I should have considered the food thing in advance. I hadn't noticed any restaurants or markets on the drive and we hadn't thought to bring provisions from Hua Hin. I had been raised to serve a tray of cheese and crackers shortly after the guests' arrival, but this was probably just the sort of thing Kosiya had dispensed with when he relinquished his worldly attachments. I decided that if anyone should come off as the American Princess, disrupting the usual mealtime routine, asking for free food when none had been offered, it should be Greg.

"I guess I can hold out a while," he conceded, stretching out on the porch with *Midnight's Children*. I gazed at the magenta blossoms drifting on the surface of the pond. It really was a beautiful, serene spot. It was almost like the Swiss Family Robinson exhibit at Disney World. If only Thai Monk Land had a straightforward snack bar.

Kosiya leaned over the railing of his porch. "I go swimming every afternoon at this time," he called. "You and Greg can come with me, if you like."

"Yes! Great! Greg, get your bathing suit on!" I was glad to see that Kosiya had a beach bag, too. I had been afraid that our suntan lotion, camera, sarongs, and books might strike him as contagion from the material world. Quadriceps quaking, we descended the hundreds of stairs to the road.

Before we stepped onto the shoulder, Kosiya draped himself in a larger cloth, fashioning a sort of cape and a skirt with a more respectable hemline. "The abbot doesn't care, but there are a lot of old-fashioned people around here," he explained. "They like their monks to look a certain way." The petrol-fumed air shimmering above the blacktop felt about twenty degrees hotter than the temperature uphill. We passed the skeletons of several new buildings under construction. "It's going to be a Club Med," Kosiya told us. We stepped over a low chain onto a dirt access road. Kosiya pointed out a long Quonset hut. "That's where the construction workers live with their families." I was horrified. The sun beat down on the corrugated metal roof and sides of the double-decker barracks, a windowless tube open only at the ends. It would be like being cremated!

"Do they have electricity?" I asked.

"They have nothing." A little boy playing on the blazing, hard-packed ground noticed us and gave a shout. Immediately, a small herd of children rounded the side of the building, running full-tilt toward Kosiya. Laughing, he dipped into his bag and handed the first boy a small packet of gummy candy discs. They looked delicious. I wondered if he had more. The little boy hugged him and raced back toward the barracks. The other kids were hopping up and down, barely able to contain their excitement as more treats were handed out: a bag of candied rice cakes, some rambutan and mangoes, banana leaf parcels, servings of *pad ped* and curry, a couple of plastic-wrap bladders filled with iced coffee and fastened with rubber bands. Kosiya dispensed this booty equitably, waving goodbye as his last customer skipped off, a green coconut bouncing against his knobby knee. "When I make my morning alms rounds in Hua Hin, they give me more than I can possibly eat myself. A monk should sustain himself on simple food, but some of the shopkeepers try to outdo each other. They think they will make more merit by giving more. They cheat and steal and curse each other when they get drunk, but they think they are good Buddhists because they give me half a fried chicken." Greg's stomach growled.

"What else do they give you?" I asked as we walked onto a gorgeous, deserted beach.

Kosiya took off his longer wrap, letting it flutter fetchingly behind in the wind. "Oh, candles. Incense. Bus tokens."

We came across a jellyfish the size of a pizza, high above the tide line. Kosiya prodded it with a stick. It was like a lava lamp or a melted paperweight or something, colorful bubbles and stars suspended in the goo. Kosiya looked at it for a long time, pulling it off of the sand on the end of his stick. "Wow. It's pretty, huh?" I asked, trying to look reverent. Greg spread his sarong on the sand, unzipped his daypack, and shaded his eyes with Salman Rushdie.

"I'd like to meditate on it," Kosiya said. "There's an important Buddhist sutra, do you know it?" I shook my head. "You observe decay, meditate on a corpse as it wastes away." I wondered what the jellyfish would smell like a few days from now. Maybe it was edible. Maybe we should tell the construction workers' kids to come and get it. "It's a beautiful meditation, to watch the flesh putrefy and fall away. Few people are willing to accept that impermanence is our natural state. Last year, I found a dead seagull on the beach and sat with it for three days."

"God, that reminds me of one of my favorite movies. *A Zed and Two Noughts*, have you heard of it? That's okay, nobody has. It starts out with this horrific car crash in which two women and a swan die in front of a European zoo. It turns out that the women are married to twin brothers who work in the zoo, but the brothers are so estranged they don't even look like each other anymore, and to the best of their knowledge, their wives had never even met. So anyway, one of the brothers becomes obsessed with what's happening to his wife's body after the funeral, so he sets up a time-lapse photography lab. He starts out with an apple, but then he moves on to a dead bird and an angelfish and a dalmatian, and, if I'm recalling correctly, eventually he bribes a zookeeper to whack a zebra for him. Periodically, the camera swoops through the lab at night with all the cameras flashing at different times as this urgent music swells, *ba buh ba buh ba buh ba buh tweet tweet tweet tweet.* Like that. But then sometimes, the director shows a sped-up film clip of just one of the animals, so you see—this is going to sound really gross—for instance, okay, the dalmatian starts getting discolored and his lips pull back and then little clouds of insects swarm in and out of him, so it's almost like he's dancing, you know, their movements reanimate his corpse and then eventually he sort of collapses and then he's just bones. And for those sequences, they play this really funny music, really busy, like an LP played at 78."

"It's incredible to me that a scene like that exists in an American film."

"English, actually. *A Zed and Two Noughts.*"

"How does it end? Do his observations give him a new perspective?"

"Oh, well, both brothers fall in love with this French woman who was in the accident with their wives, who has to have both legs amputated and she gets pregnant and the twins start looking like twins again and then the French woman dies, I think, and the twins go to her childhood home, this sort of overgrown country estate called L'Escargot. They lie down naked on a platform and inject each other with something that kills them as the time-lapse films play on a screen hanging over them. But here's the really funny part: As they're lying there, still warm, these snails come out in droves to lick the salt off their bodies. They start climbing all over the platform and they fuck up the film projector and that crazy sped-up music starts up again and there's a close-up of this one snail whirling around on a record player and, well, anyway, I think you'd really like it if you get a chance to see it . . ." I trailed off, ashamed to have used the F-word in front of a Buddhist monk when a simple "screwed" would have done.

"Extraordinary. What was the name of the other you recommended?"

"*Swimming to Cambodia?*"

"Yes. Next week, I'm going to visit my parents in Amsterdam. Perhaps I will have a chance to see both films." I smiled as Kosiya waded into the ocean, the unwound sash of his orange loincloth floating behind him. I felt proud to have extrapolated the Buddhist principles from a little-seen art film. Wouldn't a Dutch video clerk be surprised when a guy looking like a brunette van Gogh in an orange toga plopped that double feature on the rental counter?

"What was all that about dead seagulls?" whispered Greg.

On the walk home, Kosiya showed us the turnoff for a beachfront seafood restaurant. "If you're hungry, maybe you can eat dinner there. I hear it is a bit expensive, but it will save you from having to go back to Hua Hin."

"Yes, that sounds good. I don't think we want to fool with catching the bus at night." Greg asked Kosiya if he'd join us as our guest, but he said he never ate after four o'clock. No wonder he was so gaunt. I remember reading an interview with the supermodel Cheryl Tiegs in my grandmother's *Good Housekeeping* magazine, where she said the exact same thing.

We were the only customers in the cavernous open-air restaurant that night. Picking at my prawns, I wondered about all the uneaten fish spoiling in the kitchen, waiting for Club Med to open. Deterioration was much more palatable considered in the context of indie film. "So are you glad we came?" I asked.

"Ye-e-e-esss," Greg drawled conditionally, knowing that nothing was to be gained from saying "no." Why was it, I wondered, that with all my boyfriends, I had never once managed to hook up with a fellow groovy, someone who would have loved immersing himself in Buddhism without the distractions of electricity or food on demand? Actually, Wylie, with his ponytail and clove cigarettes, might have been open to the experience. His father was Japanese—maybe he was Buddhist. I couldn't remember now. Less than nine months after my return from Paris, Wylie was gone, vanquished by the one who sat across from me now, holding his tongue. Religion had come between Greg and me in the past because he wouldn't stop making fun of Christmas carols.

After a nearly sleepless night tossing on the thin straw mat and battling kamikaze mosquitoes in the stifling pitch black of our shuttered cottage, Kosiya woke us at four to accompany him on his alms round. He coached us as we waited sleepily for the bus. "You may notice that when I accept alms from a woman, I don't allow her to touch me. Instead, she puts her alms directly in my bowl. So, Greg, you can touch me, but Ayun, not you. It's nothing personal. It's just, as I said yesterday, some people expect their monks to observe the old ways. It's important to remain proper. When I receive the alms, you can put your hands together in the *wai* to say thank you." The bus driver wouldn't let Kosiya pay. The three of us touched our palms together politely. "Sometimes I have to pay, but never with this guy. We get a special discount on Thai Airways, too. Monks pay 10 percent of full fare, wherever they fly."

Hua Hin, at five in the morning, was otherworldly, shrouded in mist. Most of the businesses had metal grilles pulled over their entrances, but the proprietors were up, waiting behind sidewalk tables heaped with individual portions of that day's offering. We followed Kosiya as he went from table to table, wordlessly receiving the booty. Some of the narrower alleys we had to ourselves, but on the main drag, we waited in lines six men deep. Kosiya received his alms in a handsome lacquered bowl. When it threatened to brim over, he dumped the take into an orange cotton shoulder bag Greg had been entrusted with for the morning. I followed, taskless, a smiling public relations person. I was glad when Kosiya pulled a second bag from his wrappings, and Greg gave me the first to lug. The scene was decidedly foreign, and yet the drill was familiar. It was as if every kid in the neighborhood had decided to go trick-or-treating as a Buddhist monk in saffron robes. In this context, I was suspicious of Kosiya's contempt for the shopkeepers who tried to make extra merit through fancy donations. Where I came from, households glad-handing fun-sized Snickers were accorded the extra respect they deserved. Why would an old lady who stingily dropped single turds of off-brand penny candy into our plastic pumpkins be equally deserving of our love? Like some sugar-crazed third-grader, I couldn't wait to get back to Wat Khow Krailat to inventory the loot.

Kosiya invited us to his cottage for breakfast, spreading the morning's haul along the wooden porch railing. He ate sparingly, but Greg and I dug in with relish, eager to sample all of our favorite dishes from this Buddhist smorgasbord. In the middle of this feeding frenzy, the laywoman showed up toting a metal tiffin tin. Kosiya thanked her perfunctorily, waiting to lift the lids until she had left to clean the bathroom. "Does anybody want some of this?" he asked, displaying an uninspiring pile of white rice and a separate compartment of grayish, boiled vegetables. We shook our heads, our mouths full. Kosiya seemed excited only by the durian, a large medieval mace of fruit, whose stink is legendary. Although its fans rival the French asparagus devotees who arrange their vacations to allow attendance at the first spring harvests, its excremental stench earned a permanent ban from the lobby of Singapore's famous Raffles Hotel.

Although I enthusiastically wolfed down cheese reeking of vomit or unwashed feet, fruit that smelled like shit was a frontier I had heretofore felt no compulsion to cross. Kosiya cracked the armored rind with a hunting knife, dug out a hunk of butter-colored pulp, and offered it to me on the tip of his blade. I hesitated, embarrassed, unable to shake the feeling that one of us was responsible for the sulfurous cloud of silent flatulence that floated between us. "Its taste is heaven," he confided. Okay, what the hell? One courtesy bite of this dirty diaper and I presumed I'd be off the hook. Except I couldn't stop at one! The flavor was irresistible, a sort of delicately sweetened mascarpone that dissolved discreetly on the tongue. The Raffles Hotel was fucked in the head not to recognize durian as a treat to be eaten with the best silver! I couldn't wait to have a dinner party to force all my Chicago friends to try it.

After breakfast, Duncan roared up on his motorcycle, as rough around the edges as ever, but slightly less grumpy thanks to the giant joint he pulled from his pocket and passed around. Too stoned to follow the conversation, I marveled at the confluence that resulted in me smoking pot with a Buddhist monk from Surinam, a belligerent Kiwi bar owner, and Greg. It hit me that even more interesting combinations occur unnoticed every day on public transit, but before I could spiral down that paranoia-inducing corridor, Kosiya asked if I'd like to see his passport photo. "Sure," I said, eyes pinwheeling. He flipped to the first page, where a Christlike fellow with a flowing beard and hair longer than mine stared haggardly in black and white. "Oh my god, Kosiya, is this you?"

"Yes, when I was a *sadhu* in India. For seven years, I followed Lord Shiva. Would you like to see my trident?"

Duncan snorted. "Kosiya, mate, you're a fucking head case!" Kosiya giggled as he carefully stowed his passport. "Buddhism, Hinduism—it's a crock is what it is!" Duncan announced, flicking an ant off the railing.

"You know what Marx said," Greg interjected, his eyeballs an alarming strawberry hue.

"That religion is the opiate of the masses?" Duncan asked. I was amazed by his coherence. I was mired at that level where Karl becomes Groucho becomes Ellen, one of the ninth-graders who shared my first Paris hotel room. She spelled it differently but wouldn't it be wild if she were the Marx Greg was talking about? I tried to keep hold of the thread as Duncan and Kosiya regaled us with tales of another monk friend, the incorrigible Johnny White Robe, who was Agent Oranged in Vietnam. Kosiya was moved to speak at length on the true nature of Buddhism. His words eddied past my ears, ruffling the blossoms of the flame trees and sailing out over the ocean. I wondered if I dare ask him to crack out his alms bag again. We had barely touched the candy.

After a long nap, it was time for Kosiya's swim. Again, we

unloaded the day's remaining alms on the urchins who lived crammed in that metal oven. This time I noticed the sign staked not far from their temporary quarters, showing a boxy high-rise of the variety that lines Miami Beach. What would happen to Kosiya's little friends when construction was completed? One of their mothers came out, bearing a baby on her hip, to thank Kosiya for sharing his ongoing contribution. Instead of speaking to her, he laid a hand on the baby's head and cooed. She headed back to the communal barracks as happily as a fan who's bagged an autograph. I mentioned that I had read that touching people on the head was an insult here. "Is it okay if you're a baby?"

"It's okay if you're a monk," Kosiya smiled. "Actually, I am a baby. I can't speak or read Thai. All of my food is given to me. If I get in trouble or need something, I rely on my faith that others will help me. Like a baby, I entrust myself to the universe."

"When I was in Spain, I had to pretend to be a can opener," I said. "It was the only way to make this man who ran the refreshment stand understand what I wanted."

"How do you act like a can opener?" Kosiya asked. I demonstrated, opening my mouth wide and pretending to puncture a tin lid with my front teeth. Raising my hands to chin level, I spun an invisible can, growling in girlish approximation of a humming motor.

"Why didn't you just do this?" Greg persisted, squeezing imaginary handles together with his left hand, while turning a crank with his right.

"I was electric."

Again, we were the only bathers on the expansive beach. Like the Club Med scouts, I could see the appeal. There was no coral to cut vacationers' feet, no debris littering the sand, no stinky fish smell like on some of Bali's most popular beaches. The big jellyfish remained, unchanged, but one jellyfish is not the stumbling block that hundreds of jellyfish are. The water was warm. The sky was blue. I could have stayed there forever. I was surprised when Kosiya and Greg wanted to leave after a couple of hours. "You guys go on without me."

"You're sure you don't want to come with us?" Greg hesitated.

"I'm perfectly happy. Go. I've got my book and the sunscreen. I know the way back. See you in an hour or so." As their retreating figures dwindled, I took my book down to the water's edge. It was my Club Med moment, sprawling in the Gulf of Thailand, passionately reading, my savage tan becoming more ferocious with every lazy minute. I could just make out the plinking of hammers from the far-off construction site, so faint that the effect was pleasant, like a neighbor's lawn mower on a summer afternoon. I closed my eyes, savoring the sensation of the blood-temperature saltwater lapping at my legs. Maybe this was the key to Buddhist practice, to set yourself up in conditions favorable to living in the moment. Watching the cheerful orange-and-black blotches the sun released behind my eyelids, I endeavored to get through a few rounds of my loving-kindness meditation.

May all beings of the world be filled with loving-kindness. May they be free from physical suffering. May they be free from mental suffering. May they—

Wait a minute, why were the hairs on the back of my neck bristling? I opened my eyes and whipped around just in time to see a slim, shirtless man running from the spot where I'd left my sarong, practically cartwheeling in his haste to make a clean get away. Damn, I knew it! "Hey!" I shouted as I leapt to my feet, already running through the laundry list of things he was stealing: my shirt, my pants, a hundred fifty baht, my shoes, a disposable panoramic camera my stepfather had given me, the skull-print scarf that made me feel like a badass. "Wait! Don't take my stuff," I yelled, pounding after him. All I could think was that I'd sooner die than parade past the construction workers' barracks in a bikini. I could just see myself climbing the hundreds of steps to the monastery in two tiny handfuls of underwired black nylon, only to encounter the old abbot at the top. "Wait! Please!" The smooth, brown back disappeared over a small sand dune. I followed, as fast as my out-of-shape, recently dislocated legs could carry me. Cresting the dune, I nearly plowed into the thief, who seemed confounded that I had followed him. We grappled briefly, me intent on reclaiming my britches, him freaking on the possibility that his MTV Beach Party wet dream was coming true—albeit in a slightly doughier version—without having to emigrate to America. When I started bleating like an air horn at a football game, he popped me a glancing blow to the forehead and hightailed it down one of the dozens of rabbity sand trails leading through the scrub.

I marched back to the monastery, castigating myself for charging after the thief on his own turf, voluntarily leaving the relative safety of the exposed beach. What a booby! Man, I couldn't believe he had swiped the striped cotton shirt I'd just bought in Bangkok after searching through racks of similar merchandise, not stopping until I'd found the prettiest, palest one. Maybe I could get Greg and Kosiya to come back with me to see if he had dropped it on one of the paths. Oh, forget it. It was like an ant farm back there. My head throbbed where a miniature Japanese eggplant was beginning to swell. Now instead of a pleasant early dinner at the seafood place, I'd have to fill out forms at the police station. God only knew how long that would take if reporting a stolen bike ate up the better part of an American afternoon. No one was home at the construction workers' place, thank god, as my attempt to recover my clothes had met with only partial success. I felt like a fool facing the oncoming traffic in my Chinese pants and strapless top.

"Djoo have fun?" Greg muttered automatically as I stomped through the door, his eyes fastened on *Midnight's Children* in an attempt to evade the long description of Buddhist awakening he feared was coming.

"Yeah, it was okay, except this guy stole most of my stuff and flirted with the idea of raping me when I begged him to give it back."

"What?" Greg barked, jackknifing to a seated position, his pale green eyes sparking with outrage.

I repeated myself irritably, reassuring him that I was fine despite the lucky goose egg on my forehead. We sought Kosiya's advice on going to the police station. He told us that it was a long hike from the wat and the odds of catching the perp practically nil, especially since the distinctive blue mandala tattoo above the man's right nipple was as popular with the soldiers on the nearby army base as American flags and the Tasmanian devil were with their American counterparts. My decision not to pursue the matter owed less to Buddhist attitude than the sticky residue of sand and saltwater on skin that had nourished hundreds of mosquitoes the previous night. Itchy and bitchy, I allowed my mind to grasp at the basest of creature comforts: ceiling fans, beer, used-book stalls, poste restante, the reruns of *Twin Peaks* we had stumbled across in Lake Toba. Two days at a Thai monastery had not sufficiently pumped up my spiritual resources to the point where I could "let go and let God," to use a phrase oft quoted by a friend in Alcoholics Anonymous. Needless to say, Greg couldn't have been happier, especially when I suggested that we take off the next morning after Kosiya's alms round. I thought about the shed of decomposing Buddhas, still unswept, its impermanent occupants not yet meditated upon. The old abbot as yet unmet. The five noble truths, the eightfold path, karma, dharma—I hadn't drawn a bead on any of them. Oh well, I still had the little booklets Kosiya had given me on the train, one of which recommended putting a "smile on your dial." Buddhism appealed to me much more than the religion conferred on me as an infant, when, dressed in antique white lace, I was dipped like a tea bag into St. Paul's baptismal font. Unlike our monk friend, however, I couldn't commit years to claiming a better fit, especially if it meant missing the evening meal and rising at dawn to make breakfast for men, who would fill up on their trick-or-treat bags no matter what nourishing dish I prepared. I was less a spiritual seeker than one in search of a shirt to replace the one that turned out to be impermanent in my lucky, lucky life.

On Living Dangerously

Greg and I landed in Saigon just two weeks after President Clinton lifted the embargo. Budget travelers were beginning to pour in as the Vietnamese government eased restrictions on where foreigners could go, how long they could stay and how they could get there. The American War, as it's referred to there, was a big draw. We took a room in an ugly, many-storied hotel, a relic of the R & R era, and took a spin through the large nearby market. Amidst stalls selling vegetables and pajama suits, vendors did a brisk trade in Zippo lighters etched with Snoopy, peace signs, and such sentiments as "If I had a shack in hell and a farm in Vietnam, I'd sell my farm and go home." These items came with an oral assurance that they were the genuine article, the former property of luckless American GIs. Given the quantity of their stock, I estimated that every American killed in combat had dropped a minimum of five lighters. Even though I knew they were fake, I kind of wanted one, but Greg insisted on absolute purity. If we needed to set something on fire, we would use wooden matches like the Vietnamese. After the market, we retired to Kim's Café.

Kim was an enterprising Korean woman in her early twenties. Sensing an imminent influx of young Westerners, she had opened a restaurant that featured banana pancakes, French fries, a message board, and other amenities that backpackers accustomed to Kathmandu and Kuta Beach expected. Long tables set up on the shady sidewalk accommodated hordes of travelers who spent hours over glasses of Vietnamese drip coffee, boasting about where they'd been and razzing anyone who lighted his cigarette with a genuine GI Zippo. A dozen urchins milled around, relentless in their attempts to sell postcard booklets, candy, and gum. Dirty and tough as hell, they squabbled amongst themselves as to who had dibs on a certain customer, somewhat like the pampered divorcées who staffed the tacky Michigan Avenue art gallery that had recently fired first Greg, then me. As we watched, a dust-colored eight-year-old with a scar on his forehead slammed one of his gang to the pavement and then went after an Irishman seated nearby. "Why you no buy from me?" he demanded darkly. The corners of his mouth turned down in a dead-on impersonation of a disappointed tot, causing much glee amongst the younger members of his crew. "You promise."

"Piss off," the disloyal customer growled, rather heartlessly I thought. The child grabbed his ragged crotch with one grubby paw, waved his middle finger at the Irishman and danced away spitting a string of oaths, among them *"lính xiao,"* which we were told is Vietnamese slang for "Soviet."

"What's he selling anyway?" I called, hoping to take things to a lighter plateau.

"Who, that little criminal? He's got himself a shitload of grass rolled up in cigarette packets. Nice life he's got for himself, eh?"

"Grass? You mean like—"

"Marijuana," the Irishman drawled with a passable John Wayne accent. The crowd tittered. I pressed on.

"Is it, you know, safe?"

"Guess so," he replied, returning to his conversation.

Greg and I put our heads together, whispering furiously. "Uh, excuse me," I called to the Irish guy. "Do you know how much he's selling it for? Is his price about what it should be?"

"Dunno. How much does a joint go for in the States, then?"

On Scarface's next lap, Greg called him over and, for roughly two dollars, purchased a Marlboro hard pack well stuffed with what looked like cigarettes, filters and all. "You need more, you buy from me," the young dealer said, socking Greg in the arm. Sensing blood in the water, the other children swarmed around, brandishing scenic views of Vietnam, but Greg and I were already on our feet, barely able to contain our excitement. We headed to the hotel's roof, where we fired up one of our "cigarettes" with Cockfight brand wooden matches and peered through a chainlink fence at the grimy city. Colorful laundry waved like flags strung between dismal apartment buildings, while eight stories below, a steady stream of mopeds and bicycles whizzed along. Many carried women in traditional *aó dàis* and conical straw hats, protecting their fair arms with opera-length pastel gloves.

Smoking pot is a good vacation activity for me as it amplifies my natural inclination to lie on my side, eating. I'm incredulous that some people want to go out and have fun when they're stoned. In that state, I prefer to hunker in a familiar room, wondering why the number five can be counted on to assume the shape of a slightly irregular pale blue square with a fuzzy black dot in the center that reminds me of my maternal grandmother. By contrast, the number two invariably becomes a dark orange, masculine parallelogram. Isn't that fascinating? Happens every time, no matter where I might be in the world. And I'd smoked a place or two around the world.

Years before, when Isaac and I had crossed from Singapore into Malaysia, I had seen a billboard depicting three hanged men. This roadside eye catcher had been erected as a warning, though I caught a subtle whiff of chest beating, too. *Here's what we do to any bonehead we catch with drugs!* The threat was far from idle. Several people had been executed for dealing and smuggling earlier that year. Lonely Planet's *South-East Asia on a Shoestring* warned travelers that foreign status would not exempt them from the harsh punishments meted out to anyone possessing illegal substances—the kind of harsh that leaves the mortician scrambling to conceal the rope burns on your neck.

I had believed the horror stories. Long before I'd bought my first backpack, I'd known what life was like in a Turkish prison, courtesy of *Midnight Express*. In that movie, a hyperventilating American budget traveler, played by Brad Davis, tapes himself into a belt of hash bricks in the Istanbul airport's men's room. A phalanx of screaming, uniformed men bust him on the tarmac. He is tossed in jail, where he spends the remainder of the film getting tortured, although he does meet a nice Scandinavian inmate who is totally gracious when Davis doesn't want to be his boyfriend. His father and girlfriend have no luck wrestling the corrupt system, possibly because he wasn't wrongfully accused. The whole film made quite an impression on me, especially the long-sleeved, embroidered gauze blouse the girlfriend was wearing on the airplane as she wondered what the hell was taking Davis so long in the men's room. Before the credits finished rolling, I had resolved to travel to a place where I could buy a blouse like that, and to refrain from smuggling hash while there.

Under the shadow of the noose, I had found it easy to avoid trouble in Singapore. I'm not the type to spit gum on the sidewalk or vandalize public property with spray paint, and I'm too much of a good girl to smoke a joint if it would make my host want to kill me. Traveling with Isaac, I'd stayed straight in Malaysia and even parts of Thailand, where strategically posted flyers importuned backpackers to go to the local jails on visiting days. Western inmates, imprisoned for drug use and trafficking, relied on this emotional and practical support. Bring food and toiletries, the signs had instructed, as well as cigarettes, which were serious scratch on the in-house black market. In Chiang Mai, a large northern city not far from the Golden Triangle, I had dutifully packed a plastic bag with bananas, candy, and a few packs of 555 cigarettes. I'd imagined myself gripping Brad Davis's hands through the iron bars, delivering a message from Amnesty International.

At the appointed hour, a guard led visitors into a narrow cinderblock corridor. A few feet beyond a waist-high wall was a cage running the length of the room. Moist and sort of stinky, the place put me in mind of the tapirs' winter quarters at the Lincoln Park Zoo. I made a mental note not to mention this similarity within earshot of the inmates or the armed guard. A door opened at the far end of the cage and the prisoners trooped in, single file. They were all men. As in a Virginia reel, we were partnered with whomever wound up directly across from us in the row. I was paired with a Pakistani guy with neatly cut hair, a sport shirt, and dress slacks. He complained that his daily serving of rice gruel contained ground pork that, as a Muslim, he couldn't eat. I asked him what he had been eating. He shrugged and asked me if I had brought him any cigarettes. He asked me about America and what I did there. I've had livelier conversations at alumni events. After a while, I gathered the nerve to ask what he was in for. "Forging signatures on stolen traveler's checks," he told me, "but I am innocent!" I was disappointed that my prisoner fell so short of groovy. If we had been partnered in a real Virginia reel, the lines would have rotated, giving me a crack at the shaggy, emaciated Brit in floppy Chinese trousers a few feet away. At the end of an hour, the guard reappeared to usher us out. "I'll tell other travelers to come visit you," I called to my inmate. He shrugged again.

After a couple of months in Southeast Asia, I had arrived at a foolproof personal policy regarding drugs. If it was green, smelled like pot, and belonged to another backpacker, you could smoke some, as long as you were on or near a beach. The cities were threatening places where environmentally unsound vehicles hunted pedestrians with no regard for traffic signals. Even the monks had an edge. The beaches were mellow havens where the locals had plenty of time to hang out, playing Eric Clapton songs on junky guitars and pumping their guests for smutty Western slang. It was the inverse of the "when in Rome" theory: When the soon-to-be-topless travelers descended, attracted by the leisurely pace and paradisiacal views, the local guys grew their hair out, acquired hippie chokers, and boned up on topics dear to the backpacker heart, like Buddhism, dolphins and where to score good doob. Sometimes it seemed that everything had been arranged specifically for the low-budget travelers' pleasure. Even the local fisherman went about their tasks with the sunny, purposeful energy of Disney World staffers.

In Koh Phangan, Isaac and I had made a bunch of instant friends smoking pot in an open-air bar belonging to a likable alcoholic named Nok. More than once, Nok had gotten so sloshed that he'd wandered away, leaving us to shutter the place at the end of the night. We hadn't exactly abused his trust, but by that point in the evening, none of us as fit to handle money. We'd insisted that strangers pay for the drinks we poured, but we were like children with a toy cash register, naming outrageous sums and dropping bills in the sand behind the counter. We'd commandeered the creaky boombox to play cassettes from home. When the bottle opener disappeared, we had used our Swiss Army knives to flip the caps off of our Singhas. We had talked ourselves hoarse, eager for everyone to know everything about our childhoods, jobs, neighborhoods, favorite music, national character, and what we would eat if a magic genie appeared to rustle up any dish we craved. Some of these tidbits permeated the ether. I have rarely laughed as hard as I did when Ian, a manic carrot-topped Cockney, described his adventures as a human guinea pig for medical experiments, including the time he appeared in the waiting room wrapped in tinfoil, terrifying a heavily tattooed fellow guinea pig by claiming that the researchers were shaving off the top layers of the test subjects' skin.

Ian had been heading to Malaysia for a festival where devotees skewer their cheeks with sharpened bamboo poles. He'd told me that he had an ingenious method for transporting his pot stash across international boundaries. He packed it into a drinking straw, sealed the ends with cotton and wax and shoved it into his toothpaste tube. He couldn't believe I'd been so stupid as to cross from Rwanda into Tanzania with a half-cup or so of marijuana twisted into a piece of notebook paper at the bottom of my sleeping bag. "That's massive!" he'd piped. "You're barmy." Too stoned to be embarrassed by my lack of smuggler's savvy, I had been delighted to count among my pals someone who said "barmy" instead of "retarded." Hanging out in Nok's bar was a bit like *Casablanca*, without the sex and Nazis.

Experience was making me bold. Saigon—nobody seemed to call it Ho Chi Minh City—was decidedly not a beach, but here I was, toking away like I was still enjoying the ocean breezes in Nok's open air bar.

"Can you believe we're in *Saigon*?" Greg asked.

I held the smoke in my lungs and shook my head. I knew exactly what he meant: the desperate crowds hanging on to the struts of helicopters evacuating embassy personnel in 1970, Nixon talking about football with young demonstrators at the Lincoln Memorial, a sweat-soaked Charlie Sheen on jungle patrol, his eyes rolling in fear. But trying to give voice to these thoughts was like following those giant ants around M. C. Escher's skeletal Möbius strip. Scarface's merchandise packed a punch, all right. We picked our way downstairs, accustomed to the jolly aphrodisiac properties of American cannabis. We had trouble getting the key in the door because the lock was melting. Seconds later we were pinned to separate twin beds and the curtains were speaking to me. *Steerumphed*, they taunted in a maddening singsong. *Don't be steerumphed.*

I keep making up words, I scrawled in my journal, fearful that at any moment my capacity for language could be reduced to nothing but gibberish. *Worried that there might have been some heroin or PCP in the joint I just smoked. I get stoned and I turn into Dr. Seuss. God, the sounds are so amplified. "Owner of a Lonely Heart" is playing, which means I'm graduating up an evolutionary step—I wouldn't have been able to recognize that fact a nanosecond ago. I am almost positive and steerumphed that there was something VERY BAD in that dope—cleaning fluid or glue.* I hooked my fingers under the elastic of the fitted sheet in case the bed should suddenly tilt upward and send me sliding into hell or the Mekong Delta circa 1968. *Oh my god, I can't believe eighteen-year-olds smoked this shit and then had to go kill people!* Considering this last statement, I added a row of exclamation points—*!!!!!!!!!!!!!!!!*—convinced that I had to get myself to a mental hospital. But how? With enormous effort, I raised my head from the mattress. Greg writhed on the twin bed opposite mine, whispering threats to the ceiling fan. *I think Greg's freaking out too.* My penmanship was deteriorating into a physician's scrawl. This was a fine mess we'd gotten ourselves into! Our first day in the country and already we required emergency psychiatric intervention. There was no phone in the room, and even if there had been I was in no condition to figure out which number to dial for the reception desk. Waiting for the maid to discover us in the morning was not an option. I wasn't sure the hotel provided maid service, and more importantly, if we went that long without help, we'd fly well beyond the cuckoo's nest. The threat of the gallows wasn't nearly as terrifying as the thought of going so far around the bend that someone would truss me up in a straitjacket. What was the Vietnamese word for claustrophobia? Where was Greg's phrasebook? Who would teach me how to say, "I'm serious, you'd better untie this thing because I'm about two seconds away from freaking way the fuck out!"? Kim from Kim's Café. She was our only hope. I could just see her, bustling around the tables in her tidy apron, her thick bangs and schoolgirl glasses making her look even younger than she actually was. I hated to do it to her, but our brains had to be saved. We had no choice but to come seething into her restaurant like a hideous tide of rolling protoplasm, goo with eyes. Kim would never be so foolish as to smoke anything purchased from a streetwise-beyond-his-years twerp with crusty knees and the mug of a seasoned knife fighter. She would develop a low opinion of me, but that couldn't be helped. The best I could wish for was that this might be old hat to Kim. Hopefully she was used to backpackers crawling in on their hands and knees at the height of the dinner rush, overdosing on Little Scarface's ditch-weed. After I'd gotten the antidote, I could laugh it off as one of those boo-boos that comes with the backpacker territory. Unless I got facial paralysis or something, it would be less shameful than a "Bali kiss," the burn a hot exhaust pipe brands onto a traveler's bare calf when she loses control of a rented minibike she doesn't know how to operate. At least I wouldn't have to skulk around the tropics with my leg swathed in gauze from ankle to hip.

Now that I'd made the choice to enlist Kim's help, I procrastinated. The idea of making it down a flight of stairs seemed even less manageable than it did a few years later when I was at home in full-blown, unmedicated labor with my first child, and the midwife, reached by phone, told me it was time to come in to the birthing center. Maybe Greg could carry me on his back. I spent two or three millennia turning my head toward the other twin bed. He looked like he was on a carnival ride he should never have boarded, flattened by centrifugal force but not happily so. He was alive, right? I remembered another flyer that was posted up around Chiang Mai on that earlier trip when I brought cigarettes and bananas to the check forger. "This Is What Happens

When Foreigners Do Drugs" was neatly hand-printed above a grisly photograph of a young male tourist who'd taken too much heroin and died. Either his eyes were blank with death, or even postmortem, you can still get red-eye from flash photography. Speaking of eyes, mine felt like falafel. My mouth was parched, too. I lay motionless, my reptilian gaze fastened on Greg's neck as I waited for the flicker of a pulse.

Like a mirror image of the iguana I was morphing into, he slowly turned to face me. "I'm freaking out," he drawled. "Are you?"

"Oh, yeah," I brayed, relieved that I wasn't the only lightweight in the room.

"Do you remember those hats I made out of Kentucky Fried Chicken buckets?"

"I do."

"Do you want to get something to eat?"

"At Kim's?"

"Yeah."

"Okay." Maybe I'd start out with soup, see how I felt and play the psych ward by ear. If the other diners' faces started spilling over their shirt fronts like candle wax, mental help was still an option. Better not to jump the gun and curry Kim's disfavor if all I was going to do was come down. I was starting to come down anyway. The curtains were behaving more normally, laughing with me, not at me.

The next morning, Greg flushed our precious stash down the toilet. It was a sign of my full recovery that I tried to argue him out of it. "We are never smoking that stuff again," he said, adding that he had been muttering to the ceiling fan because he was convinced that he was in the opening scene of *Apocalypse Now*. Did I remember that?

Incredibly, I did remember him talking to the fan the day before, but I had difficulty remembering the film, which I had seen at least three times. "Martin Sheen goes out of his mind and trashes his hotel room," he informed me dryly. A few nights later we went to a recently opened bar called Apocalypse Now, which had created quite a buzz amongst Western travelers. It was a nondescript, dimly lit room with few decorations besides the crude helicopter painted on the ceiling above the fan. Every hour, the bartender cued up a cassette of Jim Morrison singing "The End" and switched the fan to its highest speed, so that it looked like a helicopter was landing upside down. It was about as much fun as it sounds, maybe less.

On Truth

would have put Kashmir in Iran, until an American we met in Darjeeling told us that it was her favorite place in India. Her descriptions of the raj-era houseboats on which travelers stayed and the three delicious meals that were included in each night's rate overrode Greg's concerns about the political strife in the area. I furrowed my brow, nodding mutely, as if I, too, had known that there was political strife to be concerned about.

As the weeks went by, the summer temperatures in places like Varanasi and New Delhi convinced me that the primary reason we had come to India was to relax on a houseboat in Kashmir's Dal Lake, escaping the insane heat that enveloped much of the rest of the country. From there, we could fly to Ladakh, high in the Himalayas, and pretend we were in Tibet. Getting to the provincial capital, Srinagar would be arduous, but worth it, or so I thought until the rickety bus on which we were traveling hit yet another landslide. Greg and I had been in transit for forty-eight hours and my patience for the rubble, cows, stalled trucks, and the myriad other things that can block a narrow mountain pass was at an all-time low. Abandoning all hope of reaching Srinagar by nightfall, I started hating everything and everyone, except for Chitty Chitty

Bang Bang, who, Godot-like, failed to appear. This impasse was especially frustrating because we were only a couple of football fields shy of the Jawarhar Tunnel, a 2500-meter manmade burrow that supposedly made getting to Kashmir much easier than it had been in the days when British officials packed their women and children off to spend the dog days in cooler climes. My intense claustrophobia, which had caused me to freak out everywhere, from the back seat of a friend's overcrowded Honda Civic to the Cu Chi tunnels south of Saigon, occupied my attention while the road was being cleared. The thought of coming to a standstill in that unventilated, pitch-black death tube caused me to rock back and forth, repeating ominous phrases. Suddenly, there was a commotion up front. Two men had climbed onto the bus and were arguing with the driver. I noticed that the other passengers had turned in their seats, their curiosity about the only Westerners on board sparked afresh. "They are coming for you," murmured a young Sikh who had entertained us with tales of his religion and his engineering degree. Oh my god, no, a guerilla faction was going from vehicle to vehicle, routing out Americans! Were they armed? My mind raced through all sorts of sodomy and shallow-grave scenarios as the men thumped toward the back of the bus, having shouted down the driver.

"You are Halliday and Kotis?" they demanded. "From America?" Our identifying documents were in our money belts. Maybe the bandits would go away if we offered them money. How many rupees did we have between us? Maybe they would accept traveler's checks.

Laying his hand on my arm, Greg thrust his chin bravely forward and said, "That's right. We're American citizens." Jesus Christ, he was going to get us killed! A State Department guy we'd hung out with after a flaccid British-style meal at an old hotel in Calcutta had given us his card and told us to look him up when we reached New Delhi. Maybe he could bail us out of this mess, even if he didn't remember meeting us. If only we'd stitched Canadian flags onto our backpacks . . .

"We are from the *Bendamir* houseboat in Srinagar. Our cousin called from Jammu to tell us that his American friends were coming. Then when you did not arrive, we became worried because we know these roads are bad. Please, we will take you the rest of the way in our car. This bus may not be moving until morning. You will go faster with us. Please, our mother is waiting. She is very worried for you."

Amazing. Who'd have thought this latest landslide would turn out to be another link in a lucky chain of events. First we met Diana, who turned us on to the Bendamir. She had told us there were literally hundreds of houseboats from which to choose, especially now that tourism was at an all-time low, but I was happy to have the recommendation. Then in Jammu, where we'd spent the night before embarking on our final leg of the journey, the guy who ran the grim, cinderblock hotel beside the long-distance bus station turned out to be related to the people who ran the boat on which Diana had stayed. All three of our jaws had dropped when I fished out the slip of paper I'd been carrying in my money belt. "*Bendamir?* But this is the name of my cousins' boat," he had shouted, clapping Greg on the back. Small world, huh? I was as grateful to him for calling ahead on our behalf as I was to the landslide that helped his cousins locate us before god-knows-what could cause our bus to get wedged in the tunnel. What a doofus I was for assuming they were omnipotent anti-American guerillas who just happened to know my name! The other passengers looked on enviously as our new escorts hustled us up the aisle, shouting to the driver to open the luggage bays so that our backpacks could be transferred to the trunk of their surprisingly luxurious sedan. As promised, their car made good time by cutting around the larger vehicles. "Thank you so much for going to all this extra trouble," I piped from the back seat, and promptly fell asleep to their melodious reassurances that it was nothing.

I woke when the driver killed the engine on the shores of Dal Lake. Behind us rose the dusky outlines of buildings several stories tall. The men who'd picked us up urged us to hurry as we picked our way along a rickety wooden landing. Several yards away, a dugout canoe cut through the inky nothingness, riding low in the water. A withered, barefoot woman wearing child-sized flannel pajamas and a veil over her long, dark hair piloted it. While we loaded our packs into the tippy craft, she squatted silently, drawing on a long-stemmed pipe. "She is Mama," one of the men revealed.

"Thank you so much for coming to get us in the middle of the night. We appreciate it very much. You are very kind," I enunciated. I hoped she would teach me how to cook exotic Kashmiri dishes. Her lazy smile revealed jagged stumps worn nearly to the gum line. I sought to catch Greg's eye in the darkness, hoping that he had gotten a load of those choppers, too. This was the real deal, the *shikara* emerging from the cloak of night, the pipe-smoking old lady dipping her paddles into the still water, the hundreds of lily pads, their blossoms closed tight as fists.

A man waited for us on the tiny veranda of a houseboat. Reaching for my hand, he hauled me indecorously up the wooden ladder, then turned to help Greg. "Madam," he welcomed, as to my confusion the *shikara* pushed off. I had thought the men that had snatched us from the bus were our hosts. "No, they are friends."

"Oh. So, are you the cousin of the man we met in Jammu?"

"Yes, madam. Cousins," he confirmed. "Please sit." He led us to a round table in the corner of the boat's tiny living room, pulling out my chair politely. His old-fashioned show of servility made me feel clumsy and entirely too contemporary. Despite the bags under his eyes, he looked to be about our age. Maybe the three of us could become friends. "Food is coming," our new host told us, bowing his way out of the room.

"God, this is wild," I whispered, drinking in our surroundings.

"Mmm," Greg sighed, knowing he was compelled to agree before he could put his head down on the table and shut his eyes. I caught my reflection in a side window. I looked rapacious, maniacal at having arrived in such a weird, cool place. The big upholstered armchair centered on the worn rug had to date back to the lake's heyday in the 1930s. A framed letter testified to the unparalleled month one Major A. J. Pimm-Bosker had passed here. "Should you choose to avail yourself of Mr. Sayeed Achabal's hospitality, you will not be disappointed," Major Pimm-Bosker confided. "He has served my family faithfully from the third of July to the second of August, 1941, a period in which we wanted for nothing." Wow. Aside from the chair and the rug, the furnishings put me in mind of my Uncle Charlie's prefab summer cottage on a manmade lake an hour outside of Indianapolis. I noticed a Western-style toilet in a small, elevated water closet and was just about to take a peek inside the desk drawers when a door slid open in the stern. Our host entered on his tiptoes, bearing a platter heaped with French fries, grilled tomatoes, rice, and some sort of fish curry. He hovered nearby as we lit into the grub.

"Everything is to madam's liking?" he inquired.

"Oh yeah, really delicious," I enthused through a great, honking mouthful, spearing another fry with a ridiculously fancy, rosebud-patterned fork.

He tipped his head to the side, modest as a geisha. "Thank you, madam."

"So, is it your wife who does the cooking here?" I asked.

"No, madam, I am not having a wife yet," he apologized.

"Oh that's all right, we're not married either," I smiled conspiratorially, hoping to telegraph that, around us, he was free to let it all hang out. We came from a land of leather daddies and gym-toned pretty boys where, every summer, paunchy couples in rainbow T-shirts paraded up a main traffic artery, waving signs lettered "We Love Our Gay Son!"

"You must be very tired," Greg observed, as our host allowed his skinny frame to sag against the wall.

"It is nothing, sir."

"Yes. You have waited up until we arrived and now we have eaten our dinner and you must go to bed. We are very tired, too." Whenever Greg wanted to show that we meant business, he stopped using contractions. It made him sound less American. According to many of the Israelis we'd met traveling, our national inclination to be liked ensured we would be treated like pushovers. With his close-cropped hair, Greg was frequently mistaken for Israeli, a fact he turned to our advantage. Whenever the tireless touts who prowl the bazaars and railway stations came racing toward us, Greg called, "Shalom!" The touts immediately turned tail, preferring to wait for less challenging game than a recent discharge from the Israeli army.

After our meal, our host led us to the room where we would

sleep, a dark-paneled bachelor's lair featuring a couple of fluorescent paintings on leather and a brown velour bedspread. As he was bidding us good night, I urged him to drop the formality around us. "We're Ayun and Greg. What's your name?"

His lips spread into a Mona Lisa smile. "Ayub, madam," he said, gesturing for us to give him our shoes. Jesus, I hoped he wasn't going to try to polish our Birkenstocks. The boat rocked a bit as he tiptoed backward, out of our room and apparently off of the boat. I wondered where he slept.

At dawn, I rushed onto the veranda to have a look at the mist-shrouded lake. It did not disappoint. The *Bendamir* seemed to be located at a major intersection on the outermost ring of houseboats. *Shikaras* swished around the corner, some laden with packages of cookies, soda, and cigarettes, like floating door-to-door newsstands. Their occupants were gorgeous, slim, and fine-boned, with tawny skin and supermodel eyes in shades colored contacts can only dream of replicating. The women wore flattering tunics over matching trousers, in soft fabrics the color of a wren. It was easy to imagine spending an entire month on Dal Lake, never budging from our houseboat, reading novels, eating fries, playing cards. I leaned back against a ruffled chintz pillow, propped my feet on the rail, and admired the wooden gingerbread framing our veranda. The other houseboats I could see had it too. "Isn't this great?" I asked, when Greg stepped out, blinking in the morning light. "It's so Three Bears. Aren't these padded benches cute?"

"Did madam sleep well?" Ayub called from the living room, where he was laying out a breakfast of scrambled eggs, toast, and more grilled tomatoes.

"Yeah, great, thanks. How about you? How did you sleep?"

"Also well, madam." I wondered if he had forgotten my name. Well, he would see it when I filled out the guest registry, a triplicate form required by the Indian government.

"Hey, Ayub, do you think we could maybe eat our breakfast out here? It's so beautiful." What little energy he'd acquired overnight seemed to drain out through the base of his spine, but he reloaded his tray and tiptoed it onto the veranda. As much as I enjoyed the ghost-of-the-raj aesthetic, the extremes to which he took his servility made me feel like a big creep. I found myself wishing he'd break out a hacky sack, like the young guys running guesthouses all over Bali. Poor Ayub was so uptight. When he finally left us, having satisfied himself beyond all shadow of doubt that breakfast met with our approval, he was practically *en pointe*.

Greg poured coffee from a metal teapot into bone china cups. "Instant?" I asked with crossed fingers.

"No, I think it's real. Hey do you think that water's safe?" He pointed to the two plastic bottles Ayub had set on one of the benches. They were the same brand sold all over India, but the seals were broken, a big no-no, given the accounts of unscrupulous vendors who refilled abandoned water bottles at the tap and passed them off as factory fresh.

"I'm sure it probably is. It may not be real bottled water, but these guys have been in the tourist biz for years. They know to boil." My attitude toward sanitation was much laxer than Greg's, particularly when hygiene involved paying for something I was used to getting free. There was a time in my traveling past when I tried to disinfect on the cheap by carrying a seventy-nine-cent bottle of iodine in my backpack, but that practice was discontinued when I got a load of just how nasty water tastes when you try to mask the iodine flavor with powdered Gatorade.

"Did you notice if those *shikara* guys have any water for sale? Maybe I should buy a few bottles, lay in a supply."

"Greg! There is nothing wrong with this water! Boiling it kills all the weird bacteria and stuff that can make you sick. Would you like for me to find you Lonely Planet's passage about boiled water?"

"Okay, I'll drink it," he said skeptically, holding the glass he'd just poured up to the light before taking a cautious sip.

Ayub returned with the guest registry and a scrapbook filled with tourist brochures, photographs, and letters of recommendation from visitors he had squired to the local sights. We dutifully leafed through as Ayub, displaying considerably more energy than he had since our arrival, enumerated the many wonders close at hand. The current political situation made it too dangerous to trek into the scenic countryside, but we could still visit the sultan's mosque, the tomb of King Zain al-Abidin, the Mughal gardens, the Shiva temple. . . . Like most backpackers, Greg and I considered guided tours the province of package tourists who had forty-five minutes to videotape a noteworthy sight before their guide herded them back aboard their luxury motor coach, eager to collect his commission for every rug or gemstone purchased at the showroom that was next on their agenda. We were do-it-yourselfers, I explained to Ayub, and to tell the truth, we'd seen so many tourist attractions in the last few months, I was feeling kind of temple-and-tombed out.

He was flabbergasted. "But madam, why have you come so far if not to see the jewels of Kashmir? Look, the fort of Akbar, madam! Sir, I think you are knowing who Akbar is. He is a great king, a hero to my people. Madam, the Shalimar Garden, the most romantic in the world, built for Queen Nur Jahan. This means 'light of the world.'" As Ayub continued, I found it hard to stick to the rote thanks-but-no-thanks line I had perfected on dozens of would-be docents who hung around the periphery of guidebook must-sees. With mounting excitement, I deduced that when Samuel Taylor Coleridge penned the lines, "In Xanadu did Kubla Khan/A stately pleasure dome decree," he had been talking about Kashmir. The scene I envisioned was equal parts Rousseau and *Jungle Book*, tame boa constrictors hanging like hammocks between flowering trees, the pale pink air scented with perfume. Our principles had made us stingy. Ayub was offering to show us everything, at least twenty palaces, gardens and mosques, for two hundred dollars. A bargain, really. God, to think I had been on the verge of asking Ayub if he had any board games, while a short distance away peacocks and handmaidens gamboled in verdant paradise. As I went to fetch our traveler's checks, I heard Ayub reassuring Greg that most certainly his sister boiled our water for a minimum of twenty minutes before it was carried in to us.

After lunch, Ayub's father, a powerful José Ferrer doppelgänger in an off-white skullcap and pajamas, chauffeured the three of us across the lake in the family *shikara*. Perhaps sensing that our two-hundred-dollar investment was beginning to gnaw away at me, he praised the first stop on our itinerary, the Shalimar Garden, as an oasis of tranquility, with spectacular flora particularly restful to a lady's delicate sensibilities. I told him that I couldn't imagine a place more restful than the Bendamir. He smiled as if he didn't understand.

We hurried past the armed soldiers crouched behind a sandbag turret and hailed a beat-up cab, which dropped us off at a parched expanse of crumbling low walls and dead plants. Uh-oh, this was not how I pictured Xanadu at all. The greenest specimens were weeds poking through the broken ornamental walkways and dry fountains. Where the walkways disappeared altogether, the ground was rubbed bald. I tried not to look at Greg, who is constitutionally unable to enjoy a garden unless someone tells him that it's covering a major battle site of the Civil War. Ayub trailed us by several feet, flicking cigarette butts onto the crabgrass. We tarried in the garden for far longer than its paltry pleasures warranted, trying to justify our expenses with quantity if not quality. Next, Ayub insisted that we drive by a bridge of some renown, which in terms of excitement ran a close second to the railroad trestle spanning Indianapolis's Broad Ripple canal. "Next we will visit the Nishat Garden, designed by Nur Jahan's brother," he yawned.

"Actually, if it's okay with you, could we just go back to the houseboat?" I asked. "We're kind of tired, still."

Back in our bedroom, I started freaking out. "Oh god, Greg, how could we have signed over two hundred-dollar traveler's checks like that? What a horrible mistake! It's like every safety failed." I curled into a fetal position on the brown velour spread, despair lodged in my stomach like a poisonous ice walnut. Oh, it was so much money, almost half the monthly rent for our one-bedroom apartment in Chicago! You could fly from Bangkok to Calcutta for two hundred dollars. In Sumatra, we had stayed in a bamboo cottage on high stilts, with a front porch overlooking a waterfall, a huge bed and orchids growing out of the bathroom walls for only four dollars a night! We almost didn't take it because the going rate was three dollars! We could've stayed there nearly two months for what we had forked over to Ayub. Oh god, if only I could roll back the clock! How could we have been so stupid?

"Those gardens sucked," Greg commented, lying rigid as a corpse beside me. According to our dog-eared Lonely Planet, admission to almost every tourist attraction we had signed on to visit was free. I whimpered as I read that you could hire a *shikara* to take you on a leisurely all-day circuit of the lake, including stops at all five Mughal gardens for sixty rupees, about two bucks. Our chain of great luck wrapped itself around my neck and dragged me way, way down. We'd been duped worse than the poor suckers who bet on public transit shell games. I felt like I might throw up. If only we were still sweating it out in New Delhi.

"Do you think there's any chance he would give us our money back if we explain that we made a mistake?" I moaned.

Greg sighed heavily, resigned to reality. "We could try, I suppose, but it doesn't seem likely." I curled against his side. Although I knew every item in his backpack, I clung to a fragile hope that he might have a magic wand concealed in some overlooked pocket. I dreaded confronting Ayub.

"What if we say I'm sick? I could say I've got some disease that comes and goes and when it acts up I have to take it very easy. Sightseeing would be out of the question." Greg patted me consolingly, my wretchedness convincing him just this once to overlook my penchant for lying my way out of a bad situation.

The next morning, Ayub could not hide his mistrust as he inquired after my health. "Madam is still feeling ill?" he asked.

I murmured a wan confirmation, doing my best to seem uncomplaining, like Beth in *Little Women*.

"Perhaps this is because madam is not used to our food. I will tell my sister to make only the plainest things." This did not bode well, as the previous night's meal had been a sad follow-up to our arrival dinner, consisting largely of rice and a tureen holding some sort of bland, overcooked sea cucumber thing.

"No, no, she needs to eat to keep her strength up," Greg insisted, as I seized a slice of hot buttered toast for medicinal purposes. "But more importantly, she needs to rest, which I'm afraid means we won't be able to visit all the wonderful places you've offered to show us . . . which is why we are asking for a refund of the money we gave you."

Ayub turned his back on Greg. "It is diary, madam?" he asked bluntly. I once heard that the best way to blow off work with no questions asked was to phone your manager and tell him you had explosive diarrhea, but clearly this tactic would get me nowhere with Ayub.

"No, it's not so much that. It's something I have to live with. It happens at home, too. When it happens, I really just have to take it easy. I wish I could go, but I know from experience that it would be a really bad idea."

"Madam needs a doctor?" How far was I willing to take this charade?

"She just needs to rest," Greg said firmly.

"But sir is still wishing to visit the sights of Kashmir."

"I'm not going to leave her," my gallant announced. When I dislocated my knee in Bukittinggi, he disappeared with the bullfight boys for hours, an arrangement that suited me just fine, as it allowed for many uninterrupted hours with my other boyfriend, Somerset Maugham.

"But sir, why should you pay because madam is ill?" Ayub

argued. "My mother and sisters will care for her. Then tomorrow, she will be better and can join us for all of our activities."

Exasperated, we practically shouted that I wouldn't recover by tomorrow or the next day. If I wanted to make that flight to Leh, Ladakh's capital city, I would have to adhere to a strict regimen of rest and eating. Without warning, Ayub applied his palm to my forehead. I immediately shrunk back, whispering, "Please, my head! It . . . hurts. . . ."

"We are asking you to return our two hundred dollars," Greg announced conclusively. Ayub countered that he would have to consult with his father. "He's going to make his dad the heavy," Greg predicted, hearing the sliding door squeaking along its runners. "I wouldn't get your hopes up."

Remarkably, the old man gave my shoulder a grandfatherly pat as he laid a large stack of rupees on the bench next to Greg. "I must keep twenty dollars because arrangements were made," Ayub remarked testily. "What can I do? I cannot refuse to pay these men because madam becomes ill."

I was so elated to hear that the consequences of my mistake were 90 percent less dire than expected that I didn't begrudge Ayub his sham cancellation charge. He lied about the gardens. I lied about my health. Good game! We both knew I had won, even though I was twenty bucks lighter. Still, I felt obliged to play the part of the invalid for the next few days. As a matter of pride, I made sure to slouch about anemically everywhere but our bedroom, which faced west onto a shuttered and apparently abandoned houseboat. The illusion that our sleeping quarters were secure was shattered when I felt our bed rocking significantly more than the activity in which we were engaged warranted.

Through the half-closed drapes, I saw Ayub's legs edging around the perimeter. Either he was cleaning the gutters at high noon or he was peeking. I decided to pretend I hadn't noticed, since we were his captives until that plane took off for Ladakh. If we relocated to new digs, we would forfeit the price of a week's accommodation, for which we had paid in advance. Rubes.

Having scrapped the guided tour, it would have looked pretty shady if we bundled ourselves off to the jewels of Kashmir without Ayub. Exploring Srinagar was out of the question, as clashes between the soldiers and militant separatists could turn the city into a shooting gallery at any time of day or night. Besides, I was too "sick" to gallivant around. We were stuck on the houseboat, as crazy as caged baboons, especially since the flight we'd assumed we'd take to Ladakh was fully booked, which meant another week of Ayub's hospitality. Dying for a change of scene, we borrowed the *shikara*, claiming that the fresh air out on the lake would be good for me. The canoeing badge I had earned at camp and Greg's boyhood experience on the ponds of Cape Cod proved no match for the wily *shikara*, which spun in circles, like a wild pinto itching to dump the arrogant humans who sought to control it. At least our wild ride gave us a good gander at the name plaques nailed low on each houseboat. What a revelation to learn that we were staying on the *Chip-n-Dale*. Rather than go on a hunt for the real *Bendamir*, we docked so Greg could race, tight-cheeked, to the WC. "He said he boiled it but he didn't," he croaked some ten minutes later, hobbling toward the bedroom, as bent as an old man. "I've been drinking shit water!" His lower lip trembled as, wracked with guilt, I headed to the veranda to buy a factory-sealed bottle from the first *shikara*-newsstand that happened by. Perhaps I had been premature in assuming that the game ended when I thought it did.

The all-rice diet I prescribed for Greg's illness did nothing to staunch the constant issue of his bowels, but at least it spared him from the depressive effects of the daily menu. It felt like a long time since we'd seen a tomato, let alone a potato. Feigning an interest in Ayub's sister's recipes, I wrangled an invitation to the kitchen, a self-contained firetrap that looked from the outside like a beaver's dam. The dark, smoke-filled interior was an exclusively female domain. Ayub's two sisters squatted on the floor, tending pots set on a portable gas stove. Mama lay on her side, nursing on a giant hookah. When her pipe went out, one of her daughters crawled over with a match, fondly stroking her long hair before returning to work. The youngest girl smiled warmly as she pointed first at her mother, then at the hookah. "She like." It did seem like Mama had a pretty sweet deal. Now that her adoring daughters were old enough to take over cooking detail, she was free to spend all her time smoking in a recumbent position. The ravages of a life-time's lack of sunscreen and fluoride did not diminish her radiance. I wanted to be Mama. Unfortunately, our complete lack of common language, and possibly my animosity toward the family's all-important son meant that I could never penetrate this womanly world. When I tried to lift the lid from one of the pots, the youngest sister playfully smacked my hand away. Was she afraid that I would burn myself, or that I would discover some awful sea-cucumber-related secret? I had no way of knowing.

"Uh, last night, what we eat? You good cook! What cook last night?" I tried, forgetting that I was the one who was supposed to be fluent in English. An uncertain smile on her face, the oldest sister opened a burlap sack in the corner and displayed some dried beans. It was astonishing how tasty they looked. What I wouldn't have given for a big bowl of vegetarian chili from the Heartland Café with a side of cornbread and a big-ass beer. Noticing the lusty looks I was giving her beans, the older girl placed a couple of them in my hand, folding my fingers closed so that I would know they were mine to keep. Pointing from my fist to my mouth, I announced hopefully, "I like!" The sisters giggled, thinking that I was about to stick dry beans in my mouth. I couldn't figure out how to ask for chili without sounding imperious. "You cook" seemed way too memsahib, even if modified with "please." Although Isaac and I had once commandeered the cooking facilities of a Thai guesthouse to make a fellow traveler's twenty-first birthday "cake" out of pancakes and powdered Milo drink mix, something told me if I tried to make chili for the girls, I'd burn their kitchen down. Given Mama's hookah, it was a miracle the place hadn't gone up in flames already. The image of the inferno activated my claustrophobia, which sent me scuttling onto the dock, straight into Ayub. "Hey Ayub," I asked casually, as if all our past deceptions were water under the bridge, "do you think you could get your sister to cook us some of those beans she was showing me?"

"Beans." He gazed out across the lake as if making a mental note to smack his sister for divulging the location of the family valuables. "Madam, as you wish."

"I wish."

That night a handful of beans was mixed into the sea cucumbers. I isolated them into a distinct pile, but they'd been contaminated with the bland, yet offensive taste that had been displeasing diners on the *Bendamir*—oops I meant *Chip-n-Dale*—for years, possibly as far back as Major Pimm-Bosker's day. He may, as he wrote in his letter, have had a very relaxing time, but I was no longer in a mood to consider as reliable the culinary opinions of a British military man.

What I wouldn't have given for a VCR. I couldn't think why I had ever criticized those travelers who spend sunny afternoons in the cafés lining Bangkok's Khao Sahn Road, watching triple features of straight-to-video action schlock.

The morning of our departure, I woke with butterflies. Soon, Ayub and his boat and the sea cucumbers would be tiny specks on the ground. His father paddled us across, instructed a cab driver to take us to the airport and paid our fare with a wad of bills from his own pocket. "I am sorry for my son," he mumbled, just before the cab pulled away from the curb.

"It's okay! No problem!" Greg and I gabbled. "We had a great time! Kashmir is so beautiful!" Americans.

Everything went swimmingly until we hit a traffic jam a half-mile from the airport. Christ, what was it this time? Landslide? Accident? The morning commute? Passengers disembarked from the vehicles ahead of us, heading toward the airport on foot. When a soldier banged on our trunk, the driver opened it and refused to take us any further. Hoofing it, we reached a table set in the middle of the road, where more soldiers examined people's documents and luggage. I had nothing to hide, but still felt nervous, much more so than I had when I crossed the border from Rwanda into Tanzania on Christmas day with that hash tucked in my sleeping bag. Compared to Ayub, the soldiers were so manly and threatening, gruffly pawing my folksy Hindu souvenirs. One picked apart my toiletry kit as if disabling a bomb. The super-absorbency, applicatorless tampons I had stocked up on in Chicago threw him for a loop. I suppose they might have looked like white cotton bullets lined up in their box, but if he'd been trained to recognize Walkmen, blow dryers, and Game Boys, shouldn't he have had a better working knowledge of feminine hygiene? I opened my mouth, but he shot me a silencing look and passed the box to another soldier, who undid a cellophane wrapper, shaking his head. Even the toxic shock warning sheet's diagram of how to prop your foot on the toilet for easier insertion offered no clue. "It's for ladies," I blurted. "Bleeding ladies." The soldiers narrowed their eyes, still not getting it. "For *ladies* who *bleed* every *month*," I said, pointing to my crotch for emphasis. They blanched, blushed, and waved us on. Greg looked a little pale, too.

Inside the airport, our luggage was taken and tagged by a reservations clerk who instructed us to identify it on the tarmac once we had cleared a personal security check. Men were examined near the gate. I joined a line of women waiting to be checked behind a temporary partition. Air India employees in skirts and blazers ran their hands over the female passengers' clothing, asking that baggy clothing be pulled back to prove no contraband was concealed within the folds. Finally, the matron ahead of me stepped forward for her turn. The moment the examiner touched her gown, she shouted indignantly, rearing back like a spooked thoroughbred. The employees' attempts to reason with her were met with a vehement head-shaking refusal and a gesture that may have been a devout Muslim woman's version of flipping the bird. The examiners scowled and shrugged, causing me to worry that they might deal with this problem by going on an extended tea break. Instead, they summoned first a supervisor and then a passenger who had already cleared security and boarded the plane. Murmuring soothingly, she talked the older woman through the pat down, but could not convince her to lift her *burqa* in front of these strangers. Fingering the tiny Buddha head strung around my neck, I inhaled deeply trying to believe that it only *felt* like the plane would take off without me. I noticed a couple of blond girls in patchwork Balinese trousers waiting their turn to be frisked in the line that now snaked past the check-in desk. "Could you do me a favor?" I called. "I think my boyfriend's probably wondering what's taking so long. He's a white guy with round glasses and medium brown hair. Could you tell him I'm next in line? Or if you don't see him, ask an Air India guy to see if he's waiting for me on the tarmac? His name's Greg and he's on the flight to Leh."

"*Leh!*" one of the Air India employees shrieked, dragging me ahead of the woman in the *burqa*. She yanked my floppy vest aside, unceremoniously hitching my skirt to the top of my thighs as she used her free hand to grope me with all the delicate finesse of a plastered linebacker. "What is the matter with you?" she yelled. "That flight is leaving in less than five minutes! Did you think the plane would wait all day for you to decide you are ready to go?" She shoved me toward the glass doors, and I ran, wondering where the woman in the *burqa* was going.

"Wait!" I screamed to the worker wheeling the stairs away from the plane. "I'm supposed to identify my backpack so it can be put on board!"

"There is no time for this," the Air India woman shouted from the doorway, appalled, motioning for the steps to be replaced. As soon as I got on, the flight attendants closed the doors, leaving me to find my seat, the only empty one, next to the terrified-looking white guy with round glasses and medium brown hair. As the engines jumped to life, I pressed my nose to the window, grieving because I couldn't see anything on the tarmac resembling the beat-up navy blue pack I'd been schlepping around for years. Could this be the final link in the chain, the endgame of an elaborate ruse that started when the hotel manager in Jammu claimed as kin the honest family who had hosted Diana on their houseboat? Perhaps if I hadn't cancelled the jewels of Kashmir tour, Ayub wouldn't have sent the lady in the *burqa* to create the bottleneck, and my backpack would have made it onto the flight. Soon we were airborne, Dal Lake glinting in farewell before it disappeared from sight. Greg, as was his custom, clawed my triceps, whimpering in anticipation of a fiery crash. The jagged peaks of the Himalayas passed so close below, it looked like we were cruising a few inches above a giant meringue pie, which was almost enough to distract me from the realization that my birth control pills were in that bag.

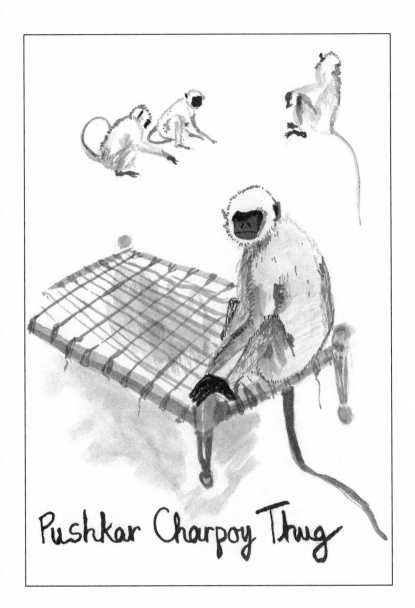

Pushkar Charpoy Thug

On Wildlife

The best thing about our Pushkar digs was the band of black-faced white monkeys who hung out on the roof. Pushkar is India's second holiest city, and don't think those monkeys don't know it. Thanks to their address, they enjoy complete immunity. No matter how calculated and deplorable their antics, the devout must treat them as Brahma's favored lap dogs. We spent many entertaining hours watching the monkeys hurl fistfuls of tiny, white candy onto the heads of the pilgrims who had come to make *puja* on the banks of Lake Pushkar. I suppose it was a mitzvah of sorts, since the candy played a part in the religious ritual. It was made from sugar, rose essence, and water taken directly from the lake, according to the young Brahmin who made his living coaching backpackers through the *puja* ceremony. His friend helped Greg through a *puja* in honor of his late father, Stanley, who had nearly died of dysentery bumming around India some twenty years before his sons were born. I selected my maternal grandmother, Elva Brockway, to be the beneficiary of my bungling attempt at Hindu observance, mostly because the candy's taste made me nostalgic for the violet perfume she gave me as a child. Laying aside the question of reincarnation, I couldn't help thinking that Gran, a Hoosier Presbyterian whose most exotic excursion was a spin on San Francisco's Rice-A-Roni street car, would have been scandalized by these heathen ministrations. Picturing her clutching her pocketbook firmly to her chest, I launched a cardboard boat bearing a flickering candle across the surface of Lake Pushkar as, behind me, a monkey the size of an outboard motor swiped more packets of candy than he could carry.

The monkeys weren't the only creatures to share the ersatz patio outside our quarters, a small adobe room built directly onto the flat roof. The family who owned this house, living in the downstairs rooms that surrounded the parquet courtyard, had a small, tan dog, a friendly-faced mutt whom everyone ignored. Homesick for Jambo, our contemptuous pet cat back home in Chicago, we adopted the eager-to-please little fellow, whom we called Doggiepants. I think Doggiepants was relieved to have some human allies, since the monkeys used him as their whipping boy. He'd be napping on the *charpoy*, a surprisingly comfortable wooden cot with a mattress of crisscrossed strings, when three or four monkeys would bound over the wall and shamble up to him in the time-honored tradition of bullies the world 'round. As we watched, one of the simian toughs—always a medium-sized henchman, never the biggest one—would grasp Doggiepants by the ruff and fling him unceremoniously overboard. Like a terrified freshman unsure if he was free to go, Doggiepants would tremble at a safe distance as the monkeys lounged, chattering on the string bed with a dozen of their pals. "It's okay, Doggiepants," we'd croon, gathering him into our arms. "They'll go away soon and then you can have your spot back." We weren't foolhardy enough to challenge the usurpers on his behalf. We were three times their size, but they outnumbered us. If they whistled, hundreds of long-tailed, opposable-thumbed relatives would come flying from the neighboring rooftops. They were buff, aggressive, familiar with the terrain, and beloved of Brahma. They were unparalleled specimens of grade-A prime ass kicking monkey flesh. Greg and I adored them. We loved Doggiepants, too, but he was like we were: weak.

Pushkar has a well-earned reputation as Rajasthan's favorite backpackers' haunt. While Jaipur has exquisite miniature paintings and Jodhpur has forts, Pushkar has ease. It's easy to navigate on foot, its narrow streets all leading back to the lake. Restaurants are plentiful, as are stalls where even the most tentative bargainer can snag a silk blouse cut from a secondhand sari for less than a buck. Naked *sadhus* patrol the streets, as dignified as elderly lions. It's an Indian vacation within India, a temporary reprieve from the big city *baksheesh* and the exhausting tourist hustle of other picturesque spots. Pushkar gets a fair share of Indian visitors, too, devout Hindus, some of whom are but cremated remains. Varanasi, the famous city on the banks of the Ganges, is the primo ash-scattering spot, but according to both Lonely Planet and the Brahmin who conducted the *puja* for Gran-Gran, Lake Pushkar was good enough for Gandhi, and that, my friends, is good enough for me, particularly if you toss in a couple thousand monkeys.

The dark side of Pushkar's legend, which in my case turned out to be absolutely true, is that you will get sick there. It caught me by surprise. Having remained relatively healthy for five years as a succession of traveling partners liquefied internally, dropping weight by the bucketful, I had decided my bout with malaria in Tanzania had left me impregnable to any number of bugs. It also seemed to be the origin of my insomnia; to this day my nights are miserable, moth-eaten affairs. Sadly, my intestinal get-out-of-jail-free-card expired on the roof of the Brahmaputra guesthouse on the shores of Lake Pushkar.

If I might be allowed a note of scatological explanation: All travelers undergo some transformation of their customary bowel function, otherwise how could they join in the lurid shit-story one-upsmanship that passes for polite mealtime conversation with others of their ilk? I was no exception, even after Africa laid me low. There is a difference, however, between the garden-variety tummy trouble one encounters on the road and the miserable, cramping, everything-I-eat-comes-pouring-out-my-ass experience that I endured in Pushkar. It's a testament to that city's easygoing quality that I was still able to spend a couple of hours every day exploring its petal-strewn streets. When it was time to stay within certain toilet range, I returned to our room on the roof of the Brahmaputra to snuggle with Doggiepants and lean on the foot-thick windowsill, gazing at pilgrims prostrating themselves on the blue-tiled landing of the temple next door. Once, an enormous, milk-colored ox found his way out onto the temple's ghat and wreaked havoc by leaning on the faithful. They scrambled away shouting before he could crush them against an ornamental pillar, but no matter how hard they whacked him on the buttocks, he refused to leave. He reminded me of my stepfather's dearly departed black lab, a loyal beast whose intelligence I always found somewhat overestimated. That dog used to lean against me so heavily on the dock of Art's summer home in northern Wisconsin that I invariably wound up in Lake Superior, another paperback novel waterlogged to thrice its original size. Doggiepants aside, my temperament marked me as a cat person. If you ask a cat person to choose between cow and monkey, the bovine loses every time, unless the judging takes place in a barbecue pit. Looking at that ox's loose hide, I doubted he'd make good eating, even if his mental thermostat was set to poultry. A furious matron in a lime-green sari had him by the nose ring, screaming directly into his nostrils, and the dumb ox just stood there, swishing his tail. Any one of the monkeys vaulting overhead would have torn her head off for such insubordination. Nandi the bull might have been Shiva's trusty vehicle, but Hanuman, king of the monkeys, was Vishnu's right-hand man.

"Why do you think it is that there are a bazillion temples to Ganesha and barely any to Hanuman?" I asked Greg.

"A bazillion?" he questioned dryly.

"You know what I mean. Hanuman's the coolest, man! When Rama's brother-in-law kidnapped Sita, that monkey saved the fucking day! He flew around with an entire forest on his arm!"

"Remember those swimming monkeys in Ubud?" Greg interrupted. Nonsequiturs like this are the norm when one person bears the daily conversational burden that at home is shared by at least a dozen. Beaming, I nodded, breast-stroking furiously in place. Greg, a far more accomplished mimic, upped the ante by climbing a tree, diving into a drinking trough, holding his breath for the underwater crossing and popping up at the far end, his eyes wild, his wet fur plastered close to his body.

"How about Hanoi?" I giggled. Greg pretended to pedal a miniature bicycle around a circus ring. When his comrades broke ranks, he seized the moment to hurl his bike at his whip-cracking trainer, a valiant rebellion, considering that he was still chained to it by the neck. "Oh my god, I thought I'd die. We were the only ones laughing."

"Or that juvenile who put his foot on me?" Greg recalled, returning to the Monkey Forest. Nibbling an invisible peanut, he planted a companionable bare foot on my upper back. Knowing my cue, I looked around slowly. Startled, Greg snatched his foot back, amazed that he had been so forward with a fully grown male of the hairless species.

"Or the one who stole the cherries?"

"He was such a thug," Greg remarked admiringly, having imitated both the rubber-faced bandit who helped himself to a heaping armload of fruit from a vendor's cart and the victim, shaking his fists as the thief sat impassively on a telephone wire, spitting the pits onto the man's head. "Where was that? Manali?"

"Dharamsala," I said, wiping my eyes.

The whitewashed walls shook as our resident troop swarmed up the steep stairs that led to the roof of our rooftop cubicle, launching themselves toward some mysterious group appointment. "What time is it?" Greg asked, groping for his watch. "Four? How are your guts? Do you think you could handle one of those *bhang lassis* your Brahmin guy was telling us about?"

I fished out the business card my *puja* master had handed me— the Sunset Café, his brother-in-law's place, the most beautiful garden in Pushkar, he had vowed. "I think it's worth a try, as long as we can walk very slowly."

We followed the map on the back of the card to a formidable, whitewashed dwelling. A restaurant had been set up in the back, which as promised, was shady, green and very tranquil. We ordered fruit salad and, feeling a bit shifty, *bhang lassis*. These yogurt shakes, the Indian take on hash brownies, got on the menu because of the *sadhus*, who sometimes find that an ascetic lifestyle and wandering around naked is not enough to induce spiritual visions. A holy man bellying up to the bar for a marijuana smoothie struck me as totally legit in a way that two obviously godless, backpacking Good Time Charlies calling for the same beverage did not. If our waiter was offended by our order, he didn't show it. "Small or large?" he asked before disappearing into the kitchen. Half an hour later, he returned with our fruit salads, which were not the usual anemic specimens, but generous platefuls sprinkled with coconut and freshly squeezed lime. We spent the next hour wondering if he'd forgotten about us and wishing that some other travelers would show up, since after the initial appreciative shock wore off, the unnatural quiet of the garden felt oppressive. I made two runs, no pun intended, to the spacious ground-floor toilet. Finally, our waiter reappeared, bearing two tall glasses on a cocktail tray, which seemed absurdly formal given that he was crossing his family's back yard. Upon inspection, the *bhang lassis* showed evidence of a chef's touch. Thick and flecked with green, they were garnished with an attractive spoonful of chopped cashews. The long wait had dampened my madcap mood, but ever since puberty, when I grew out of my picky eating habits, I have been con-stitutionally unable to waste food, especially if I'm paying for it. While technically beverages, the *lassis* served in this establishment clearly belonged in the meal-in-a-glass category. It was like drinking a pasture.

"Wow, it's really grassy," Greg choked. "You feel anything?"

"Not yet. You?"

"Unh-unh."

The Brahmin who had knelt with me beside Lake Pushkar entered, noticed our order, and gave me a big thumbs-up. I was confused. I didn't know much about Brahmins, other than they were top caste, favored a particular shade of periwinkle for home décor, wore strings on their upper arms, and weren't allowed to clean their own toilets. I doubted that it was kosher for them to drink pot, or serve it to paying guests for that matter. Maybe this young fellow was just another ambitious, tourist-hustling, Western-fucker minus the beat-up guitar and groovy duds. "You have come to the Sunset Café," he said, shaking our hands warmly. "Very good. You have met my brother-in-law?" The waiter waved from the doorway. "Is it not the most beautiful garden in Pushkar? Are you enjoying these drinks?"

"Yes. Very, uh, fresh tasting. Green."

"Mmm," he nodded. "This is because of the ganja."

It smelled like the real thing, but neither of us was feeling the expected effects. Oh well, even if they threw the contents of their lawnmower bag into a blender, it didn't matter. We had passed a pleasant enough afternoon and the Brahmins seemed like nice enough guys. I wasn't all that hepped up to be rip-snorting high anyway. Promising to refer other backpackers, we pushed through the heavy wooden doors onto the street, where the mind-altering substance he had just consumed in the large size hit Greg like a semi barreling down the exit ramp, heading for Cracker Barrel. He turned to me, shifting his mandible demonically, his eyes brighter than embers. "Holy shit! Are you as stoned as I am?"

"No," I said, steering him firmly by the elbow. He pranced alongside, alternately giggling at or flinching from the standard Pushkar scenery, the sandalwood beads festooning the bangle-wallah's stalls, the open sewers, the savage white stripes painted across the holy men's noses. "Keep it together," I muttered as he clapped his hands at a monkey seated on a low wall. The monkey shot him the disdainful glance of a prom chaperone, disgusted by the student's sloppy intoxication.

"This is some crazy shit," Greg howled in amazement, ducking to dodge an airborne hazard visible only to him.

"Okay, here we are," I said, pulling him into Brahmaputra's court-yard. The family's grandfather, an intellectual-looking fellow with long white hair and beard, horn-rimmed glasses, and a big, bare belly hanging over his sarong, gave us a dignified nod. "Greg. Greg, listen to me. Do you want to use the bathroom? Because we're right here and once we get you up the stairs, I don't know how easy it's going to be to get you back down." I pointed him toward the toilet and then played with the little boy who lived on the premises while Greg whispered and chuckled to himself behind the door. I had never seen him like this before, though he came close two years later, on our wedding night. I was afraid that he was going to emerge with his pants around his ankles. Apparently, the illustrious old man was used to such monkeyshines. He remained seated on the portico, gazing unflappably across the darkening water when a lesser man might have fallen all over himself trying to protect his grandson from the bad element. I managed to get Greg up the stairs and into bed, where he jiggled and sang and generally behaved like someone higher than Sputnik. Finally, he started to come down. Just as he stretched out, exhausted, the *bhang lassi*'s latent properties struck me. "Greg! Hey, wake up! I'm feeling it!" But Greg, spent, rolled on his side, unable to keep his eyes open after a wan "bon voyage." I am unable to remember much about the next few hours, other than an impression of ripples on the lake and monkey tails flipping around in the moonlight. Compared to our psychotic meltdown in Saigon, it seemed to have been an agreeable few hours. At last I, too, lay down for sleep.

• • •

The next thing I knew, someone punched the heavy double doors to our room wide open. I jerked upright, too disoriented to wonder why the medieval-looking bolt hadn't been fastened the night before. A giant monkey strode in on his knuckles, testicles swinging, contemptuously surveying the scene. "Greg," I peeped. Groggily, he lifted his head a quarter-inch off the pillow and went back to sleep. "Shoo! Heeyaw," I ventured, clutching the sheet to my unclothed bosom. The monkey strutted over to the windowsill and knocked a packet of incense to the floor, as if to say, "Fuck you, girlie. I saw you out there fumbling through your stupid American *puja*." Oh no, he was a hood! The door gaped open, admitting a pearly predawn light. How long until the others of his band came streaming through? All quiet next door at the temple. No signs of life from the family downstairs. It was up to me to defend our territory. I grabbed one of Greg's rubber flip-flops from under the bed and chucked it toward the monkey, missing by a mile, thank god. I don't like to think about what he would have done to me had I scored a direct hit. "Go on, get out of here," I pleaded, lobbing the second flip-flop. The monkey scratched his ass, seized both shoes, and loped out of the room.

"Greg! Greg! He's got your shoes!" I screamed as Greg finally woke, just in time to see the monkey's powerful hindquarters disappearing through the door.

"What the fuck is going on?" he demanded over my shrill instructions to get his clothes on, a giant monkey had made off with his shoes. Still not understanding what had transpired, Greg leapt to his feet, pulling on a pair of white, elastic-waist trousers as he stumbled outside. I sat for a minute stunned, then rifled through my backpack for something I could throw on quickly. Naked beneath a wrinkled sundress, I tripped to the threshold in time to witness a tense standoff between Greg and his adversary, who squatted on the *charpoy*, gnawing a flip-flop. Doggiepants cowered in the far corner. Greg took one step toward the *charpoy*, looking, I must say, very lean and handsome in his casual, beachy bottoms. The monkey sprang from his perch and Greg tottered backward, crossing his arms in front of his face. The monkey streaked past, not slowed for a second by the rubber sandals clenched in his black paws. Greg started laughing in disbelief as he headed up the steep, banisterless stairs, following the monkey to the flat roof over our room. Doggiepants and I rushed to the center of the lower roof, but Greg and the monkey had disappeared into our blind spot.

"Be careful," I tittered, just as Greg reappeared, running as if his life depended on it. He held his arms out like a tightrope walker as he started down the stairs, his knees pumping past his waistband in his frenzied effort to escape. To his left, it was a sheer two-story drop to the tiled floor of the family compound. Awareness of that danger slowed his descent. Fangs bared, the monkey gained on him with the effortless muscular coordination of a natural predator. In the quiet before sunrise, the sounds of the chase were weirdly amplified by the painted cement stairs: the panicked *slap-slap* of Greg's bare soles, the monkey pushing off with his handlike feet, the macho rippling of those simian glutei. "Run!" I shrieked, unable to stifle my laughter. It would have looked less funny had Greg's pursuer been a cheetah or a ferocious hippo, but there was something great about that monkey's indignation. *Boy, you think you're evolved just because you're wearing pants? I'll show you who's the boss around here!*

Greg leapt the final three stairs, thudding flat-footed to the roof. For some reason, the monkey drew up short. He probably reckoned it was beneath him to polish off such unworthy opponents. He held his ground, glaring, as Greg and I raced hand in hand to the safety of our room, Doggiepants hot on our heels. We remained there, bolt firmly in place, until we heard the family stirring below us and the legendary Pushkar sickness reasserted itself. Miraculously, the *bhang lassi* had worked temporary tonic effects on my motility, stoppering me up for an entire night. Cautiously, I stuck my head out. All clear. Scuttling toward the loo, I noticed Grandfather still racked out on a *charpoy* positioned in his favorite lake-view spot. I was glad the scuffle upstairs hadn't disturbed him. He'd probably grown accustomed to overhead brawls between monkeys and the guests who paid to sleep on his roof.

We headed out to shop for a new pair of thongs to replace the ones the monkey had stolen. This was the second pair of shoes Greg had had nicked in India. He complained that he felt conspicuous galumphing around in white socks and bulky black athletic footwear from home. Could it be that India was pushing Greg Kotis toward something resembling fashion consciousness?

When we returned from our expedition, we found that the monkey had left a calling card, perhaps a warning of the kind of misfortune sure to befall anyone foolish enough to tangle with him twice. The mangled upper portion of a flip-flop lay on our doormat, chewed well past the instep. Greg leaned down to pick up his souvenir, cradling it gently like the sacred relic it was. "Look," he intoned, "you can see the teeth."

We examined the ruined shoe, whose twin would be discovered later that evening, abandoned in similar condition on the upper roof. I fully believed that the missing part had been eaten. "God," we chimed in unison, "monkeys are so cool."

On Dress

Greg granted me a temporary stay from donning the Lawrence of Arabia costumes he had commissioned from a tailor in Jaisalmer. In flapping Chinese pants and a sleeveless Thai blouse purchased because it was precisely the same Brahmin blue as the paperback cover of Milan Kundera's *Immortality*, I dug my toes into the sand to climb the dune. The late-afternoon desert was unlike any landscape I'd encountered, certainly nothing like my paternal grandmother's condo complex in Tucson or the extreme-sports playground of Joshua Tree National Park. Familiar desert plants like aloe, saguaro, prickly pear and mesquite were nowhere to be seen, the only vegetation tufts of parched grass, cropped nearly to the ground by hungry camels. Strangest of all were the ridges the unimpeded wind combed into the dunes, causing me to feel like someone had shrunk me and deposited me in one of those tabletop Zen gardens, from which all the rocks had been removed. It almost seemed a shame to mar nature's artistry with our footprints, especially when maneuvering to the top required such effort. After only a couple of yards, I was winded, crawling on all fours like an animal, but I had to admit, the breathtaking view did justify jellied calves and painful flashbacks to Mount Kilimanjaro. The desert unfurled beneath us, a vast, bumpy carpet with the vacuum tracks still visible. In the near distance, the camel drivers busied themselves around the bunkhouse, hauling jerry cans, watering their animals, and drinking tea around a small fire. The sun sank toward the horizon, turning everything pink. Spreading my arms wide, I intoned, "This . . . . is . . . . the . . . . *desert!*"

"Is that some famous quote?" Greg asked. I then explained about my boyfriend in college who forced me to watch *Lawrence of Arabia*, which he loved but I found excruciating. To me, the pain of sitting through it was encapsulated in an early scene where Omar Sharif turns to Peter O'Toole, taking several weeks to deliver his line:

"This . . . . is . . . . the . . . . *desert!*"

"Are you serious? How could you hate *Lawrence of Arabia*? It's one of the greatest movies of all time."

I knew then we were in for a rough ride.

That night, rather than sleep with the guides and other camel trekking tourists in the grim bunkhouse that served as desert base camp, I insisted on dragging our blankets into a small hollow scooped between the dunes. We first tried sleeping on one of those glorious peaks, but it was freezing cold up there and every time the wind blew, the shifting sands bit into us like red ants wielding nettles. At the foot of the dune Greg dropped off quickly, but I stayed awake, watching a sky so starry it was planetarium overkill. How, I fretted, would I make it through the next few days? While I had no prior camelback experience to go by, I had plenty of residual equine anxiety, a throwback to summer camp when I was the only camper not gripped by intense horse mania. As my cabinmates whooped and hollered, I clung to the mane of the broken-down nag peer pressure had seated me astride, praying that the other girls wouldn't persuade the counselor to let us canter. I had since ridden an elephant, a gentle creature trained for the Chiang Mai tourist trade, but even on Miss Boonchoo's massive, benevolent back, I couldn't shake the feeling that I was in constant danger of slipping off. I've got this thing about being trampled.

With no trees or buildings to slow the dawn, the sun went from a blood-red rising ball to a blinding three-million-watt bulb in less time than it takes to pee. Our driver sent his assistant, a sweet nine-year-old boy, to get us to shake a leg. "Soon hot," he shouted over his shoulder, as we stumbled after him, kicking up sandy plumes. Ducking into the bunkhouse, we changed into the trekking gear Greg had purchased: identical white cotton pajamas and enormous gauze turbans, maharaja orange for him and screaming maharani pink for me. The tailor who had knocked these outfits out in under an hour had sworn that this was what the camel drivers wore to protect themselves from the sun. "Much cooler than T-shirt," he had promised. Watching Greg preen before the tailor's three-way mirror, I felt alarmed. Usually he was the one suffering from his mate's outlandish garb, skulking a few feet behind as I traipsed out of our apartment in a full-length vintage kimono, a ceramic peace medallion the size of a Nerf ball, or the Masonic fez that was my souvenir from the Chelsea flea market. Of all places, why here, where groups of young men stared from a distance that facilitated breast and heiner tweaking, would Greg suddenly gravitate toward eye-catching getups guaranteed to call even more attention to us?

"Maybe I'll just wear the shirt and trousers with my regular hat,"

I said, checking to see how blatantly my underwear showed through the thin fabric.

"What?" he cried. "The turban pulls the whole thing together! You can't not wear the turban." I stood at sulky attention while Greg swathed my head in twenty feet of brilliant azalea gauze, which immediately drooped down over one eye. With any luck, we wouldn't be the only foreign trekkers dressed like trick-or-treaters. Stepping into the blinding morning, we were met with great hilarity by the drivers. They stopped tying supplies onto their camels' wooden saddles to better enjoy the spectacle. Greg puffed out his chest, cinching his fanny pack around his waist like a Rajput warrior's sword belt. I willed myself invisible as we walked toward our driver, passing other trekkers dressed in what passes for backpacker sportswear. Never have I so longed for a pair of cutoff sweats and a Hard Rock Hanoi T-shirt. At least Greg and I were going alone, just the two of us with Fonzie, the camel driver, and Khaled, his boy-assistant. I would have died of shame had I been forced to ride alongside the cool kids, garbed as Dorkimus Maximus.

Fonzie cracked an engaging grin as he studied us, shading his eyes with one hand. "You bought these clothes in Jaisalmer? Good, this is same what we wear." It was true, but I envied the faded nonchalant gray of his well-worn bottoms. He held off on the turban and top until the last minute, completing his chores in a stretched-out, pale blue tank shirt that gave him a sort of surfer flair. Slender and curly-haired, he was a handsome guy, even with a sparse, squirrelly moustache. Khaled, mutely attaching nylon reins to the camels' wooden nose pegs, wore a much-laundered, long-sleeved dress shirt and a piece of blue fabric as a sarong. I wished our duds weren't so brand spanking new. We looked every bit as silly as pampered executives arriving in Kenya for their Abercrombie and Fitch safari, ludicrously overequipped with big-game hunter vests, battery-operated compressors to inflate queen-sized air mattresses and bush hats advertised in the *New Yorker*. I would gladly have traded our entire water supply for permission to change into a sundress. Greg seemed untouched by embarrassment, watching Fonzie rewrap my turban, eager to master the mid-forehead wrist snap that was the key to turban-stability. He helped distribute the supplies between our three camels, carefully studying the knots Khaled used to anchor bundles of bedding and lentils to the beasts' backs.

I knelt in the sand, hoping I would get the most picturesque one, whose plaid saddle blanket was edged with a salmon-colored ruffle. She looked the friendliest, though perhaps I was deceived by that frill. All three of them seemed like bizarre inventions, better suited to science fiction than to exotic, three-day-long pony rides. I couldn't bring myself to look her in the face, partly because I'd heard that camels' foul-smelling sputum could blind you if they spat in your eye, but also due to the cruelty of that wooden plug staked through her nostrils. The urban primitive movement was just gathering steam, and as a subway-riding city dweller, I'd seen my fair share of septum piercings and oversized jewelry whose purpose was to stretch. Still, I couldn't help noting that those were modifications humans inflicted upon themselves by choice. I reckoned that if I were an animal and some two-legs drove a chunk of wood through my nose, I'd feel pretty fucking stoked to get payback. I wouldn't hesitate to buck any brightly turbaned turkey making a show of steering me by yanking on a nylon cord.

"Is it okay if I pet her?" I asked Fonzie.

"It's okay, yes. You can pet."

"Hey girl," I crooned. "My name's Ayun. What's y—" Her muscular neck dipped and rose like the cables of an elevator as she rearranged her head to face me, honking with disapproval. She flattened her ears, baring a topsy-turvy collection of broken, brown teeth. Oh man, I shuddered to think of the consequences of those infectious choppers clamping down hard on my thigh. She sneezed threateningly, tagging me with a prodigious stream of camel snot. Fonzie bounded over to beat her on the neck and snout. Semichastened, she shot me an imperious look, batting her long eyelashes as if to say, "I'm prettier than you."

We were the last trekkers to get started because, when one of our camels stood up, his heavily weighted saddle slid all the way around until it hung upside down beneath his belly. The camel farted and chewed his cud as Fonzie, cursing, reloaded him from scratch. Finally, we too were ready to depart. "Okay please," Fonzie said, as Khaled forced Ruffle Blanket to her knees by hanging on her muzzle. Swinging a leg over the camel's broad back, I realized I would be riding with my legs completely abducted at all times. "Here, reins." With no further instructions, Fonzie cracked my ride on the rump and she rose, unfolding like some sort of nifty space-saving device. With her legs fully extended, it was a distance of at least nine feet from her hump to the ground. There were no stirrups and, for that matter, no pommel on the tower-shaped wooden saddle. It seemed to have more in common with a lobster crate than with the leather models my fellow campers had so lovingly tended. I looked around for something to hold on to that might prove more substantial than the slack nylon ropes. Maybe by slipping my hands between my legs and under the old quilt that served as a cushion, I could get a grip on the saddle's wooden frame. I seemed to recall Laura Ingalls racing an unbridled, bareback Indian pony across the prairie on the cover of one of the later *Little House* books, her hands tangled in its blowing mane. The best Ruffle Blanket had to offer were a few sparse bunches of coarse hair that formed a dotted line down her neck. Perhaps my best bet was to bond with the creature. "Who's a sweet old baby?" I whispered. "Who's the best camel girl in the whole world? That's right, you are! You don't have anything to worry about because I'm not going to hit you or jerk on your reins. If you're thirsty, I'll give you lots of yummy water to drink. Does that sound good to you, pretty lady?" It was like talking to a piece of furniture.

Greg whooped happily as the surly young male he had been assigned rose to his feet. With the casual grace of a man who knows his way around a dromedary, Fonzie mounted the one he would share with Khaled, barely waiting for the boy to hop behind him sidesaddle before setting the animal in motion. Greg's camel and mine followed suit, their soft feet slapping like pancakes across the hot sand.

It didn't take long for the nausea to register. I recognized the symptoms immediately. I hadn't been this seasick since Malaysia three years earlier when Isaac and I hitched a fishing boat to Tioman Island. I spent most of that crossing hanging over the bow beside a gorgeous Greek girl, both of us puking our guts out. The undulating camel precisely mimicked the pitch and roll of that rickety fishing boat, except, I immediately decided, this was worse. Then, I had another person with me to hold my hair back and ensure I didn't fall overboard. No matter how horrible I felt, I knew that in a short while I would stagger to the solid ground of an island so lovely it was the setting for Bali Hai in the Hollywood version of *South Pacific*. Barfing in a bikini was humiliating, but could it compare to spewing one's breakfast all over a camel's neck, whilst costumed as Omar Sharif?

"Greg, wait up," I called weakly. "I think I'm going to be sick." But Greg was too far to hear, lost in a boyish adventure fantasy, experimenting with different rein grips and scrutinizing Fonzie's authentic camel riding chops. Our saddles were the equivalent of infant car seats. Fonzie didn't have one, resting instead against a small bundle of supplies, his legs drawn up and hooked around the hump. Khaled kept his ankles crossed demurely beneath the hem of his sarong, as he rode without holding on. My own legs banged helplessly against Ruffle Blanket's sides, chafing through the pajama pants. My delicate lady parts fared no better, the folded quilt affording scant protection from the wooden saddle struts that knocked into me at a rate of thirty blows per minute. At least the pounding provided a distraction from my distinctly green gills. Instead of thinking about throwing up, I could fixate on a story told by my cousin thirty years earlier: She had been playing on a seesaw when the girl on the bottom got off without warning, sending Cindy crashing down, still astride the board. "Blood came out where I pee," she had gravely—and indelibly—informed me. Whimpering, as sweat prickled beneath my turban, I plucked at the crotch of my thin drawstring bottoms, wondering whether, were I to lose my balance, I should cup my privates in my hand, like a man.

Up ahead, Greg barked with cowboy pleasure as the others broke into a trot. "Please, no," I whispered when Ruffle Blanket lurched after them. My teeth knocked against each other, the saddle spanked my ischial tuberosities, and my vision joggled crazily. It was like riding in a rumble seat. "Slow down!" I shouted, throwing my arms around that furry neck. "I'm going to fall off!" I heard Greg signaling Fonzie, and suddenly, we were walking again. I drooped forward, resigned to the nausea. Maybe they could lash me on like supplies, or like a recently captured bad guy. If only I could bag out now. Would-be mountaineers were felled by altitude sickness all the time. Surely there was no shame in admitting that camel-induced motion sickness was too strong to fight. We hadn't been gone more than an hour. Gingerly, I peeked over my shoulder. There was no sign of the dunes on which we'd slept the night before, only shimmering waves of heat. Maybe I would be able to find my way back to the starting point on foot, but more probably I'd wander in circles until I expired from dehydration while crawling toward a mirage. My stomach contents churned, but I willed myself to consider carefully before waging a campaign to abort the mission. There was a chance my misery was mostly psychosomatic, a commitment to the actor's craft. Unenthusiastic to begin with, had I cast myself as a Camelback Camille, an agonized martyr, deserving of pity? Perhaps if I could conjure up a more gung-ho attitude, the nausea and crotch pain would evaporate. I picked my head up.

Fonzie drew alongside. "Now we must go fast," he said, preparing to whack the reins against his mount's neck.

"No, I can't."

"Yes, this too slow because we have far." He gave me his gravest Omar Sharif look. I squinted, doubtful that we had anything to gain from a swifter pace except more sand and the open display of my stomach lining.

"I cannot go fast," I said giving each word a conclusive weight.

"Fast is fun," Greg urged, a goofy smile lighting his face.

"Greg, listen to me. I feel really, really sick to my stomach right now. I swear to god, if he makes me go fast . . ." My bottom lip trembled. It was hard not to feel sorry for myself, especially knowing that the ridiculous headdress was undermining my pathos.

"Okay, we can take it slow for now," Greg said kindly.

"Slow no good," Fonzie insisted. "We have far!"

"Yes, yes, I know what you are saying, but for now we go slow," Greg told him, holding my ground. Khaled stole a shy glance at me. Haggard and devoid of dignity, I met his eye, hoping that at least the child would understand the depths of my wretchedness. He covered his lips with his hands to stifle a giggle.

We plodded on, fanning out so that Fonzie and Khaled took the lead, with Greg in the middle and me lagging far behind. Like her rider, Ruffle Blanket was a dawdler by nature, but this shared tendency was not enough to change my low opinion of her. Her stupid rolling gait was to blame for my stricken condition! I closed my eyes, tensed my thighs and willed myself to believe I was lying quietly in the plaid hammock in my grandmother's side yard. "Ayun!" Greg shouted. "Hey Ayunee!" Grudgingly, I opened my eyes. "Take my picture!"

"Sick," I whimpered, knowing there was no chance of him hearing. Greg struck a heroic pose as I pawed limply through my daypack for the Nikon. With trembling hands, I lifted it to my eye.

"Get closer!" I shot him a harassed look. Having forced me on this vomitrocious excursion, he was disturbing me on the closest thing I had to a sick bed, in order to record him having the time of his life. I focused on the Gandhi glasses he had purchased on the advice of a backpacker we'd met on the River Kwai. He'd praised India as a ridiculously cheap source of prescription eyewear and over-the-counter Valium. "Get the camel in there!" As if there were a chance the fucking thing might not make it into the frame. Gritting my teeth, I fired off shot after shot until the Grand Pooh-Bah was satisfied that his likeness had been duly captured. "Now I'll take one of you," he offered, holding out his hand for the camera.

"Maybe later, if I start feeling better," I said testily, thinking, "Hey buddy, I'll let you take my picture when we're back in Jaisalmer, wearing normal clothes and having a beer in a peaceful sandstone *haveli*."

It was a great relief when a small tree appeared on the horizon. Fonzie announced that we would break here for lunch. Khaled forced Ruffle Blanket to her knees, but I couldn't dismount without assistance, so cramped were my inner thighs and battered pubis. Greg, too, appeared permanently bowlegged, tottering over to the small patch of shade under the tree as Khaled and Fonzie stripped the camels of their loads. "Man, it's really fun, but it's killing my balls," he confided. I pulled off my sweaty turban, then lay on my back, legs in the air like a bug's, trying to enjoy every moment of this glorious motionlessness. Khaled squatted shyly nearby, building a small fire with sticks he pulled from a supply bundle. He put lentils and chopped onion into a dented aluminum pot, along with some water from a jerry can so heavy he could barely lift it. Meanwhile, Fonzie stripped down to his blue tank shirt and made dough for chapatis. He asked Greg to teach him some good curses in English, happily running through the repertoire he had gleaned from other tourists. The smell of Khaled's dal and the chapatis roasting on a beat-up grill revived me. Famished, I wolfed down the simple meal, certain that it had given me restorative camel-riding powers.

I was wrong. After an hour-long break for lunch, only two things had changed: Now it hurt to get on the camel as well as off, and the sun had reached charbroil. Fonzie had bandaged me back into my turban, this time adding a sort of muffler so that only my eyes were exposed. The gauze scent over my nose and mouth made me think of hippie import stores. What I wouldn't have given to be in Moondancer or the Mexican Shop, fingering flimsy embroidered blouses tagged "Made In India," instead of actually *in* India *on* a camel. As if she could read my mind, Ruffle Blanket simultaneously belched and lifted her tail to litter the sand with a half-bushel of camel apples. My stomach pinched, longing to be so free. Again, I dropped my head to my chest, as lifeless as poor, dead Grandma Joad, crossing the California border tied to the top of the family truck. In a way, Grandma Joad was luckier. She was beyond feeling.

A commotion up ahead pulled me from my nauseated self-absorption. Opening my eyes, I saw Greg hanging on for dear life as his mount bombed away full-throttle. As a precautionary measure, I pulled on Ruffle Blanket's reins until her snout pointed to the blazing, desert sun, but she showed no inclination to bolt after her more spirited colleague. Khaled jumped to the ground as Fonzie galloped after the runaways, a thrilling matinee idol of yore. Heading them off at the pass, he dismounted, and after a few botched attempts, managed to seize the dangling reins. Shouting what I suspected were some very foul oaths against the entire humped species, Fonzie drew back his hand and slapped the camel hard, right across the face, as if challenging him to a duel. For the next hour, Khaled led Greg's camel by the reins, humming a little tune as he walked in front. Despite this infantile arrangement, Greg wanted his picture taken again, badgering me until I dug out the Nikon. A part of me hoped I would puke all over it. Perhaps then he would register the damage this hideous camel business was wreaking on my digestive tract.

The sun was low when we stopped for the day and laid out our bedrolls at the base of a dune. I couldn't see much of anything besides sand, but within minutes of our arrival, a half-dozen children materialized. The oldest, a doe-eyed beauty around Khaled's age with a nose ring and a sheer veil over her long, wavy hair, pulled a sprig of greenery from her *salwar-kameez*. Smiling mysteriously, she didn't seem at all worried as Ruffle Blanket's discolored choppers grazed her palm, greedily gobbling up the exotic snack. The other kids were scruffier and much younger, their hair bluntly hacked as if they cut it themselves. A five-year-old hauled a toddler sibling on her hip as she surveyed our every move. Their older brother produced a headphoneless Walkman, using his hands to ask Greg what it was. "Oh, this is a radio. It makes music," Greg explained, singing snatches of various tunes until the kid understood. "But you need headphones. Do you have headphones?" The boy looked perplexed. Greg cupped his ears, then pointed to the headphone jack and flipped open the empty battery hatch. "You need batteries, too. Uh, four AAs. Until then, I'm afraid it won't work." He handed it back with an apologetic smile. The kid thought for a moment, then ran to Fonzie.

"He say, how much you give him for this?" Fonzie asked, brushing chapati flour from his tank shirt.

"Oh, no thank you. It's very nice, but I don't need it. Tell him I have one, back in Jaisalmer."

Fonzie conferred with the kid. "He says he make you good price."

"I'm sure he would but I don't need."

Dejected, the children strolled away, depressed by their inability to sell the strange object. Fifteen minutes later, they returned, lugging jerry cans to water the camels. The pretty girl balanced hers on her head. The others hauled the heavy jugs in tag teams, rotating the five-year-old's baby brother between them. The Walkman boy showed me the Walkman. I shook my head. Fonzie gave them a couple of chapatis and sent them away as Khaled tended stoically to the small fire. I wondered if he wished he could go play with them.

Fonzie wanted to know if I felt better. I told him that I was having trouble adjusting to the waves of the ambulating camel, but on solid ground I felt fine, if a little sore. He laughed, understanding. "Bottom hurts, yes? Legs, too. Come, I will give you massage."

Previous experience had taught me that, just like thousands of my male counterparts, I much preferred my bodywork to be performed by a nice Thai lady. The grandfatherly fellow in Sumatra who wished to rub my affected knee with *jamu* stood alone in his therapeutic intent. There's really no such thing as a free back rub, if you receive my meaning. Still, I figured, what hanky-panky could Fonzie have in mind with Greg stretched out on the dune a few feet away, trying to read in the fading daylight? I flopped onto my stomach, groaning with pleasure as the heel of Fonzie's hand pressed into my aching buns. He seemed to know what he was doing. Maybe in a country where male friends promenaded hand in hand, camel drivers didn't feel inhibited from soothing each other's ouchy glutes at the end of a long day's ride. It was impossible to imagine American camel drivers doing the same—the straight ones, anyway. Khaled, heading off to scour our dinner dishes with sand, made a laughing comment. Fonzie now straddled my heiner, working his thumbs alongside my vertebrae. I took a deep, cleansing breath. When he came to my bra, he indicated that he could progress if only I would reach beneath my shirt to unhook the strap. Fair enough, I supposed, though I was beginning to wonder how long this treatment would continue. I was holding my water until nightfall, figuring that only darkness could give a girl some privacy in this treeless, bushless wasteland.

"How's the massage?" Greg inquired.

"Great," I grunted. "Fonzie's a natural. You should have him work on you next."

Greg returned to his book and Fonzie ran his fingernails lightly over my ribs, not stopping when he came to the sides of my breasts. I decided to consider this an accidental blunder into anatomical no man's land. Several years earlier on a beach in Bali, I had permitted a matronly masseuse to untie my bikini top, flip me over and knead my gazongas as if she were mixing up some homemade bread dough composed of equal parts sand, coconut oil, and human flesh. Any accusations against Fonzie would be gender-based. The thought of kicking up a ruckus gave me the heebie-jeebies, especially since Fonzie was brown and I was white, Fonzie was poor and I was poor by choice in the richest country in the world, Fonzie knew the way out of the desert and I . . . *whoo*, okay, it was getting a little too close for comfort. I giggled, flinching. "You are ticklish?" Fonzie laughed. "Okay." He immediately pulled up stakes, relocating to my grievously wronged legs. It hurt so good, to quote my Hoosier homeboy John Cougar Mellencamp, but now in addition to my bladder being full, my guard was up. He worked down my hamstrings to my calves, then knelt between my legs, prodding the meat on the inner thighs. Having spent almost the entire day with my drumsticks locked in wishbone position, this struck me as entirely valid if a bit torturous. I sucked in my breath, vowing to meet the pain full on.

"Everything okay?" Greg asked.

"Yeah," I snarled through gritted teeth. "My legs feel like they're on fire but in a good way." I tried to concentrate on the cooling sand beneath my cheek, the good desert smell. A little beetle scurried a few inches away from my hand, intent on making it to his destination before total darkness fell. The bells Khaled had tied to the grazing camels' necks clanked mildly as the wooden clappers struck their copper sides. Closer to home, several fingertips snaked across the outer reaches of my . . . I froze. Underpants and insubstantial cotton trousers did not adequately disguise the contours of my body, as Fonzie and I both knew. A situation like this called for reinforced Teflon tap pants equipped with a spring-loaded mallet. Sadly, I'd left mine in Chicago. Yep, here they came again, those sneaky fingers, brushing up against my forbidden fruit. I waited a half-second to see if Greg would react, then scrambled to my hands and knees.

"Thanks, that's enough," I snapped, a bit of Nancy Reagan creeping into my tone.

"Finished with massage?" Fonzie asked, not believing that anyone would cut a friendly freebie short.

"It's his turn now," I announced, pointing to Greg. Unsure what had just transpired but sensing something fishy, he dutifully crawled to the spot I had abruptly vacated.

Later, when our guides had taken their blankets a little distance away and I had drained several quarts of urine into the sand, I asked Greg if he had noticed Fonzie getting a bit fresh during my massage. "Oh, is that what was happening?" he groaned sympathetically. "Sorry, I couldn't quite see for sure."

"It's okay."

Subtle deviations from the script often go undetected. Nobody ever attempted a stealth raid on Lawrence of Arabia's vagina, though if I recalled correctly, in *The Sheltering Sky*, wasn't a turbaned Debra Winger abducted by Bedouins when their leader realized he'd forgotten to pack any womanly companionship? Debra cleaved to him pretty quickly—he was much hotter than John Malkovich—but I was less confused by her affection for her Bedouin love master than why those camels didn't make her the least bit urpy. I guess some girls are just cut out for desert trekkin'.

Hanuman ~ Hunky Monkey!

On Culture

Finally, somebody older than eighteen thought our ragtag theater company was hot shit. Consecutive bookings with almost all of our expenses paid allowed us to cobble together a two-city world tour. Immediately following a gig at the U.S. Comedy Arts Festival in Aspen, Colorado, we would fly to Romania, where the NeoFuturists would appear as part of the International Festival of Young Professional Theater Artists. Stuffing my backpack with the heaviest sweater and the shortest black cocktail dress I owned, I wondered if there was a chance our act might be picked up for a sitcom and whether the Romanians would be disappointed when they saw we were neither professional nor young. I would celebrate my thirtieth birthday our first day in Sibiu, the Transylvanian town that played host to the festival.

Aspen was a blur of free DoveBars, free bottled water, and dance parties free to anyone sporting a laminated badge on a yellow nylon cord. Before arriving in Colorado, my life on the stage had never involved corporate underwriting. The hard labor and brutal conditions of low-budget theater had never bothered me. Squeezed into our single dressing room, hunting for a missing prop amid the half-empty coffee cups and balled-up street clothes that littered our folding table, I cracked jokes about the delicious mint I had found in the urinal whilst swabbing the grimy bathrooms with a mildewed mop. Due to the loyalty of our overwhelmingly teenaged audience, we were able to pay ourselves a pittance, but the real prize was the opportunity to perform three nights a week in strange two-minute plays we had written ourselves, for characters who shared our names, home lives, and liberal political views. The invention necessitated by our poverty drove our aesthetic. Aiming flashlight beams directly into the audience's eyes, we held toilet paper tube megaphones to our lips to denounce the fatty excesses of better funded, more mainstream entertainment. Dead flashlight batteries were a constant source of aggravation and accusation.

In Aspen, it quickly became apparent that we were the smallest fish in the pond. The industry folk swarmed around a handful of fast-track young standup comedians. I no longer needed to worry that one of the other NeoFuturist women would get more airtime than I in the hit cable series based on our long-running late-night show. To Hollywood types, we weren't just an undergroomed collective from the aging Slacker generation, shouting about reproductive and gay rights through toilet paper tubes shipped all the way from Chicago. We were invisible. This lack of interest was actually a great blessing because it freed me to enjoy the great bounty of free food. I couldn't get over it. Not only could I help myself to a bottle of water from the ice tub in the performer's club, I didn't have to refill it at the sink! In full view of the organizers, I could crack open a second bottle, leave it half-drunk on the bar, and stick another in my pocket in case I got thirsty during a free screening later in the afternoon.

Tickets, drinks, buffets and swag, as it's known in the industry, rained down. On our first day, we were each issued a sturdy black tote with the U.S. Comedy Arts Festival logo, a swag bag in which to stow the ear warmers, fanny packs, sunglasses, and windbreakers that also bore the official imprint. After years of toil, presenting our show became secondary to acquiring complimentary chair massages and baseball hats printed to match the tote bag. When we asked for directions to the hot springs located a couple of hours away, a festival organizer whipped out her chunky black cell phone and arranged for us to use a festival hatchback free of charge! I jab-bered our thanks, dazzled by the ubiquity of these newfangled contraptions that were more walkie-talkie than pay phone. It didn't occur to me to be anything but slavishly grateful. Over breakfast, I was shocked to hear other, more worldly participants knocking the quality and quantity of the freebies. Veterans of the comedy festival circuit, they had just come from Toronto, where mountains of shrimp, top-shelf liquor, and handsome ripstop satchels were the order of the day. "This sucks," one of the funnymen groused, frowning at his eggs Benedict, which had arrived free of charge. I nodded sympathetically, wondering if his sour demeanor owed more to his award-winning shtick, Aspen's allegedly sub-par swag, or the fact that HBO had just cancelled his show. "They drag us all the way out to this fucking mountain in the middle of nowhere to treat us like *this?*" He flashed a bitter smile around the homey breakfast room of our B & B. "We must really be the dregs if they've got us staying all the way out here. Everybody else is on the strip. In a hotel. With room service. Where did they put David Sedaris?"

Gripped by warm feelings for our benefactors and their corpo-rate sponsors, I began praising our accommodations, in particular the hot tub on the back deck. After a lifetime of Jacuzzi-less midwestern winters, I could not sit idly by as this jaded ingrate disparaged the munificence that paved the way for me to wear my bathing suit outdoors in March. Rather than take an aggressive tack with a celebrated acidic wit, I channeled a born-again Christian friend from college, who habitually cast her eyes ceilingward to thank God for such gifts as her musical abilities, her handsome boyfriend, and hot chocolate in the student union on a frigid January morning. I tell you, Melissa never praised Jesus like I praised that hot tub to the complaining standup at breakfast. To my relief, he didn't cut me in half with one swoop of his critically acclaimed tongue. He smiled as if indulging a toddler who has drawn a yellow line that she claims is a giraffe. "That's a refreshing point of view," he remarked. "You'll learn."

"He's wrong," I thought many times throughout the festival, particularly while shaking my tail feathers in a too-short cocktail dress at the Ritz. Beloved yellow laminated badge! It bought me free entry to the lavish closing-night festivities at the Ritz! *The Ritz!* I kept returning to the ladies' room to admire the marble expanses, the golden fixtures, the buffet of grooming products, and myself growing more alluring with every no-charge Heineken. So what if our scrappy, low-budget show had cast nary a ripple with the Hollywood suits? So what if a rising television star had elbowed me unceremoniously off the dance floor to give the photographers a clearer shot of her boogying with a life-size cardboard cutout of Mr. Jenkins, the mascot of Tanqueray gin? For a week, I had wined, dined, and hot-tubbed in the land of the free. I had no desire to be one of the wealthy women I saw toddling around Aspen's quaint streets in snug black ski pants, mink head wraps, and expensive, year-round tans. Why aspire to pay for your pleasures when the fare was waived for even the lowliest jester aboard the king's gravy train? The seasoned comics were making themselves miserable hunting for holes in a bulging feedbag.

Thirty-six hours later, I was stuck in a blizzard on a country road in Romania with five very crabby, sleep-deprived comrades, a fetching volunteer translator, and a driver who kept getting off the bus and wandering away. The bus, a real Department of Corrections special, was unheated. We unpacked and put on every scrap of clothing we had brought, winding sweatshirt turbans around our heads, but it didn't help.

Diana, who had been nursing a cold since our arrival in Aspen, started bearing an uncanny resemblance to a skull. She bore her discomfort stoically, as does someone who is entering a long tunnel and running toward the light.

Lusia needed to eat. She wasn't just peckish or merely ravenous. Her therapist had intimated that Lusia's psychological well-being depended on a strict adherence to regular mealtimes, and with no cooler on board she was dangerously overdue. At one point in our sixteen-hour odyssey (the trip from the airport in Bucharest to the festival town of Sibiu is supposed to take slightly less than five hours), we came upon a funereal, nearly empty disco. We pulled over in hopes of procuring something for Lusia to eat, but the kitchen was closed and the few patrons playing slot machines in the lobby grimaced as slush dripped from our chunky boots onto their red wall-to-wall carpet. The bartender wouldn't even give Lusia a glass of orange juice, no matter how much American currency she waved around.

David, hearing the translator Simona's views on gypsies, was preparing to out himself in solidarity. I recognized the way he started exhaling through his nostrils, like a bull. I suspect that Simona was under the impression that she had never met a gay person, and to the best of my knowledge, David had yet to meet a gypsy. After much discussion and research, we had decided to keep David's sexual orientation our little secret. "They don't like The Gay in them parts," David rationalized, as eager to save his hide as we were not to risk ours by defending his. He couldn't coax himself so far back into the closet, however, that he was willing to cut a juicy monologue he'd written for himself on the subject of gay rights. After all, the theme of this year's International Festival of Young Professional Theater Artists was "tolerance." Bolstered by years of preaching to the choir, we figured that an audience almost entirely composed of homophobic non-English-speaking Romanians would see the light just moments after they saw our two-minute play and rush out to embrace their gay brethren. Either that or they'd storm the stage to tear David and anyone who dared protect him limb from limb. He managed, barely, to keep from spilling the beans to the gypsy-phobic Simona. At five in the morning, when Lusia's search for food and the driver's exhaustion led us to a rustic shed where truckers could buy vodka and tea, David was befriended by a gang of rough, middle-aged men. "I want to fuck you!" one of them roared, pounding him on the back as David was treated to another shot. Could it be that our research was so totally off base? Only later did we figure out that the trucker was maxing out his English vocabulary in the service of killing David's brain cells—to fuck him *up*, as it were.

Greg—as in my boyfriend Greg, not Other Greg, the founder of the NeoFuturists—squirmed with discomfort. Romance dictated not only that he had to share a seat with me, but also that I could attempt to warm my feet by nestling them in his crotch. It didn't work, but I clung to the few shreds of hope available to me. For all I knew, we could be stranded on this isolated, icy road for days. We had all the makings of the Donner Party. It was a pity that Diana, our skinniest member, was in the worst shape. If I'd gotten to pick, David would have made a far juicier meal.

Other Greg was acting weird. Every time the bus ground to a halt behind a long line of vehicles all mired in the snow, off he hopped, as cheery as a Saint Bernard puppy. This was a man who routinely swore he couldn't sweep the theater floor because he didn't know where we kept the brooms. The snow worked on him like an intoxicant. Suddenly, he was the red-cheeked manly man, eagerly straining against the rear end of a stalled van. Even when it was our turn to get a push, he refused to get back on, breezily informing us that he could run faster than the bus could travel in those treacherous conditions. We told him that we were sure to get bogged down again when we stopped to let him reboard. He loped joyously away, a Saint Bernard with a purloined roast.

Did I mention that it was my thirtieth birthday? Yes. At midnight, Greg cajoled the others into a dirgelike rendition of the birthday song. I spent a goodly portion of my thirtieth birthday on an unheated, foodless bus in the middle of Frozen Nowhere, Romania, with my sleep-deprived, starving, miserable friends, the happiest of whom could not be induced to stay in the vicinity. It was even more memorable than my twenty-ninth birthday, which was flat-out great.

• • •

We rolled into Sibiu as the midmorning sun joined the newly fallen snow, creating that particular glare that always makes me carsick. Ugly, Soviet-style buildings loomed over a fairy-tale town square. I almost screamed when Simona pointed out our hotel and we drove past it without stopping. The festival headquarters at the University of Sibiu were deserted, save for a man with a broom who was not inclined to be helpful. After almost an hour, the festival promoter appeared, looking pissed. He distributed booklets of vouchers that entitled us to eat in the student cafeteria, which was not open at this time. "Ask him if we can get something," Lusia demanded. "I've got to eat!"

The promoter shook his head. "I am sorry, it is not possible."

"You don't understand," Lusia rasped, grinning like a fiend. "I don't have a choice." Oh my god, her therapist wasn't kidding about her mental health hinging on regular meals. I thought back to the dining hall in the basement of Northwestern's Willard Hall, with its long self-serve table of economy-sized cereal containers, at least a dozen varieties. Surely, the U. of S. had something that stayed set up all the time like that, some kind of brown bread bar, or a bin of root vegetables. This fellow had the key in his pocket, but he wouldn't give it to us! He was trying to oppress us! That wasn't the Aspen way! We had traveled thousands of miles in blinding snow to teach his people about tolerance, and he wouldn't bend the rules to give us cold cereal or its Balkan equivalent!

"I am sorry. There is nothing I can do. Please, now it is time for your hotel." Muttering curses and complaints, we trudged back on the bus.

Despite its prime location in the center of town, the Hotel Bulevard lobby had none of the main square's storybook charm. As

Simona checked us in, some bronze-skinned people in leather pants got off the elevator. "I'll bet they're part of the festival," Other Greg wagered. We approached them with hands extended, bursting with the need to share highlights of our bus ride with fellow artistic souls. They tossed their dark ringlets and smiled apologetically. "We Greek," they said, pointing to their chests. "Greek."

My Greg pawed through the festival program. "You Greek?" he said, scanning the offerings, which were printed in Romanian, the familiar alphabet scattered with a confusing array of slashes, triangle hats, and *accents aigus*. "Ah, here we go! *Antigona.* That's the Greek tragedy, right?" he asked. Ho, ho, not so high and mighty with his degree in political science from the University of Chicago now! I had spent an entire quarter focusing on Greek theater in my acting class, preparing for this moment.

"Mm-hmm," I affirmed, as condescendingly as I dared.

"Wow, you're putting on *Antigone?*" Other Greg whistled. "I have to say, that's really great!" I couldn't tell if he was being sincere.

"Yes," one of the Greeks volunteered. "*Antigona.* Greek." He put his arm around the buxom woman at his side. "She Antigona."

"Wow!" we all said. "We'll have to hang out."

The Greeks nodded, we smiled awkwardly for an eternity and they escaped into the glare. "Let me see that program," I said. What if none of the other companies spoke English? There were presenters from all over Romania and a Bulgarian group presenting Ionesco's *The Bald Soprano.* Come on, Ireland! Come on, Australia! Nope, we were the only native English speakers. Japonica, that must be Japan. At least there were no French ensembles in attendance. The NeoFuturists could continue believing that I was fluent in French. After thirteen years of study, I should have been, but mostly what I remembered were lessons absorbed in second grade, when we played a game with variously painted chairs. When it came to colors, French was my second language. *Oui, bien sur, rouge, bleu, vert, jaune.* . . .

We were given three double rooms equipped with twin beds, fake wood dressers, and battered armchairs. I tried to rally Greg to push our beds together, but he, mindful of my inability to curb my feet's heat-seeking nature, refused. "Goddamn, it's freezing in here," he said as he got in the bed along the far wall, still wearing his coat, hat, and gloves. Reminded how much my thirtieth birthday was sucking, I curled up under the giant lion's head that decorated my synthetic plush blanket and slept through another huge chunk of it.

I woke several times in the next eight hours, parched as a bone, but, too cold and tired to leave the bed, fell back into an unrefreshing jet-lagged daytime sleep. I finally got up when someone knocked and wouldn't go away. It was David, wearing a blue wool cap and brandishing several Catholic icons trussed up in newspaper and rubber bands. He'd been sightseeing for hours and had postcards to prove it. I opened my mouth to inquire after the health of Diana, his festival roommate, but my tongue had turned into felt. Two smudged drinking glasses sat on the dresser. I headed into the bathroom and turned on the tap.

"You'd better not be drinking out of that sink," Greg called.

"Well, what am I supposed to do? I'm thirsty!" Greg's slavish devotion to hygienic precautions in foreign countries never fails to bring out the rebel in me. I have eaten skewers of unidentifiable meat from questionable street stalls because I wanted to prove by opposite example that he was behaving like a fussy old lady. But I had to admit there was a good chance he might turn out to be right about the dangers of drinking Romanian tap water. After all, he'd been on target with the suspect water onboard the *Chip-n-Dale* in Kashmir. This time, I might be the one to pay for my mistake. I tried to imagine performing with a case of explosive diarrhea. It would be a shame if the trip were ruined by an avoidable bout of green apple quickstep. Still, shouldn't the birthday girl get to do whatever she wants? You'd think, given the duddy nature of the day, Greg would have allowed me a couple of swigs from the faucet as a consolation prize.

"Better not risk it, Ayun," David seconded. "Especially since you and Lusia may have to take over Diana's parts. Here, you can have some of the bottled water I bought while I was out."

Feeling grouchy as hell, I accepted a pull from the heavy glass bottle David extended. Jesus Christ! I've never been to Utah, but I can't imagine the Great Salt Lake would taste much different. It was like licking the bottom of the popcorn bowl. "This is mineral water," I accused.

"It was all they had," he said, shrugging. "You don't *have* to drink it."

Fixing him with the evil eye, I polished off half of the bottle. "Before rehearsal, we have to change money and stock up on bottled water, the *regular* kind," I told Greg. Aspen had turned me into an Evian-dependent tenderfoot by hooking me on the stuff, making it free and readily available even when what came out of the spigot posed no danger to me. I wondered if globetrotting Romanians feared drinking from the tap when they went skiing in Vail.

"I want to make sure we've got enough time for David to take me to the hat maker where he got his hat," Greg said, his priorities clearly, if wrongly, placed.

"You go with Lusia, Ayun. She needs to eat," David suggested, checking his watch.

"Wait! Don't we all want to eat together?" I asked, hoping to salvage some semblance of a birthday celebration.

"We want to get hats."

The student union was a good twenty-minute hike from the hotel. The air in the joyless dining room was redolent of flatulence. Lusia and I took trays and joined a long grub line of gray-faced students in acrylic sweaters. "Do you think these will get us whatever we want?" I asked her, squinting at my vouchers. She nodded hopefully. At the head of the line, a matron (as in prison) handed us plastic bowls of dishwater broth and jutted her chin in the direction of the cashier. "Is there anything else?" I ventured, searching in vain for an alternative selection—steamed hamburgers, corn dogs, institutional spaghetti and meatballs, anything! The matron emitted a guttural sound that sent us scuttling to the cashier.

"Well, this bread looks okay, anyway," Lusia said, helping herself to a couple of dark slices from the enormous bowl by the register as I tore off a voucher. Something was wrong. The cashier was trying to tell me, but I, of course, didn't understand.

"It's okay, we are from theater festival," I reassured her in a vaguely Eastern European accent.

She repeated herself, as if that might jog my memory and remind me that I did speak Romanian. I smiled confidently and pushed the voucher toward her. The meal was far from appetizing, but as one of the perks to which a young professional theater artist was entitled, it had the ceremonial value of a U.S. Comedy Arts Festival fanny pack. I would have it! "It's okay," I insisted. "American."

The cashier looked around wildly. We were creating a bottleneck. She collared a tall boy, chattering to him urgently, as Lusia and I tried to look nonchalant. Boy, would they feel foolish when they saw us onstage! "The head of the festival gave us these vouchers," I informed the boy, smiling pleasantly. "Maybe she's unfamiliar with them." The cashier gestured to the voucher emphatically, raising her voice.

The boy pointed at Lusia. "She says you have to pay for bread."

"But we have these," Lusia whimpered, displaying her voucher booklet like a losing Monopoly player offering her laughable nest egg for Boardwalk.

The boy examined the vouchers. "Yes, is okay but for one bread only." The cashier snorted out a loud observation for the benefit of the growing cluster of onlookers.

"But I don't have any Romanian money yet," Lusia pleaded. The cashier crossed her arms and raised her eyebrows, unmoved. Sadly, Lusia returned one of her bread slices to the big bowl.

Later, Simona showed us the way to Teatrul de Stat Radu Stancu, the theater where we would perform the next night. Diana, her eyes sunk deep in a face the color of pussy willows, insisted on rehearsing with us, lying on the black stage floor whenever it wasn't her line. When we emerged, exhausted after a couple of hours rehearsing, a cluster of teenagers were waiting in the lobby. A tall, freckled boy with bristly orange hair stepped forward, clutching a festival program to his chest. "Excuse me," he said with a little bow. "I am thinking that you are NeoFuturists company from America." His friends pressed close behind him, their faces avid.

Delighted by his formality, we congratulated him on his assumption. Beaming, he produced a pen. "Please, if you will put your name here for memento."

We all autographed his program, complimenting his English. The other teenagers scrutinized our signatures, sounding out each name in turn. Their spokesperson introduced himself as Radhu. He made us repeat each of his friends' names, patiently correcting our pronunciation until we got it right. A bashful girl named Channi whispered something in Radhu's ear. "She thinks you are the prettiest girl," he told me. "Also Lusia and also Diana." Lucien, an extroverted seventeen-year-old with a gleaming brown bob and the goofy vibe of a second banana, clapped our men's shoulders, robustly, like David's trucker boyfriend. "You are my friend?" he demanded, cracking up only after he saw that his intensity had produced its desired unnerving effect. "Yes, friends!" he howled. "It's cool!"

Radhu wouldn't let us go until he'd made a short speech on behalf of himself and all his pals, about how freedom was wonderful, as was America, and how they wouldn't be able to sleep or eat that night, knowing that soon they would see our magnificent performance. The teenagers flanked us like an honor guard as we crossed the street and headed uphill toward our hotel. Channi, who spoke little English, tucked her hand into the crook of my elbow. "Where do you guys live?" I asked.

Channi giggled. "She lives down there," Radhu said, pointing back the way we had come. "She is my—what do you say?"

"Girlfriend?" I ventured.

Radhu shook his head violently. Lucien's ears pricked up at an English word he understood. "Girlfriend?! Oh, it is romantic! Love and then fucking. This means girlfriend, yes? Ayun, you are my girlfriend. Diana, my girlfriend, Lusia, all my girlfriends."

"She is my neighbor," Radhu said, mortified that his vocabulary resurfaced too late to prevent calamity.

Over our new friends' shoulders, David caught my eye and raised his eyebrows, spooning invisible soup toward his gobbling, empty mouth.

I nodded imperceptibly, cocking my head at the hotel lobby. "Okay, guys, it was great meeting you! We'll see you at the show!" I turned to go. Radhu seized my hand.

"My heart is filled with joy that the NeoFuturists have come to my town to perform for us in English. I hope we will be true friends forever."

"Yeah, me too. Okay, see you tomorrow!" The NeoFuturists went into the hotel. The teenagers followed. Torn between the desire to part company and the wish not to offend, I fled to the elevator behind Other Greg and Lusia. Greg, Diana, and David stayed in the lobby, weaning our admirers from the mesmerizing wattage of our celebrity.

"What's the deal? Are those kids going to shadow us everywhere we go?" Other Greg grumbled, voicing my very thoughts, thus freeing me to pay lip service to benevolence.

"Oh, Greg! They're just excited because we're American. They'll get over it. Besides, they see us as role models. Didn't you hear what Radhu was saying about only now being able to speak freely, that his parents still freak out if they hear him criticizing the government in their own home? Lusia, what's the matter? Why are you making that face?"

"You guys, I need to eat, but I, I, I don't think I can handle any more of that cabbage soup or whatever it is." In my experience, unpalatable spates in the chow department came with the traveling territory everywhere except Aspen, oh golden complimentary cornucopia. I fondly recalled lusting after brownies and twice-baked potatoes in Africa with my frat-boy friends, but Lusia was beyond taking comfort in a postmortem of the U.S. Comedy Arts Festival's superlative club sandwiches. All I could do was pat her back and refrain from breaking down myself.

"I'm thirsty," I complained when Greg reappeared, having gently pried himself free of our fans. "The only things those kiosks sell is that super-salty seltzer water. Lusia has to eat again and I need real water."

"I'd give it fifteen minutes," he said, looking meaningfully at our closed door. The teenagers, having taken it upon themselves to make sure he made it safely to his room, were milling about the corridor, hoping that one of us might re-emerge.

What I wouldn't have given for a hot tub and a bottle of ice-cold Perrier. I felt a brief kinship with the cocksure standup who'd found so little to recommend Aspen's swag, but then I got hold of myself, grimly gloating that our current conditions would send him running, crying for his mama.

I got another taste of the rock-star life when I showed up at the theater the next night, an hour before we were scheduled to take the stage. Despite freezing temperatures, a huge crowd had gathered, not so much milling as pushing insistently forward as if that would guarantee admission. Simona had told us that all of the festival events were free, so attendance was high, no matter what was showing. Because advance reservations were not accepted, people arrived early, ready to fight their way inside. There was a distinctly Altamont edge to the bundled hordes pressing against the glass lobby doors. What if David's gay play sent them over the edge? I decided I would run behind the velvet curtains at the first murderous cry.

"Oh my god," we muttered to each other. This was not the same thing as the *Oh my god, did you see the size of that crowd, I am so psyched, you guys, we are going to kick cheerleading butt and make it to the national semifinal rounds for sure!* energy we had experienced when peeking through the curtains before other gigs. This was more of a powerless-to-stop-the-impending-train-wreck "oh my god." When the ushers opened the doors, people charged in, knocking each other over as they bolted for front-row seats. It was perhaps as close as I'll ever come to the running of the bulls in Pamplona. When the theater was dangerously stuffed with spectators seated on each other's laps, in the aisles and astride the rafters, the staff locked the doors, reinforcing them with their bodies, lest the luckless ones try to force their way in. Stepping tentatively onstage, we were greeted with a wall of sound. It was insane. Other Greg began his prologue, explaining a complex system of audience participation that could baffle even native English speakers. Emboldened by the crowd's roar of approval, he executed a saucy little hop. Baryshnikov in his prime never heard such screams. I squinted past the lights into the blur of faces. I could make out Lucien perched on a stairway rail. He gave me a thumbs-up, his face shining like someone receiving Olympic gold.

For the next hour, we could do no wrong. Nearly every one of our thirty short plays inspired the crowd to ecstasy. And funny! I'd never gotten so many laughs, especially when addressing capital punishment, gun control, and reproductive rights. As far as teaching tolerance, our pupils seemed amiably disposed to parrot any theory we felt like pushing, the way football fans will oblige the announcer by doing the wave on demand. Having endured the brutality of a recently deposed regime, they saw us as ambassadors from the Great Rock Candy Mountain. You don't argue with the guys who know the way to the lemonade springs and the cigarette trees. Even David's gay play turned out okay, if a bit of an anti-climax. Remember that *Far Side* cartoon, the one about what we say versus what the cats hear? Perhaps the somewhat poetic nature of the monologue worked in our favor. David was wise not to go the "Hey, I'm a homosexual, come and kill me" route. We all breathed a sigh of relief at our curtain call, which was operatic, lavish—much more generous than we deserved.

We spent the next few days wandering around, perpetually trailed by our teenaged groupies. I'm ashamed to say that we started con-cocting elaborate dodges to escape their adoring company, like John, Paul, George, and Ringo dressing as garbage men or pastry chefs to sneak through a rioting crowd of young girls. We were also great favorites of the gypsy children, streetwise panhandlers who, to my great surprise, actually sported colorful aprons and mounds of jewelry, lacking only tambourines and pet monkeys to complete their storybook effect. "You're confusing gypsies with organ grinders," my compatriots told me as, clutching our valuables, we raced away, the children pattering after us, giggling, "Money me money me hungry me money!" Like Garbo, I started holing up in our room, dreaming of American sinks and garden hoses, anything that produced an endless supply of potable water. On one of his strolls around town, David had discovered that a dirty, understocked department store was the cheapest source not only of religious icons, but also of the mineral-deposit-heavy seltzer that was sold in place of bottled water. Resigned to the idea that Romanians felt, as I so recently had, that if you were paying for water, it should taste significantly different from the stuff that flows from the tap for free, I made morning and afternoon runs, buying as much as I could carry. Drinking it only made me thirstier, but there was no alternative. Even in the hotel's bedraggled dining room, where you paid extra for butter and jam, the only alternative to saltwater was soda pop. One morning Greg ordered orange juice and was presented with a can of Fanta. After less than a week, our cheeks were taking on an unhealthy pallor. I kept checking to see if my gums were receding. Rather than suffer the cabbage stink of the student union, we had renounced our vouchers and now paid full price to get scurvy. In Romania, oranges are not the only fruit. Apples are the only fruit, and they cost as much as a car.

In the evenings, we ran with the bulls, taking in the other festival offerings. Dully watching these plays unfold in mysterious languages, I ruminated that my time would have been better spent watching American police dramas dubbed into Romanian in my room, had the hotel had TV. Once, I arranged to sit beside Radhu so he could whisper the gist of the action. "He is wanting her to marry him, but she is reluctant. This other man, I am not sure who he is supposed to be. It is not a very good play, I think," Radhu murmured apologetically in my ear as Channi, Lucien, and the others stared at the actors with absolute concentration, haggard with the desire to understand. My tongue had again turned to flannel when the play finally ground to its conclusion. The actors trooped out from the wings, holding hands and smiling graciously.

The audience leapt up, beating their palms together in a frenzy. Roses exploded as they hit the stage. It was exactly like our curtain call, except that this company, being Eastern European, knew the culturally approved method for accepting their accolades. They dragged it out, as the audience expected and wanted them to. We had cut it short by exiting the stage before the applause could peter out. I could have milked a cow in the time it took these guys to get through their bows. Five times they snaked offstage, then back on again, while the crowd stayed put, clapping rhythmically. At home, at least half a dozen people could be counted on to trundle up the aisle well before the applause died of natural causes, hurrying to the parking garage ahead of the after-theater rush. In Aspen, a couple of cell phone–wielding bigwigs in the choicest reserved seats had left indecorously, soon after Other Greg's prologue. As the Romanian festivalgoers flagellated their palms, my Greg shot me a disgusted look. I read him loud and clear. Cheering at length for a bad play was immoral, like voting for Bush. Maybe it was all in the spirit of tolerance.

On our final day, after a few laps around the town square with the teenagers, Diana, now fully recovered, announced that she thought it would be nice for us to treat them to lunch. We had been entertained in their homes, wedged between the spindly curio cabinets that clogged their humble apartments. Their fathers had poured us endless rounds of *tuica*, the high-proof national plum brandy, as their mothers proudly showed us baby pictures. David had even made a spur-of-the-moment decision to stay out all night party hopping with some of them. The next morning, when Lusia reported that he hadn't come home, we immediately assumed the worst, anxiously debating whether or not to ask

Simona if gay bashing was a crime in Romania. It was only proper now that we should host our own farewell luncheon, with the teenagers as guests of honor. We were given a large, round table in the hotel dining room by an imperious older waitress who didn't bother to hide her suspicion that her young countrymen would stiff her on the bill. Radhu looked stricken. "No, no, it's on us," Other Greg said, as expansively as Daddy Warbucks.

One of the younger boys, whose name I never learned, chewed his lip and made some comment to the others. "He says this lunch cost more than his father earns in a month," Radhu translated. Funny. I had just been thinking what a cheap date this was. A little over two dollars a head bought homemade soup, cutlets, vegetable side dishes, bread, dessert, and an ample supply of that sodium-rich fizzy water. The teenagers' eyes were round with the wonder of this fancy experience. I wanted to tell them that we didn't usually eat this way at midday, but stopped myself when I realized my customary cup of coffee and carryout sandwich from the local convenience mart ran about the same as a new pair of shoes in Sibiu.

That night, we returned to Teatrul de Stat Radu Stancu, which the Greeks had taken over for their production of *Antigona*. They were presenting it in ancient Greek, and, although I had no idea how that differed from modern Greek, I was excited. Having failed in my junior-year acting class to find anything vital in the nearly unperformable ancient text, I was intrigued. The players wore masks and long, pleated robes. Their movements were stately, some might say deathly, and I soon discovered that ancient Greek sounds very similar to a suburban Sunday afternoon, when all the power mowers come out at the same time. Brave Antigone had barely reburied the corpse of her dishonored brother when the young Romanians who had stormed the barricades to get in headed for the exits. Watching their migration, I was baffled, until I realized that all of the other shows had been in Romanian, or a similarly easy-to-grasp Balkan language. I can't speak for the Japonica, having missed their production of *Misterul Celor 10 Crime Din Kawachi.* The NeoFuturists were American, so we could have pretended to be a choo-choo for eight hours and they would have stayed, loving every minute of it. But this monotonous droning, issuing from inscrutable, hard-to-tell-apart masks, was more than they could brook. I felt bad for the actors, who soldiered on, despite the tidal wave of departing patrons. At last, Antigone was dead, Creon undone by his hubris, and the chorus so grief-stricken that its members hurled themselves to the stage floor. Their voluminous costumes rendered them of indeterminate gender, but when the chorus member nearest me fell, a great cry rose up from the audience—and it wasn't lamentation. Unsheathed by a robe that had ridden up to its owner's waist when she collapsed was a glorious, golden Greek ass, as plump as a peach in a pair of thong panties. Every eye in the theater was drawn immediately to its radiance. This was the reward for the polite schoolboys who had refused to join their restless friends in the flight up the aisle. The actors who were still standing had about five minutes' worth of lines remaining. They said them, but they were drowned out by a ruckus that surely rivaled the one that met the Beatles, although this one was created by swooning males.

Talk all you want about tolerance and freedom and cultural exchange. Those buns were the high point of the festival for those boys, some of whom, like Radhu, would be denied admission to the state-sponsored university despite exceptional intelligence.

Others, like my boyfriend Lucien, had been army-bound from the cradle. They were young and high-spirited but justifiably fatalistic, too. They knew their nationality had given them a bum deal in the world-on-a-plate department. On their behalf, I praise the faceless Greek actress who heard the uproar, but committed to her choral prostration. Truly a young professional. An amateur would have broken character long enough to flick her skirts back over those excellent hams.

Channi wept because her father had upheld her curfew on this, our last night together. "She says her heart is breaking," Radhu told us. I knew just what she meant. It's amazing that I lived past eighteen when my high-school boyfriend left for Purdue two weeks before I started my freshman year at Northwestern. Lucien volunteered to see Channi home safely, his face a comical hybrid of tender concern and wolfish self-interest. The rest of us went for a last hurrah at an all-ages disco, where revelers in pullovers patterned to excess executed limp dance moves beneath a paucity of Christmas lights. I got very drunk and had a tête-à-tête with the teetotaling Radhu, whose grasp of world politics was light years more mature than mine.

Bright and early the next morning, Simona collected us from the lobby. With twelve hours until we were scheduled to depart, tensions ran high. We worried that we would miss the plane if we didn't break for the bus in a dead run the instant that it pulled up in front of the hotel. Unfortunately, Lusia had placed some calls to her boyfriend in Chicago. She had used her calling card, but the desk clerk insisted there was a surcharge for calls placed from the hotel's phone. "Thirty-five bucks," Lusia growled indignantly, widening her stance. "Thirty-five bucks!"

"Lusia, just pay it!" we pleaded. "Do you want us to be stuck here for another week?" Her objections didn't strike me as unreasonable when I did the math. That extortionary phone fee would have bought our teenagers lunch, dinner, ice cream cones, new hats, disco admission for a year and round-trip bus fare to Bucharest to see us off. Groaning, "I'm totally broke now," Lusia reluctantly paid up and climbed onboard. The bus driver burned rubber, nearly mashing some gypsy children who were heading for the morning shift in the town square.

"Do not make a sad face, Lusia. We have food this time," Simona consoled, distributing white pasteboard boxes tied quaintly with string. My hangover was doubly bad due to dehydration. I hadn't felt this woozy since the morning after I tied one on at the Ritz, when the festival organizers rustled up a minivan to speed us to the Denver airport, a freak snowstorm having closed the runways in Aspen. Oh, Aspen, dear Aspen. The minivan came with a cooler, thoughtfully stocked with great quantities of that well-known hangover remedy, Diet Coke. If only I had one now. Expecting the worst, I peeked inside my boxed lunch. Picnic food! What a relief! A hard roll, a wedge of cheese, a packet of mustard and, what's this, a hunk of homemade sausage, its casing bristling with hair, the same kind of hair that you see growing on a pig. Swallowing hard, I pressed my forehead to the window's cold glass and didn't open my eyes until we reached the airport. My extended rock-star moment was ending, just slightly ahead of my thirst.

On Freedom

My only previous experience of being kicked out of a bar was when, at nineteen, I drunkenly entered Shannon's Roaring Twenties, a strip club in my hometown, clutching an imaginary microphone and claiming I was on assignment for Channel Six. Now, thanks to Glasgow's strictly enforced No Children In Pubs rule, I got the bum's rush every time I ordered a drink. The ordinance might have ensured regular customers a measure of peace, but it laid to waste my fantasy of enjoying a sociable pint while my eleven-month-old daughter perched on my lap, amusing herself with cardboard bar coasters. "It's to keep alcoholics home with their families," a young bartender apologized. "If they could bring the wee uns with 'em, they'd have no cause to leave the pub." I could see the logic, but not how it applied to me. Sleep deprivation, coupled with the imperative to get the kid out before the cigarette smoke hung too heavily, ensured that I would be gone after one or two quickies. I had no desire to tie one on. I'd learned that lesson six months before when, overstimulated by adult company at the new tapas bar around the corner from our East Village apartment, I'd downed more than my fair share of our second pitcher of sangria. A troop of admiring flamenco dancers took turns dandling Inky on their bright satin knees as I boozily rehashed the good old days with my far less soused, childless college friends.

It wasn't so much the beer that drew me to the pubs as the convivial atmosphere I remembered fondly from when I'd performed in the Edinburgh Fringe Festival a decade earlier. Now, trudging through the clammy July mist, Inky fooling with my hair from her backpack carrier, I peered longingly through steamed-up windows behind which World Cup fans screamed for blood.

Just shy of one, Inky was a seasoned domestic shoestring traveler. At four weeks, she lived in a tent on Bread and Puppet Theater's farm in rural Vermont. Overriding Greg's objections to the strong August sun on her virgin skin, I carried her into the ring for her Domestic Resurrection Circus debut before she could hold her head up. There were obligatory visits to the grandparents in Cape Cod and Indiana. We spent two months in Chicago, acting in one of Greg's plays and crashing with various friends, enlisting many others as unpaid baby sitters. Incorporating a baby into these adventures was not without stress, but I figured it beat sitting around a miniscule tenement apartment, wondering what stay-at-home mothers did to fill their long days.

So when our good friend Karen announced that she would wed her Scottish beau toward the end of a performance workshop her company taught every summer at Glasgow's Centre for Contemporary Art (CCA), there was no question that we would go, especially since it meant Inky would get one chance to wear the fancy velvet dress her grandmother had purchased at Bergdorf Goodman before she grew out of it. When contrasted with the fetid skank of July in lower Manhattan, Scotland's cool summers seemed a wonderfully wholesome climate for hauling around a small child. Other small memories of my first unchaperoned trip abroad crowded aside sexier recollections from more exotic locales. I trailed Greg around our 340-square-foot apartment, regaling him with descriptions of mossy tombstones, a kilted street performer wielding hand puppets on his feet, and the rhubarb-and-custard boiled sweets I bought from a young Pakistani confectioner who complimented me on my Hoosier accent in a brogue thicker than Braveheart's. For English speakers traveling with a baby, I could think of no destination more hospitable than Scotland. Financially, it was a reckless proposition, but then inspiration dawned. If Greg and I both enrolled in the performance workshop, we could deduct the whole trip from our taxes! When we called Karen to tell her of the scheme, she invited us to stay with her and her fiancé, CJ, in his flat's extra room. Perfect! Our only expenses would be food and two plane tickets, since children under the age of two flew free as "lap passengers." I immediately rushed out to have Inky's passport picture taken and buy art supplies, figuring if the groom was nice enough to open his home to three strangers, one of them incontinent, for an entire month, our wedding present should be creative and laborious rather than nice and registered for.

After discussing our plan with her fellow company members, Karen called to tell us that Greg would pay full tuition, while I audited, since they anticipated there would be times when caring for Inky would preclude my participation. The terms sounded good to me, especially since Karen's co-teachers probably assumed I'd need a private place to breastfeed. Hell no! I didn't care who saw. Besides, her bumblebee rattle and a baggie full of Cheerios would keep her entertained while her mother and father immersed themselves in the kind of vibrant artistic community it's difficult to find in the States, particularly at the bargain-basement rate of one hundred twenty-five pounds for three weeks.

The morning of orientation, we bolted our breakfast and hurried to the CCA, a gallery and theater complex located right on the main shopping drag. Snooping around its bookstore the day after we arrived, I'd watched conservatively dressed families push through the glass doors, expecting them to turn tail immediately upon realizing they'd blundered into a hornet's nest of avant-garde art. Instead, they spent twenty minutes reviewing incomprehensible film loops and a series of photographs by the director John Waters, before wandering back out. Never before in my experience had the art snobs and the bovine mainstream intermingled so promiscuously. Next to childbirth, this was going to be the most amazing experience of my life!

It was our fourth day in Glasgow, and while I had not grown used to the cold rain or the skies that stayed light until 11 P.M., we were over jet lag and I was eager to commence with our justification for imposing on CJ's hospitality for such a long stay. He remained unfailingly gracious, as baby food jars crowded his cabinets, disposable diapers befouled his meticulously kept trash bin and small, sticky hands groped toward his alphabetized CD collection, but I couldn't help thinking that, in his shoes, I'd prefer to wander around the apartment naked, farting, and bathing whenever I wanted. Not only would the workshop give structure to our visit, it would introduce us to a whole new set of people, who would give our hosts a break by taking us out to pubs and dinner. I studied the others, wondering who would emerge as our close friends. The tiny

German with cat's eye glasses and a flowered schmata looked cool. "Who's this, then?" a sharp-faced Englishwoman leafing through the orientation materials at the next table asked. In the subservient manner of new parents, we introduced Inky first, then ourselves. "Aren't you sweet," she cooed, as Inky hammered a spoon against my coffee cup. "You and Mummy wanted to see what Daddy would be doing for the next three weeks!"

I was shocked at how quickly her innocent mistake proved prophetic. After we had gone around in a circle, submitting brief bios of name, nationality, and performance background, we located to a black box theater, where we were told to find partners for the first exercise. Greg nodded at a Mohawked young Scotsman in Doc Martens and a ragged, sleeveless T-shirt. As other pairs headed for the stage, my preordained partner yanked my shirt to the clavicles, eager to wash down her Cheerios with milk hot from the cow. The others began to explore radical movement, squirming and jumping, Greg and the punk spinning each other like reckless schoolgirls. My partner shat herself in the bleachers. Feeling an uneasy mixture of conspicuous and invisible, I pulled her, protesting, behind an industrial paint bucket to freshen up. Greg and Karen kept glancing my way, aware that I was falling behind the rest of the herd. I waved and smiled, miserable.

Later, when a distinguished speaker took the podium to impart her theory of "performativity," my partner burped, squawked, and trilled random bars of "Baa Baa Black Sheep." When the lecture was upstaged by the wings-*cum*-teething-rings of a stuffed bumblebee launched from the audience hitting the black floor with an impolite thwack, I knew the jig was up. Greg offered to divvy up the baby-minding responsibilities, but between the class's need for continuity and Inky's unflagging passion to go to second with Mommy, it wasn't a workable solution.

It wasn't long before the other participants forgot that I had started out as one of them, worldly, artistic, eager to make a fool of myself presenting underrehearsed, site-specific assignments in the public gardens. What did they think when I showed up for noon break with Inky and a carefully assembled lunch for Greg—that I was a mousy, clinging wifey who filled the giant void in her existence by making her family her fetish? If only Radhu, Channi, and Lucien, my number-one Romanian fans, had been on hand to tell them about my triumphant history on the international stage. The tedium and disappointment endured in the name of low-budget theater— the maddening aesthetic discussions, the utter indifference of the Aspen power brokers, the frozen, food-free thirtieth birthday in Transylvania—all this seemed downright jaunty when viewed against the tedium and disappointment of early motherhood.

"John's got a kid, too," Greg told me one day, nodding to his Mohawked buddy as the workshop participants tumbled into the CCA's main lobby, twenty minutes later than their official dismissal time. I'd spent those twenty minutes shooing Inky away from the electrical outlets and remembering the glory days when I could combat the boredom of unforeseen delays by reading or writing in my journal. If only I'd known at the time how fortunate I was, waiting at 2 A.M. on an Indian railway platform for a connection running three hours behind schedule.

"You do?" I cried, smiling so broadly I could have fit John's entire head in my mouth. "That's great! What's her name?" With luck, this fellow parent would notice that I was not waving but drowning. A cozy image sprang to mind, Inky and John's kid happily playing on the floor of his flat, while the adults lounged on battered, second-hand furniture, mugs, or better yet, empirical pint glasses in hand, listening to music and laughing with our heads thrown back. "Please let his female counterpart be as good natured and sociable as he is," I prayed, crossing my fingers in the hope of finding a confederate in similar straits, who'd make me glad the workshop was barred to me, that's how much fun we'd have yucking it up in her kitchen when we got sick of roaring around town with our babies.

His reply came encrypted in a thick Glaswegian accent. "Ah th' weeyuns nut uh gull—zwee boy, loonan blue. Sthree hears zold. Thas huh trip, huh? Doont live wut me, but I teak hum ever dee wi' ow fay. Weir goo frens, me oon loonan blue." As best I could figure, the child was a boy, already three years old to John's disbelief. Although he didn't live with his father, they were close and John made sure they saw each other every day. Only after it had been spelled twice did I realize that I had heard correctly: John's son's name was indeed Loonan Blue. With that, John borrowed twenty pence to call Loonan's mother, telling us that they both had crazy schedules that wreaked constant havoc on their already precarious child-sharing system. To complicate matters even further, his squat had no phone. "Ha boat looz mah mine train t' keep tractor ooze gut Loonan," he complained, tugging his hawk in frustration. My fledgling vision of an invitation to spend the next three weeks loafing on an extended playdate in cozy local digs went up in smoke.

Instead, Inky and I crisscrossed Glasgow's gray streets in weather ranging from fierce downpour to bone-chilling mist. I was beginning to understand why so many of the traveling parents I'd encountered in Southeast Asia had been British, collecting the dole in absentia while their children frolicked naked on the beach. As a tourist destination, Glasgow had a lot to recommend it, much more than was readily apparent on my first visit ten years earlier. Back then, Nate and I spent a rainy afternoon trudging around Sauchiehall Street with our backpacks on to avoid a left-luggage room fee, eventually repairing to Pizzaland to share the cheapest pie on the menu and about fifteen complimentary sugar packets. Angling the metallic gold umbrella I'd bought in an East Village discount store in such a way that my lower half got drenched but Inky's eyes were spared the proverbial poking out, I sighed, remembering. The delusion that, with forewarning of the limitations imposed on mothers of small children, I could have made more of my early freedom was as compelling as crying in a mirror. Had I but known, I wouldn't have been such a penny-pinching slave to convention! My succession of boyfriends and I could have blown our shoestring budgets on beer and slept in the same dumpsters that yielded our surprisingly well-balanced meals! It would have been a gas, like the first half of *Trainspotting*, before all those overdoses cast a major pall over Iggy Pop and that sleeveless, sequined party dress. "Git uh grrrrip on yur sef, gull," I admonished myself aloud, figuring it didn't matter if anyone overheard me practicing a Glaswegian accent. Mine was the mangled burr of an imposter, but at least I wouldn't appear to be engaged in a lunatic's public monologue, not with the little pitcher on my back. My sturdy inner Scot was right: Moping around wasn't going to salvage the situation. If I had to undergo existential, maternal angst, at least I was doing so in a city loaded with museums, art galleries and good public transit, where everyone spoke English, sort of.

Every morning after the other adults had departed, I loaded a bag with diapers, extra tiny outfits, a camera, reading and writing material in case Inky fell asleep, the garish collapsible umbrella, dry socks, a teaspoon, and several jars of the pricey imported baby food we were constantly replenishing at a distant health food store, since every brand stocked by the chemists and supermarkets contained strained meat—even the carrots, even the prunes. Thus weighted, we set out for the Botanic Gardens, the Scotland Street School Museum of Education, the Necropolis, St. Mungo Museum of Religious Life and Art, a pit filled with petrified stumps—any diversion that might rationalize subletting our apartment in a New York City neighborhood so interesting that bright red, double-decker tourist buses visited it hourly.

One afternoon, we paid twelve pounds to see the Dead Sea Scrolls at the Museum of Natural History. Inky fussed the whole time, perhaps picking up on her mother's economic dismay. For twenty bucks, the humble scraps of papyrus in humidity-controlled cases delivered less of a bang than leafing through my own passport. At the Glasgow School of Art's student exhibition, we took in naked torsos sculpted in beeswax and a sectioned lemon rind rearticulated with straight pins. Inky suffered a nappy blowout that stained her up to her armpits, which was actually sort of a highlight. The vintage washroom where we peeled off the foul layers and daubed her heinie with brown paper towels appeared to have been designed by Charles Rennie Mackintosh, the celebrated architect whose ubiquity drove Karen insane. While other tourists gorged themselves silly on Mackintosh, buying note cards, lap rugs and letter openers adorned with his art deco roses and idiosyncratic font, I'd been avoiding him out of respect for my hostess. The apex of Mackintosh mania was the Willow Tea Room, a second story recreation of the original. Out-of-town visitors queued like cattle for the privilege of a table near the stained glass windows designed by the master. I aped Karen's disdain for the place, as Inky had showed signs of growing out of the so-good-in-restaurants phase. It wouldn't do to have her screeching, shitting, and clawing at my boobs in front of people who had stood in line two hours for dry scones and overpriced pots of Earl Grey. We fed alfresco, in the mist, on oatcakes, baby food and McVitie's Digestive Biscuits, whose vaguely medical name was all the excuse I needed to devour an entire packet in one sitting. The chocolate-dipped versions were the healthiest.

So when Inky awarded me with an unexpected bonus nap in the Gallery of Modern Art just two hours after waking from a morning siesta, I could have wept for joy. The exhibitions were much less invigorating than the idea of the second-floor café. Lowering Inky into a space between the table and a domed front window, I chastised myself for ordering orange juice instead of wine. My seat afforded me a fine rear view of the Duke of Wellington and his horse, defending the museum's entrance in a larger-than-life sculpture. I was delighted to see that some nimble prankster had given the duke a hat, an orange traffic cone balanced perfectly atop his noble head. It would make a cheery news bite later, when Greg, unable to dredge up ample workshop gossip to satisfy my unquenchable thirst to feel included, asked what I had done with my day. I sketched the slumbering Inky in my journal, made my expensive juice last with minuscule sips and tried not to get too hung up on the older couple at the next table, grimly chewing quiche without uttering a word to each other. When Inky's eyes fluttered open, I was almost glad, hoping that she might have the power to break the neighbors' conversational permafrost. The woman watched hungrily as the little plumper reached up to pat my face after I hauled her into my lap. I smiled at her over the top of Inky's unintentional dreadlocks. With a sigh, she returned to her plate. For the next few minutes, my affectionate, toasty warm baby seemed like the best traveling companion in the world, even if she did lick all the dressing off my salad before returning the uneaten leaves to the bowl.

"Mommy's going to make a fine party for your birthday," I promised as I propped the backpack into a freestanding position and redeposited her so I could pull on my coat. I'd take a big cake to the CCA during the workshop's lunch break, I schemed, as I turned to signal for the bill and maybe do a dramatic blow-by blow retelling of her birth. Inky bounced up and down as if she could read my mind. I turned back just in time to see the thin metal strut that stabilized the backpack collapse as she flung herself exuberantly backward. Before I could move, she slammed down, banging her occipital ridge on the guillotine-sharp edge of a metal heater running along the baseboards. Oh, the screams. The other women were even louder than Inky, who indulged in a moment of stunned silence before her first ever head wound (milestone!) caused her to erupt in bloodcurdling shrieks. Without a thought to Scottish social mores, I tore my blouse wide open and plunged a nipple into the yelling mouth, ignoring a lady in a beige sweater who stood nearby, meekly proffering a handful of paper napkins. The recovery was remarkably swift to everyone's relief, especially mine and that of the man at the next table, who looked everywhere but my openly displayed rack as he remarked to his wife, "Didja noot think the wee small bairn hud chopped her haid oof, Mavis?"

• • •

The activities with which I filled my time alone with Inky drained me, mentally and physically. Every day, no matter where we were, I found myself aching to get back to the digs fled with such determination every morning. I had experienced something similar when Nate and I visited the Uffizi in Florence, except that then, gratification was postponed. The youth hostel in which we were staying was one of those hard-ass militaristic ones that locked everybody out from ten in the morning until five in the afternoon. At least now I was free to come and go as I pleased. On the other hand, Nate hadn't required quite so much of my total attention as Inky. Even when he was pissing me off, blowing unnecessary dough at McDonalds, he was capable of diverting himself with postcards, harmonicas, and our shared copy of *The Hunchback of Notre Dame.* What I wouldn't have given for Inky to leave me to my own devices like that. There were occasional blessed intervals in CJ's flat when the baby unexpectedly managed to amuse herself, scrunching the pages of a literary magazine Greg had brought from home while I lay on our pullout bed, staring into the cold fireplace, worn out from the day's long march.

The apartment was crammed with books, but it was like having stomach staples in a fudge factory. The moment I pulled a volume from one of the shelves lining the dim, high-ceilinged hall, Inky lobbed her ball at me expectantly or tried to pull herself to a standing position by yanking on the phone cord. Every time I turned around, Inky was falling down or smacking her head, usually both, the wages of learning how to walk. CJ's flat turned into a gauntlet of sharp metal edges, exposed electrical cords, and heavy bookcases that would have looked much better bolted to the walls. Having braved precarious Himalayan roads in speeding buses piloted by lunatics, it seemed ridiculous to fear a tiny, wheeled washer/dryer, but I guess the hazards seem more real when they threaten someone you love even more than yourself. She could electrocute herself! She could break it! She could pull on it so hard that it would come rocketing out of the niche beside the minifridge to knock her out the third-story window! What if she mistakenly embraced the red-hot stove, thinking it was her old pal the wheeled washer/dryer? I had been psyched that CJ had laundry on the premises. Then I discovered that the nifty little contraption took four hours to dry jeans, blowing fabric-softener-scented exhaust out an accordion tube snaked through the kitchen window while enraging the old-age pensioner downstairs, who claimed his chandelier had been shaking since noon. Our safest bet was to spend as little time in the flat as possible until the others returned for the evening, when I could sip scotch and nod off watching videotapes of *Father Ted*, an Irish sitcom about three disgraced priests exiled to a godforsaken parish named Craggy Island.

The other adults, sensing my frustration the way one senses an African elephant in the living room, tried to find ways to leaven the long hours of their absence. They arranged a playdate with a sweet boy whose father helped teach the workshop, but when Inky persisted in knocking down the tower he dutifully rebuilt using yogurt cups and plastic carryout containers, I had to question the fairness of saddling a seven-year-old with my motherly grunt work. "This is kind of boring," he confessed. Roger that, pal.

Inky's first birthday turned out to be a much more understated affair than the one I'd imagined before the gash in the little nipper's head brought me so rudely back to reality. The birthday girl watched over my shoulder as I bought her present, a board book remarkable only because the hero, a down-market version of the Hungry Caterpillar, samples a "packet of crisps." The toy store clerk had done her best to sell me a Loch Ness monster sporting a tam-o'-shanter. With three hours to kill until the workshop's lunch break, I lay in the damp grass of Kelvingrove Park, watching Inky run oral experiments on fallen leaves as I tried to relive the specifics of her agonizing birth (seven hours of pushing!) 365 days earlier. On this July 3, I had meant to write postcards to everyone who had helped us: the midwives, the friend who attended the birth, the nurses in the neonatal intensive care unit—hell, I'd have sent one to the cab driver who drove me across town, but being in labor, I'd forgotten to ask for his address. Frankly, even though I had a sack of postcards, it was all I could do to keep my eyes open, lest a baby snatcher or a broken bottle take advantage of an exhausted mother's inattention. What a dud I was. The limitations imposed by traveling with a toddler sucked almost as bad as that psychosis-inducing pot we smoked in Saigon. This was a far less dramatic way of losing my mind, more cross-country than sprint, though at least there were plenty of English speakers about this time, should I require medical intervention.

Karen had told me how once, on a long tramp through the English countryside, she'd started going into diabetic shock. Fortunately, it wasn't long before she happened upon a roadside pub, which she entered, lurching up to the bar, croaking for food. The startled counterwoman froze, thought for a minute, then bravely whispered, "Uh cood make yuh uh cheese toastie." What would a sensible matron think if I staggered toward her, begging her to entertain Inky so I could shut my eyes or read, anything to help me regather my marbles? She'd probably think I was stoned, that's what. I managed to scarf down enough digestive bikkies to surmount that hypoglycemic feeling long enough to get to Safeway, where I bought a dumpy sheet cake and, because it seemed like the kind of thing that might be worth something in fifty years, a can of Teletubbies pasta, never to be eaten. Poor little nipper, I was failing her on the anniversary of her entry to the planet. A psychic grandpa we passed en route to CCA pressed a pound coin into my hand "for the wee small honey." I told him that I'd put it in her college fund, and immediately cashed it in on a child's padded satin jacket that looked like it had traveled from Beijing to this Scottish Oxfam outpost by way of Chinatown, NYC.

With harried expressions, the workshop participants glanced from the sheet cake to their watches. Their break was short, and in the absence of lonely spouses with nothing better to do but serve them a daily picnic, most of them went down the street for lunch—far down the street, as the closest cheap option was a chip shop specializing in deep-fried haggis. Though I had a pocket of candles, I realized I hadn't mapped out any ideas for presenting the cake. My imagination always cut to the chase, in which following the special surprise first birthday performances the participants would have spent all morning rehearsing, I handed out slices and thanks for everyone's consideration. Watching several gay men who had never shown the slightest interest in the baby in their midst edging closer to the exit, I passed the buck to Greg. "Uh, okay," he stalled, shifting Inky to the crook of his arm. "Maybe we could sing to her . . . uh, why don't we form a circle?" John the Punk leapt obediently forward, encouraging the others to do likewise. A ring of thirty marched counterclockwise, singing the birthday song while Greg and Inky rotated at the hub. I wish I had had a camera or a small tape recorder to capture the moment. A young adult Inky might have enjoyed evidence of that very first birthday, when her parents spirited her away to Scotland and, instead of some dopey clown, an international cast of outré artist types provided entertainment on the spur of the moment. Condensed like that, it does sound rather exciting.

The next bright spot on my bleak calendar was the wedding. A few friends from Chicago arrived early but soon disappeared into the pubs. "Yule see them at the reception, gull," I growled under my breath, recalibrating plans for unbridled fun with the unenrolled. CJ's aunts and their friends arrived all aflutter from a small island in the northwest, thoughtfully presenting Inky with a tartan-swagged teddy bear, an example of Scottish kitsch painful to the groom. On every visit to his beloved, he'd been inundated with questions about shortbread and kilts from well-meaning Chicagoans, eager to make him feel at home by showing interest in his tribal culture. The bridal couple was too well organized to have much in the way of the panicky last-minute errands I'd been hankering to be dispatched on, but I did manage to snuff out some of the long workshop hours searching for tights to go with my small companion's velvet frock. You'd think in a country where constant infusions of tea are required to combat the chilling effects of the year-round mist, little girls' tights would never go out of season, but we had to hunt hard. Perhaps if I had worn a grass skirt or covered Inky in body paint, our search could have been considered site-specific performance art! I still had flashes of hope, when it seemed like full-fledged participation in the workshop's final days was only a matter of coming up with a workable, not necessarily good, idea.

When the big day arrived, we gathered at the Marriage Suites, the government building where all secular weddings in Glasgow take place. A mustached major-domo with the air of a retired Royal Air Force man kept things moving, preventing revelers from the day's many scheduled nuptials from lingering on the marble front steps so littered with confetti, rice, and rose petals that they looked like a Hindu shrine on Diwali. A boisterous party of kilted groomsmen bounded into waiting hatchbacks, as a horse-drawn carriage pulled up to disgorge a sort of Barbie über-bride. "Inky, look!" I squealed, wheeling around so quickly, the backpack carrier nearly knocked an elderly lady with a corsage off the top step. "Pretty bride! Pretty bride!" Perhaps we could spend the remainder of our vacation rubbernecking at the Marriage Suites. It seemed a far more exciting use of time than collecting leaves and making lunch.

"Last call for Mitchell and Christopher," the old RAF officer barked. "Closing the doors on Mitchell and Christopher!" We scuttled up the stairs before he could punish our tardiness by demanding fifty pushups. Our friend Lisa from Chicago had saved seats in front of the desk where Karen and CJ would exchange vows. Considering Inky's performance during the performativity lecture, I had held off on nursing her all morning as assurance that she'd spend the ceremony quietly suckling. It was the perfect plan, except for my dress, an impossible-to-iron, sexy, gypsy number with fraying embroidery and constantly shedding Rajasthani mirrors. Greg hated it. His willingness to embrace flamboyant nonmainstream fashion had not endured much past his Lawrence-of-Arabia period. As soon as we had returned to the States, he retired his black Speedo and the fringed cotton scarf he had used as a do-rag to avoid a sunburned scalp after an Indonesian barber honored his request to make him look like a Thai schoolboy. His wedding finery was a no-brainer: the only suit he owned, a conservative costume he had been allowed to keep after the show that necessitated its purchase closed. I chose my dress for the event with an eye toward the reception's dance floor. Its skirt possessed unsurpassed twirling potential, but I neglected to factor in the problems inherent in its tight bodice.

Inky, her pump primed, plunged a plump hand into my décolletage. A delay was sure to raise hell. I couldn't remember why for the life of me I'd been so opposed to pacifiers. The teddy bear aunts, wild with admiration for Inky's proper but princessy frock, called our names, waving from the row facing ours. Oh well, it couldn't be helped now. As the heavy doors were pulled shut, I slopped a big, naked breast over the top of my square neckline and attached Inky to it, trusting the other wedding attendees to follow the advice Lonely Planet gives travelers blundering upon Balinese women bathing nude in a stream: Behave normally, don't stare, and for god's sake, don't take pictures. In the seat next to me, Lisa destroyed the outfit she had laboriously assembled in Chicago, whipping off her fancy shawl to cover me as best she could. Shrouded in patterned chiffon, Inky emitted a loud hum of satisfaction, the sound a car makes when its battery is dead but the desperate owner keeps cranking the ignition—*Uh RUR uh RURRR uh RURRR! Uh RUR uh RURRR uh RURRR!*—causing even Karen to glance away from the dour clerk cleaving her to CJ. It's one of the few known instances when breastfeeding has been *heard* on videotape.

There's not a lot of room for creativity if you're getting hitched in a Scottish civil service. For all their artistic impulses, Karen and CJ were allowed just one brief deviation from the bureaucratic script, to be delivered by another workshop teacher, a compact fellow with an intense gaze and the proven stamina to crawl backward on his unpadded elbows for more than twenty minutes in the name of art. Matthew's speech might have lent a note of romantic eloquence to the dry proceedings, but he was drowned out entirely by a two-year-old guest, who hopped off his father's lap to do a little hornpipe in front of the photographer, coyly piping, "Photo? Photo, okay? Photo?" It was adorable. He sounded just like the enterprising urchins who haunt the beaches and souvenir markets of Southeast Asia, angling for pens, gum, and spare change. His mother, standing up at the desk as CJ's best man, crossed her eyes at her husband. His attempt to collect and muffle their son produced such a cacophony of toddler fury that the chattering solicitation of the photographer was allowed to continue as the lesser evil. I was grateful to him for exhibiting powers of disruption far more advanced than Inky's. He made me think of John's three-year-old son, Loonan Blue, who had been escorted by his mother and grandfather to see his father's final performance in the workshop. As John, shrouded in a grim reaper's cloak and flanked by two similarly hooded participants, converged on a fruit basket, Loonan kept up a running commentary in a voice like a piccolo: "Eating dinner. Joomping up and down. Time for bed. Look, it's Johnny! Hey, hallo, Johnny! It's me, Loonan! Over here! Cun I have one of yuhr apples, Johnny?"

After the ceremony, we posed for group pictures in the pounding rain, then trailed the bride and groom in a dwindling group to the university's reception hall, where the secular art shenanigans commenced unchecked. A friend of CJ had sewn himself to a stuffed wedding dress and stood, quiet as a statue, while guests slipped scrawled responses to the phrase "The First Time Ever I Saw Your Face" under votive candles at his feet. It was a good project, not so freakish as to scare away the matronly aunts in their tight permanent waves and sensible pumps. A specially produced 'zine was distributed. The workshop participants, arriving to view the post-dinner slideshow and dance to a ceilidh band, presented Karen with a kinetic hat one of them had made from screen window mesh and cotton balls. She gamely stuck it on her head, leading us in a bumbling reel that did not improve when the open bar closed. My NeoFuturist pal David and his boyfriend volunteered to hold Inky so Greg and I could dance together for the first time in a year. As we whirled past their table, I heard Edward coaching, "Now Inky, this is Uncle David and he's a man, and I'm Uncle Edward and I'm a man, too, and it's like we're married but not!" If only every day in Glasgow could have been wedding day.

The next morning, we bundled up for a day trip to Edinburgh with Uncle David and Uncle Edward, praying that on the hour-long ride, the train would outrace the torrential rain flattening Glasgow. Our attempt to wait out the storm in a gallery-*cum*-bookstore's café was thwarted when an alarm sounded and firemen shooed us all out before our sandwiches had arrived. Visibility was so poor that we couldn't make out the Edinburgh Castle. We went anyway, swaddling Inky in a Hefty bag a guard pressed on us. Not caring about things like broken umbrellas or an obscured view, she was far happier than the rest of us, whose shoes soaked through in a matter of seconds. We did manage to smuggle her into a pub, discovering too late that the Slaughtered Lamb signified not authenticity but an embarrassing "scary" theme heavy on the stuffed ravens, unappetizing polyester cobwebs, and frozen margaritas in souvenir skull cups. The waitress showed as little concern for the underage patron wearing a wet garbage bag as the cook did for his floury clam chowder. We went home after one pint, so everyone but Inky and I could pack.

My undecided plans for the week Inky and I would spend without him were a cause of great concern for Greg, who had been charting my behavior. Watching *Father Ted* with Karen and CJ, I seemed almost normal, but after a long day tromping to increasingly far-flung minor museums with no one but Inky for company, I looked like someone peering out of a semi-submerged bamboo cage. "Are you sure you don't want to change your ticket and come home with me?" he ventured, knowing odds weren't good that I'd eat my pride and a seventy-five-dollar airline penalty. "It might make it easier to fly, if there are two adults."

I reminded him that on the flight over, the British Airways flight attendants had wheeled Inky up and down the aisles on their drink cart, giving me a false impression of how easy this trip would be. For years, I'd wanted to see Findhorn, the legendary organic farming community, just so I could confirm that their vegetables were as giant as I had heard and that the bugs really did limit themselves to a special patch cultivated specifically for their eating pleasure. With advance warning, visitors were welcome as long as they were willing to work. But "work" meant wielding a hoe, not breastfeeding, diapering, and entertaining a small nonresident child who would spend her mornings stripping the tomato vines of their unripe fruit. Karen recommended a farm on the Isle of Bute that accepted paying guests. The woman who answered the phone cried, "No dear, I coodna late you coom here with a baby if you've nah gah a car. You'd die of boooooooredom!"

We ended up taking the ferry to Bute anyway, a harrowing experience owing less to foul weather at sea than to a certain someone's desire to walk far around the rain-slick outer deck. A couple of young Swedes sat smoking on their poncho-covered backpacks, blissfully unaware that the gaps between protective railings were much much much too wide. The rain was horizontal when we docked in the port town of Rothesay. The other passengers raced down the gangplank while I lumbered along like Quasimodo, an Indonesian sarong draped over the slumbering baby on my back in an effort to supplement my puny urban umbrella. By the time we made our way to the B & B the farmer's wife had recommended, our Nepali duffle bag had bloated to capacity as twenty disposable diapers soaked up the precipitation admitted by the groovy loose cotton weave. "Heavens, lookit the poor dear. She's half-drowned, aren't you?" the sturdy matron who opened the door cried as she led us to our room, a huge pink chamber with a shared toilet. Inky opened her eyes, unfazed to discover herself in a new location, all chintz and foofy valances after the austerity of CJ's bachelor flat.

While I brewed a cup of tea in the electric kettle, she went to town on the beribboned baskets of dried floral arrangements with which our hostess had fussed up the joint. After weeks of fending her off of CJ's music collection, it was a delight to let her have free rein. She flung the ruffled pillows off the bed, climbed in and out of drawers, and danced in front of the rain-streaked French doors with the wastebasket on her head. Heaven. As Inky rampaged, I huddled on the windowsill, watching the immobile bumper cars in the deserted seaside amusement park, wishing we could remain in this easy room until Inky was old enough to start kindergarten. When there was a slight break in the weather, we ducked out for provisions. A few teenagers slumped beside the ring-toss booth, complaining that this was a sucky place for a holiday. Some older ladies in rain bonnets and galoshes crowded into the tourist information office to pick at the postcard racks and dishtowels decorated with thistle and bagpipers. The subdued vibe of this inclement tourist honky-tonk agreed with me. Other visitors were disappointed that their weekend at the shore wasn't allowing for much sunbathing, gull feeding and moon jumping. But their low spirits bolstered mine, especially since I suspected that Rothesay was generations away from anything resembling a performance art workshop. The local pub had a sternly worded brass plaque on the door: No Children Under the Age of Fourteen! A family in slickers slogged wearily past, the adolescent children whining about crossword puzzles and cheeseburgers.

"Inky, babu?" I asked.

"Babu," came the cheerful reply. It was her only word and I had yet to figure out what it meant.

The man at the liquor store didn't have a bottle opener, but he showed me how to use my keys to loosen the crimped cap one ridge at a time. It took me half an hour, but the beer tasted extra delicious for being hard won. With Inky down for the night, I propped open the door to our room with five pillows so I wouldn't find myself accidentally locked out after a trip to the communal toilet. Bladder empty, I clicked through the channels of the elderly television until a rerun of *NYPD Blue*, a show I had heard of but never seen, caught my interest. "Hey, that's our playground!" I shouted, as several squad cars raced to the scene of a murder in Tompkins Square.

The next morning in the breakfast room, I told our hostess and all the other guests about seeing my neighborhood on TV. "Ooh, Nyoo York," the mother of the two teenagers playing peekaboo with Inky cried. "I'd be skeered out of mah wits!"

"Yes, you're quite brave, especially with the wee bairn," our hostess nodded as she piled more scrambled eggs onto my plate. "Dear, are yeh sure yeh would not lahk to try the baby seat?" Without waiting for an answer, she scooped Inky off of my thigh and deposited her in an eyelet-trimmed highchair printed with pastel teddy bears. Such an eyesore would have been far too gaudy and cumbersome in our minuscule East Village apartment. I paused, waiting for screams of containment, if not aesthetic outrage, but Inky happily occupied herself by dragging the amenable teenage girl onto the plastic tray by her hair. "Thass better," the older woman declared, smoothing her flowered apron over her bosom before she poured out another cup of tea. "Lets Mother be free."

Acknowledgments

Thanks to those who aided and abetted me on the road, particularly Kosiya, Kay Tipples, and Geoff Comben, wherever they may be; The Neo-Futurists, Karen Christopher, CJ Mitchell, and my mother, Betsy Harris. Thanks, too, to Todd Weeks, Drew Camens, and Jamie Ayukawa.

Thank you and spank you to the readers of *The East Village Inky* for their tireless guerilla marketeering on my behalf. Ditto the independent booksellers who have given me a leg up.

Despite her refusal to appreciate the great quantities of plastic bags I made her take to Europe, Spencer Kayden proved as athletically supportive as ever. Readers of *The Big Rumpus* will kindly note that Spencer and Little MoMo are one and the same.

Presiding in the editorial abattoir, Leslie Miller trimmed me into a much more palatable person than I was in the first draft, a service for which I am greatly in her debt. Thanks to Elizabeth Wales, Meg Lemke, Jennie Goode, and Dave Awl for implementing their expertise on aspects of this project beyond the grasp of my cavewoman brain.

Not that I can pronounce it, but thank you in every language and dialect to India Reed and Milo Hanuman, the tiny monkeys who have infested our apartment and especially their father, Silverback Greg Kotis. Onward!

About the Author

AYUN HALLIDAY is the author of *The Big Rumpus: A Mother's Tale From the Trenches* (Seal Press 2002) and the sole staff member of *The East Village Inky*, the 2002 Firecracker Alternative Book Award–winner for Best Zine. Her work has appeared in *BUST, Bitch, Utne, Hipmama* and *Brain,Child* as well as the anthologies *Neo-Solo, Breeder, A Woman Alone, The Unsavvy Traveler,* and *Women Who Eat.* She lives in Brooklyn with her family.

http://www.ayunhalliday.com